IMAGES
of America

FAIRFIELD

ON THE COVER: During the 19th and early 20th centuries, Fairfield remained a small town, housing the governmental center of Solano County and serving as the business district for fruit growers in the surrounding valleys. The 1920s aerial photograph on the cover shows Fairfield's downtown with a view towards the northern hills. The Solano County Courthouse, built in 1911, marks the center of the county's governmental complex, facing Texas Street and Union Avenue. Next to it, partly visible, is the county jail. Directly below, along Union Avenue, stands the new Armijo Union High School, built in 1914. Opposite its entrance, at the southwestern corner of Texas and Union Streets, a row of Spanish-style houses occupy the lot that will be the future home of the Solano County Free Library (built in 1931). On the left side of the lot, along Texas Street, the Fairfield Fire Department is housed in the white building. To the left along Texas Street, the front of the Capitol Hotel and the 700 block of Texas Street can be seen. The Southern Pacific railroad tracks in the foreground divide Fairfield from its neighbor and rival, Suisun. Tracks visible behind the water tower run diagonally toward the distant Northern Electric Railroad, connecting Vallejo and Sacramento. Today's Webster Street follows the same pattern. The California Pacific Packing Company, in the foreground, is one of several fruit packing and shipping companies that shipped the fresh and dried fruits for which this area was famous to markets across the country. Together, the county government and fruit industry shaped Fairfield's identity for nearly a century, until the advent of the Air Force in 1942. (Courtesy Bay Area Electric Railroad Association Museum.)

IMAGES
of America

FAIRFIELD

Sabine Goerke-Shrode

ARCADIA
PUBLISHING

ISBN 978-0-7385-2888-5

Published by Arcadia Publishing
Charleston, South Carolina

Printed in the United States of America

Library of Congress Catalog Card Number: 2004104606

For all general information contact Arcadia Publishing at:
Telephone 843-853-2070
Fax 843-853-0044
E-mail sales@arcadiapublishing.com
For customer service and orders:
Toll-Free 1-888-313-2665

Visit us on the Internet at www.arcadiapublishing.com

CONTENTS

ACKNOWLEDGMENTS

Local history is the accumulation of events and people, and their efforts to create a community. In this publication, photographs and captions tell the story of Fairfield and those who lived here and called this city home.

Over the years, many citizens recorded and preserved these stories. Without their work, this book could not have been written. Each added valuable pieces to the growing body of research on Fairfield history, just as I hope that others in the future will be inspired to add their voices, corrections, and nuggets of new research and information.

While the format of the book precludes a bibliography, I would like to mention some of the resources that were most helpful to my research. Research materials were found in many places. Fairfield's office of Environmental Affairs commissioned a "Survey of Cultural Resource Central Fairfield" in 1982, which contributed to my interpretation of Fairfield's history. Mary Higham of the Solano County Historical Society provided me with a set of Solano Historian magazines, one of the important research tools for Solano County history. Nancy Dingler also shared some of her research material with me. The work of the Solano County Genealogical Society and the Solano County Historical Records Commission proved to be invaluable. Clyde Lowe kept me straight on the information about Chief Solano. Leslie Batson added valuable insight to the chapter on Captain Waterman. Jane Loveall shared her Whitby and Richardson family genealogy and some wonderful family anecdotes. Ian Thompson opened up the Daily Republic's historical article collection and brought my attention to an unpublished manuscript by former Solano Republican publisher and author David A. Weir. Descendants of David Weir further helped with my research.

Many images were shared with me for this book. The Vacaville Museum generously provided me with access to its extensive photo collection. A sizable number of photographs in this publication come from their archives. In addition, registrar Heidi Casebolt spent hours trying to locate an elusive title photo for me. I am indebted to the Solano County Library for lending their photo collection to me. Most of these photos and the information accompanying them had never been widely circulated and they have proven to be a veritable treasure trove. Larry Melling shared his incredible Fairfield postcard collection, some of which can be found in this volume. Brian Irwin helped me with photographs and information. His excellent documentary video on Fairfield's history contains a wonderful segment on the city's recent history, a subject not covered in the archival collections.

My most heartfelt thanks go to the Vacaville Heritage Council and Jerry Bowen. Without Jerry there would have been no photographs. For months, he scanned countless images, transformed them into the correct format for this book, shared research material and knowledge—and remained cheerful and upbeat throughout. Last but not least, my thanks go to Hannah Clayborn, my editor at Arcadia Publishing, for much good advice, helpful tips, and nearly endless patience.

Introduction

For nearly 150 years, Fairfield has served Solano County, one of the seven original counties formed in 1850, as the seat of its county government. Yet despite this long time period, trying to record the history of Fairfield is a challenge. The major historic events—from Suisun Indian Chief Solano, to city founder Captain Robert Waterman, to the installation of Travis Air Force Base—are well documented. Other elements of the city's history, especially its architectural history, have also been recorded, thanks in large part to the City of Fairfield itself and to the excellent work of the Heritage Society of Western Solano County and its historical collection surveys.

Despite these efforts, grasping the essence of this town remains difficult. Beyond the enumerated buildings and the major recorded events, people create history and shape the identity of a community. So far, none of the published works really address the social aspects of Fairfield's history.

Solano County straddles the divide between the Bay Area and the Central Valley, and its seven cities reflect this in their diverse identities. Fairfield is located at the center, on the plane between the Blue Ridge Mountains and the Suisun Marsh, surrounded by lush valleys and beautiful vistas, yet separated from upper and lower Solano County by those mountains. More isolated in its early years, when it had neither port nor other easy access to larger market towns, today it is shaped by rapid growth along the Interstate 80 corridor and the influence of the large military installation nearby.

Fairfield's beginnings are linked to the name of clipper ship captain Robert Waterman, who in 1856 founded the town after his failed attempt to establish a port city at nearby Bridgeport/Cordelia. Within two years, Fairfield became the county seat and has served the population of Solano County as the central governmental center ever since.

Yet despite its political prominence, Fairfield was an artificially created city and was overshadowed by its neighbor and rival, Suisun City, for the first 75 years of its existence. Well into the 20th century, Fairfield did not have many residents. Most people lived in the surrounding valleys, using Fairfield for their bureaucratic needs. Suisun, with its port, was the commercial hub that everybody turned to for trade, commerce, and entertainment. Despite the fact that Fairfield served as the seat of county government, it didn't even have its own post office in the early years.

To this day, residents tend to link both cities together, as the names for agencies such as the original Fairfield-Suisun Airfield, the Fairfield-Suisun Chamber of Commerce, or the Fairfield-Suisun Unified School District attest. Every now and then, the question comes up as to whether the cities should be combined into one entity.

Despite the close relationship, and often outright rivalry between Fairfield and Suisun, this publication's intent has been to present solely a pictorial history of Fairfield, without overlooking the contributions of the residents in the surrounding valleys and communities. A future publication will hopefully do the same for Suisun City and vicinity.

During the late 19th and early 20th centuries agriculture, especially the fruit industry, dictated much of the development of the area. To this day, agriculture is a major economic factor in Solano County, though the focus has shifted from orchards to row crops, nursery stock, and vineyards.

The limited number of existing photographs and the length and format of the book did not allow an in-depth exploration of all facets of Fairfield's history. While extensive collections of local historic photographs exist, images were often taken by amateur photographers intent on capturing an interesting moment. Thus many important ordinary local events were never documented by a photographer. Prior to the 1860s, photographs were not common in rural California, which precludes photos of the original inhabitants, the Suisun people, before the settlement era. Later, whole ethnic groups, such the Chinese and, to a lesser degree, Japanese orchard workers, who contributed so much to agricultural growth in the 19th and early 20th century in our area, have no preserved visual representation in our local public collections. The many views of the Solano County Courthouse and the Solano County Free Library building at Texas Street and Union Avenue, on the other hand, could probably fill every page of this book.

But Fairfield had more to offer than just its governmental center. With incorporation as a city in 1903, allowing a bond measure to create much-needed improvements, and the rerouting of the Lincoln Highway through the town in 1915, Texas Street finally developed into a bustling center. Over the years, businesses such as Goosen Hardware Store, Gerevas Meat Market, Woodard Chevrolet, the Solano County Republican newspaper, J.C. Penney, the movie theater, and ice cream parlor attracted residents from the surrounding valleys and vicinities. Installations such as the Fairfield sign across Texas Street in 1925 and the statue of Chief Solano in front of the Solano County Free Library building in 1937 created visual landmarks that define the image of Fairfield to this day.

Until World War II, Fairfield retained its small-town flavor, serving its citizens, the residents in the surrounding valleys, and the county at large. The installation of the Fairfield-Suisun Airbase, later renamed Travis Air Force Base, changed this. Suddenly, large numbers of new residents needed housing. For the last 50 years, growth has been one of the driving forces in the city. The large increase in residents, many of whom have resided here for only a few years, has in some ways created a citizenry that no longer feels connected to the roots of this community. To many, Solano Mall, rather than Texas Street, has become the center of town.

Exploring our local history has helped me to become a part of this community and to care deeply about its future. Hopefully, this collection of historic photographs will inspire old-time residents and new residents alike to rediscover the fascinating history of Fairfield.

One

Suisun Indians and Californio Dons

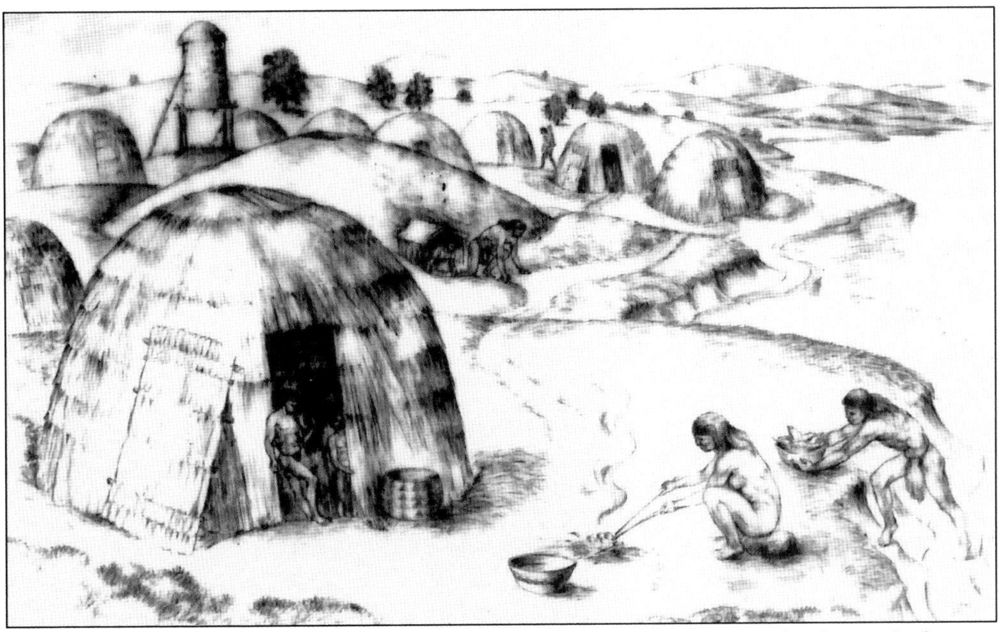

Native American Village. The original inhabitants of the area were the Suisun Indians, a local triblet of the Patwin Indians. They lived and hunted in the verdant valleys bordered by the Blue Ridge Mountains and the Suisun Marsh. The word "Suisun"—where the west wind blows—is a reminder of the strong summer winds that spring up in the evenings. Several families formed a group, moving among a number of established settlements according to the season of the year. Gathering, fishing, and hunting provided a rich variety of food sources. They crafted tule boats and fishing nets as well as baskets from willows, grasses, and vines. Land stewardship, such as the controlled burning of vegetation, helped support a lifestyle that was well adapted to its surroundings.

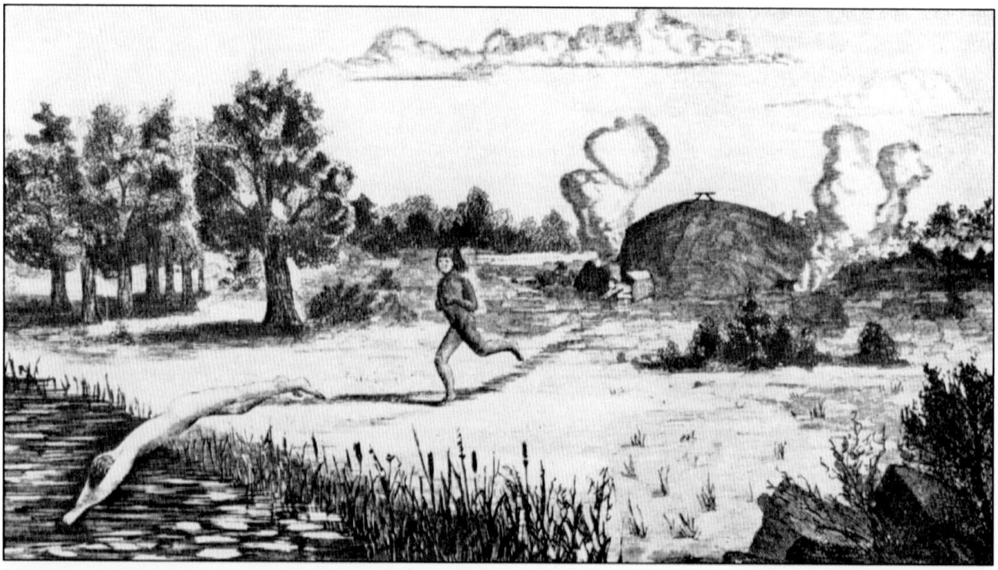

NATIVE AMERICAN SWEATHOUSE. Each village consisted of several different dwelling types. Two or three families lived together in large structures. Women retired to the menstrual house during menses. The sweathouse served as a ritual and spiritual center where village members assembled to conduct cleansing ceremonies, which included singing and dancing. At the end of the ceremony, participants plunged into cold waters nearby. Large villages also boasted a ceremonial dance house. These two images are part of a series drawn by sculptor William Huff for paleontologist Dr. Charles Kemp in the 1950s.

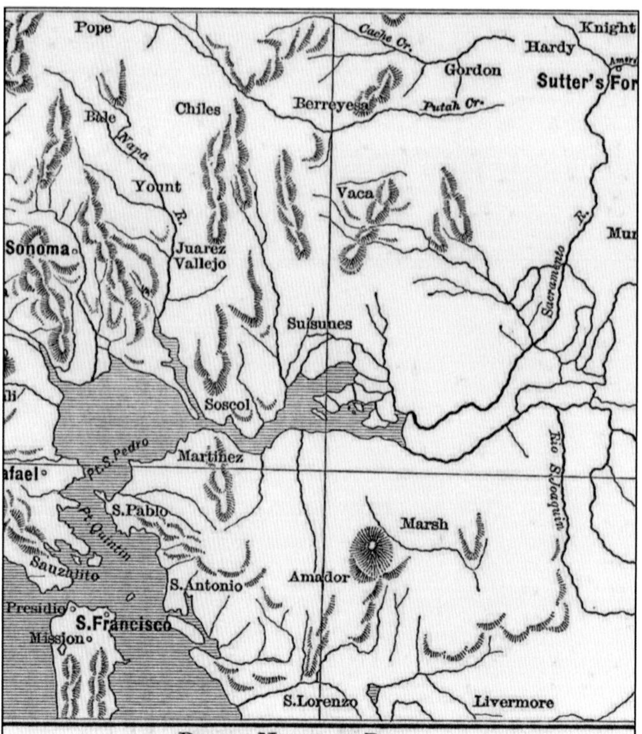

BANCROFT MAP. The advent of the Spanish missionaries destroyed the Patwin Indian culture completely. In 1817, a large group of Patwin Indians living in the vicinity of today's city of Fairfield was massacred. Survivors were taken to Mission Dolores (in the current city of San Francisco) and Mission San Jose (in the current city of Fremont) to be converted and forced to work the mission's fields and as cattle tenders. Among them was a 16-year-old man named Sina. In 1823, the last of the missions, San Francisco de Solano, was founded in Sonoma. Here, young Sina's name was recorded as "Francisco Solano-Sina-Suisun" in 1827. This map shows the North Bay Area sometime in the 1830s.

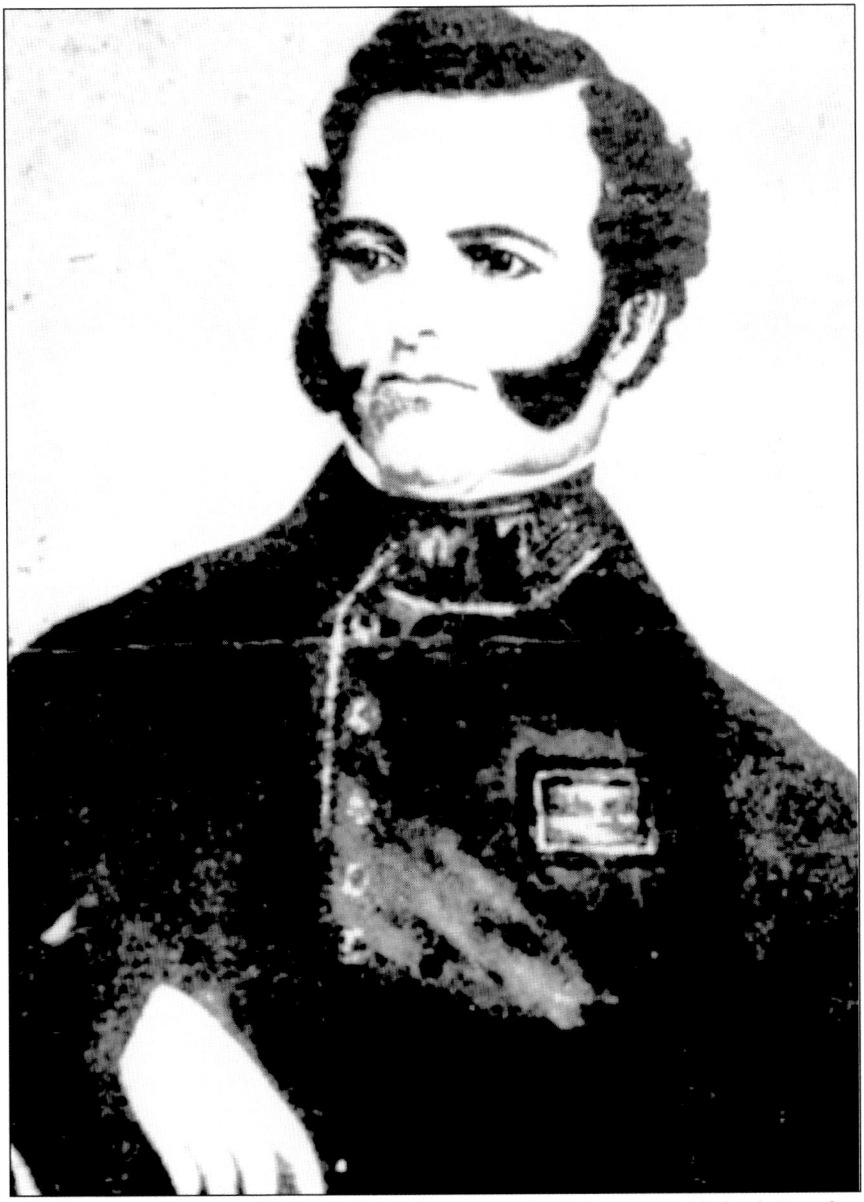

GENERAL VALLEJO. In 1824, Mission San Francisco de Solano established Rancho Santa Eulalia in the Suisun Valley, the former territory of the Patwin Indians. By 1830, Sina/ Francisco Solano lived at the rancho, supervising daily operations. After the secularization of the mission in 1835, he continued to live on the Suisun Rancho, as it was now called. From 1836 until 1843, Francisco Solano served as a captain in the Mexican army under General Vallejo, suppressing Indian revolts north and west of Sonoma. The smallpox epidemic of 1837 hastened the demise of the Native American tribes. In what later became upper Solano County, only a few hundred Suisun Indians survived the disease, for which their immune systems had no defense. Following secularization of the missions in 1835, Gen. M.G. Vallejo awarded Chief Solano, as he was often thereafter known, the provisional land grant for the Suisun Rancho in 1837, four leagues (approximately 17,814 acres) in all. This print shows General Vallejo a few years later, around 1846.

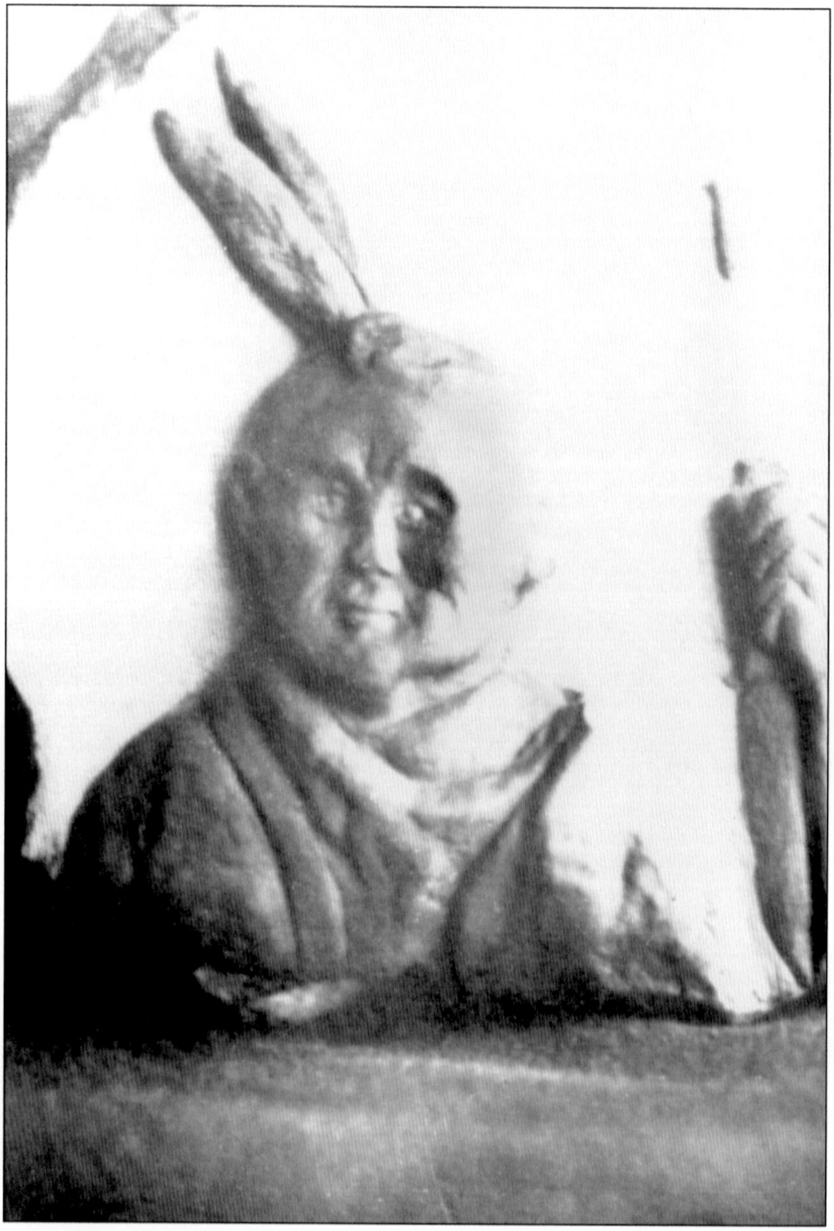

Portrait of Chief Solano. After his campaigns against local Indian tribes, Chief Solano returned to Suisun Rancho which he operated with the help of Suisun Indian farmhands and vaqueros. He erected several adobe houses and barns on his property. His own house was situated in the vicinity of the future Samuel Martin home "Stonedene," opposite today's Solano Community College campus. In May 1842, Chief Solano sold his land grant back to General Vallejo for $1,000 in coin and moved up to Sonoma, where he also owned property. After the Bear Flag Revolt in 1846, he disappeared into the wilderness up north. Sick and dying, he returned to Suisun Rancho in 1850, where Samuel Martin took him in. Legend claims that Chief Solano's grave is located near the memorial plaque on the Solano Community College grounds. General Vallejo's son, Platon Vallejo, who likely knew Chief Solano by sight, later carved this image into a piece of rock.

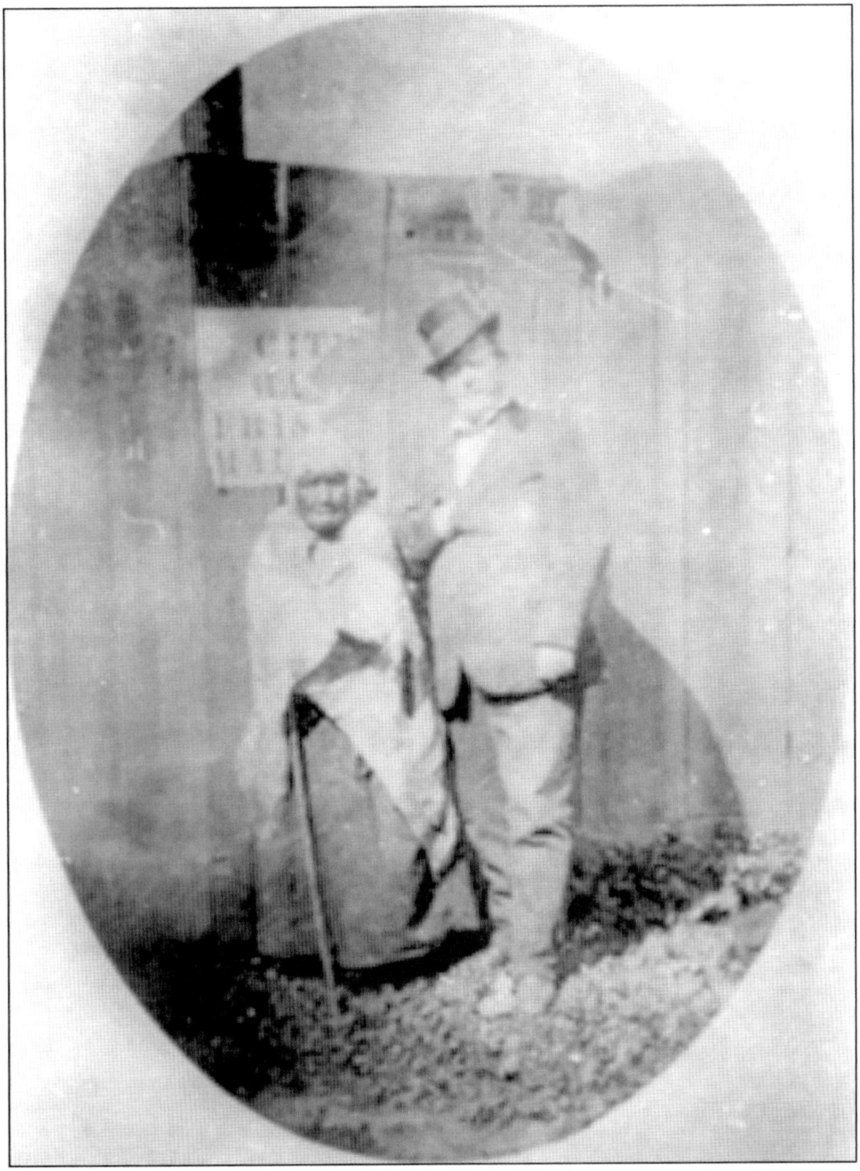

VALLEJO AND INDIAN WOMAN. In 1877, White Heron, also known as Isadora Filomena, one of Chief Solano's wives, recounted her life story. She was captured on one of the raids against local tribes conducted by Chief Solano and General Vallejo. "When Solano went out to fight, he armed his men with daggers made of flint, and lances and arrows pointed with flint, all dipped in poisonous herbs," she recalled. "I don't know whether they mixed anything else with the herbs or not. Solano's warriors did not wear coat, shirt, shoes, trousers or hat! They were not foolish enough to have anything on the body by which a white man or another Indian could take hold, but went entirely naked, with only a bunch of feathers on the head. The Indians who carried the food wore gray feathers pulled out of wild fowl. The fighting men carried lances and arrows, with white duck feathers on their head, except for the captain, who wore black feathers." While the woman seen here with General Vallejo is said to be Isadora, this seems doubtful. General Vallejo was five foot, nine inches tall and Isadora was described as five foot ten inches. Even old age would not shrink her that much.

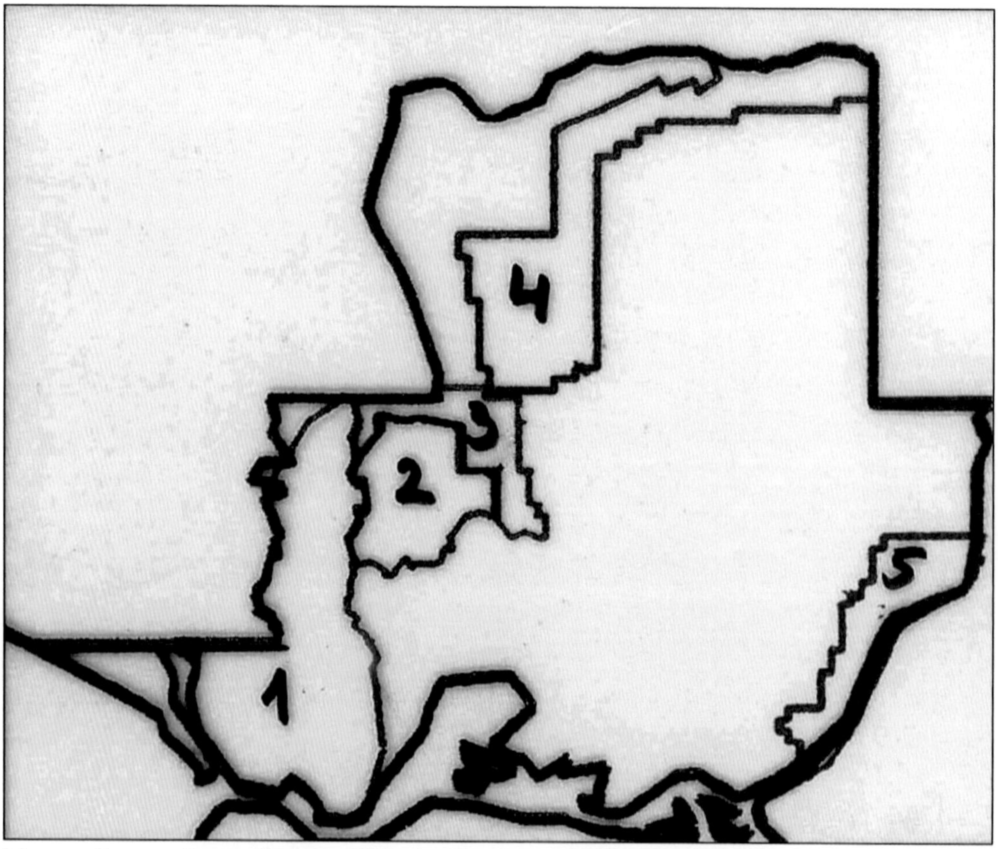

MAP OF SOLANO LAND GRANTS. The distribution of land grants brought the first non-native settlers to the area. Among them was Santa Fe trader Don Jose Francisco Armijo, who helped establish the Old Spanish Trail, also known as the Armijo Trail, which connected Santa Fe and Los Angeles, opening new commercial routes between the Southwest and the West Coast. Don Armijo may have come to this area as early as 1835. He clearly liked what he saw, as he began to petition General Vallejo for a land grant as early as November 1837. On March 4, 1840, General Vallejo awarded Don Armijo three square leagues (13,315 acres), named the Tolenas Grant (3), with the admonition that "he not molest the heathen (native Indians) dwelling there." Armijo's Tolenas grant was bordered by Chief Solano's Rancho Suisun (2) and the Rancho Los Putos Grant (4) given to Armijo's cousin, Juan Manuel Vaca, and Juan Felipe Peña. Two other land grants included the Suscol Grant (1) belonging to General Vallejo, and the Los Ulpinos Grant (5) given to John Bidwell. Don Armijo quickly built a "palizada", a temporary dwelling. He then returned to New Mexico to retrieve his wife and the five oldest of his seven children, as well as four Pueblo Indians, who eventually settled on the Armijo grant. The family made the journey in 1841. Cousins Vaca and Peña followed in 1842, bringing with them the two youngest Armijo children.

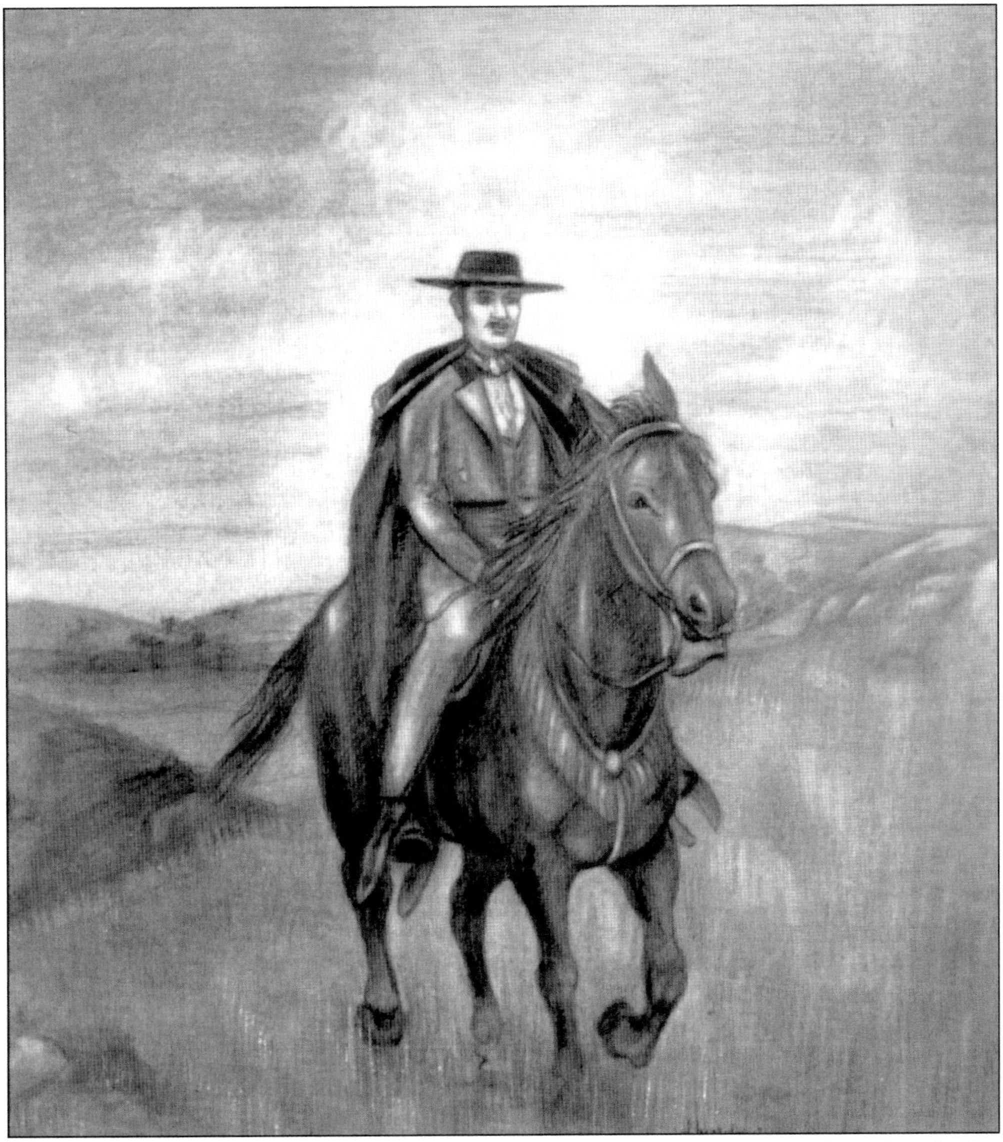

ANTONIO MARIANI ARMIJO. As yet no image of Don Jose Francisco Armijo has been found. This pencil sketch, created by J. Lundquist in 1851, shows Don Jose's eldest son, Antonio Mariani Armijo, on his horse, Fuego (Smokey). Antonio Armijo is wearing the typical costume of a Californio, as the early settlers of Spanish/Mexican descent were called. Californios generally were skilled horsemen, proud of their thoroughbred horses that could cover long distances in astonishingly fast times. Don Antonio brought his wife and children with him and settled them in an adobe close to the home of his parents. The family ran cattle and sheep. Cattle were valued for hides and tallow, but not for meat. Sheep were bred for their wool. In addition, the family planted wheat, oats, and barley. Don Armijo was also noted for his vegetables and fruit orchards, which seem to have been quite extensive and went beyond the needs of his family.

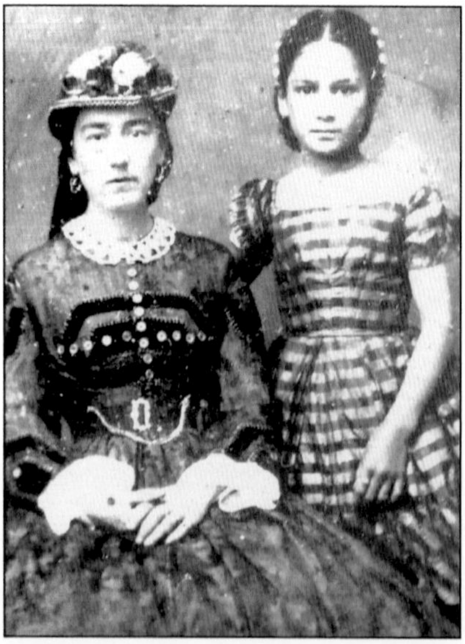

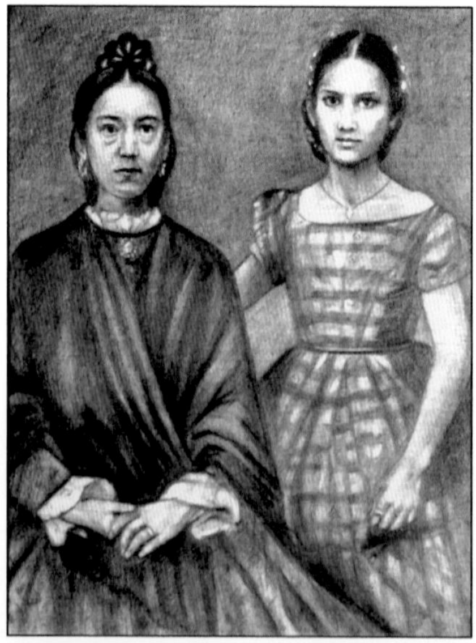

Dona Jose Francisco Armijo and Granddaughter Maria Antonia Armijo. J. Lundquist also drew the 1851 pencil sketch on the right of Dona Jose Francisco Armijo and her granddaughter Maria Antonia (likely the daughter of Antonio Armijo) by copying the tintype photograph on the left. In the photograph, both are smartly dressed in fashions of the time. Interestingly, Lundquist changed Dona Armijo's dress in his sketch by wrapping her in a shawl and changing her stylish hat to a hairstyle with a high Spanish comb, over which she would normally wear a mantilla. The Californio lifestyle was well adapted to the hot climate, with long siestas in the afternoon in the cool rooms of their adobe. Hospitality played an important part, and colorful fiesta celebrations lasting for days drew visitors on horseback from as far away as Los Angeles. Such customs and lifestyle seemed strange and even indolent to the newly arriving Anglo-American settlers.

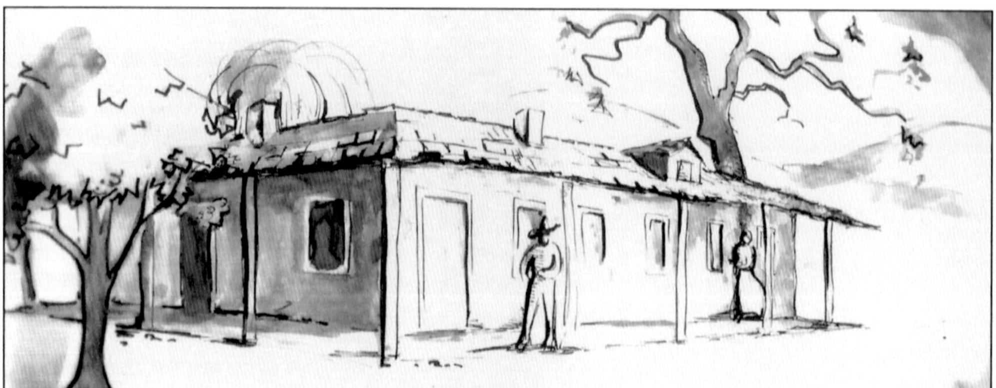

Armijo Adobe. The Armijos, like most of the early settlers, lived in adobe houses that kept rooms cool in summer and warm in winter. The Armijos' adobes were located where Rancho Solano is today. Mexican land grants tended to have loosely defined, often overlapping borders. Don Armijo had to settle border disputes between himself and Chief Solano, as well as the Vaca and Peña families. The Gold Rush brought Anglo-American settlers to the area who pressed their claims to land much more aggressively. Squatter problems occurred on all land grants over the next decades. While both Don Francisco, who died in 1850, and his son Antonio lived on their land until their deaths, in the end the family lost most of its holdings to other parties.

Two

Founding a City
Capt. Robert Waterman

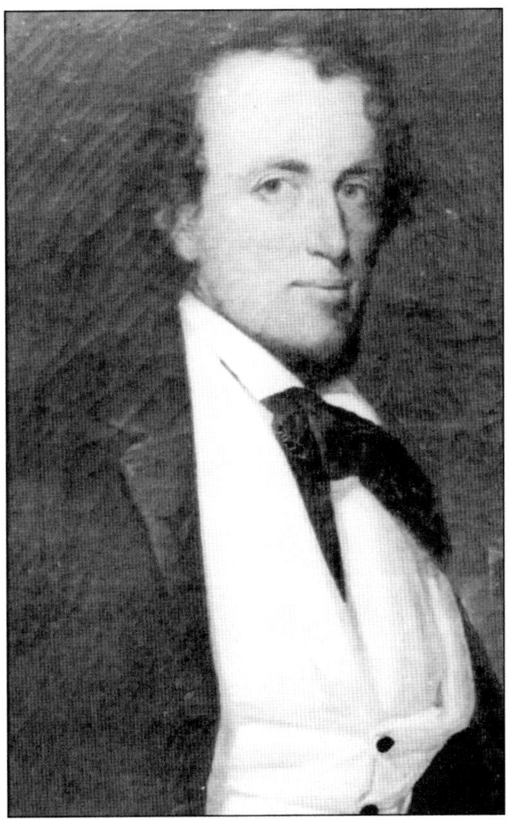

Captain Waterman in 1848, Age 40. Capt. Robert Henry Waterman was one of the famous clipper ship captains of his age. He was born in New York on March 4, 1808. In 1820, he began his sea career as a cabin boy, quickly rising through the ranks, until he commanded his first full-rigged ship in 1833. He designed the rigging of the first true clipper ship, the *Sea Witch*, and sailed her to China four times between 1846 and 1849, setting a speed record that is still unsurpassed. In 1850, he decided to retire and seek his fortune in California land speculation. Drawn out of retirement in 1851, he commanded his last ship, the *Challenge*, on its maiden voyage from New York to San Francisco. When the unruly and inexperienced crew mutinied off the coast of Brazil, Captain Waterman exercised harsh discipline, aided by a brutal first mate. Several men died during the ill-fated 120-day voyage. In 1852, Waterman and his first mate were accused of murder and brutality and underwent several trials, but were exonerated of the murder charges. However, Waterman's reputation for stern discipline earned him the nickname of "Bully Waterman."

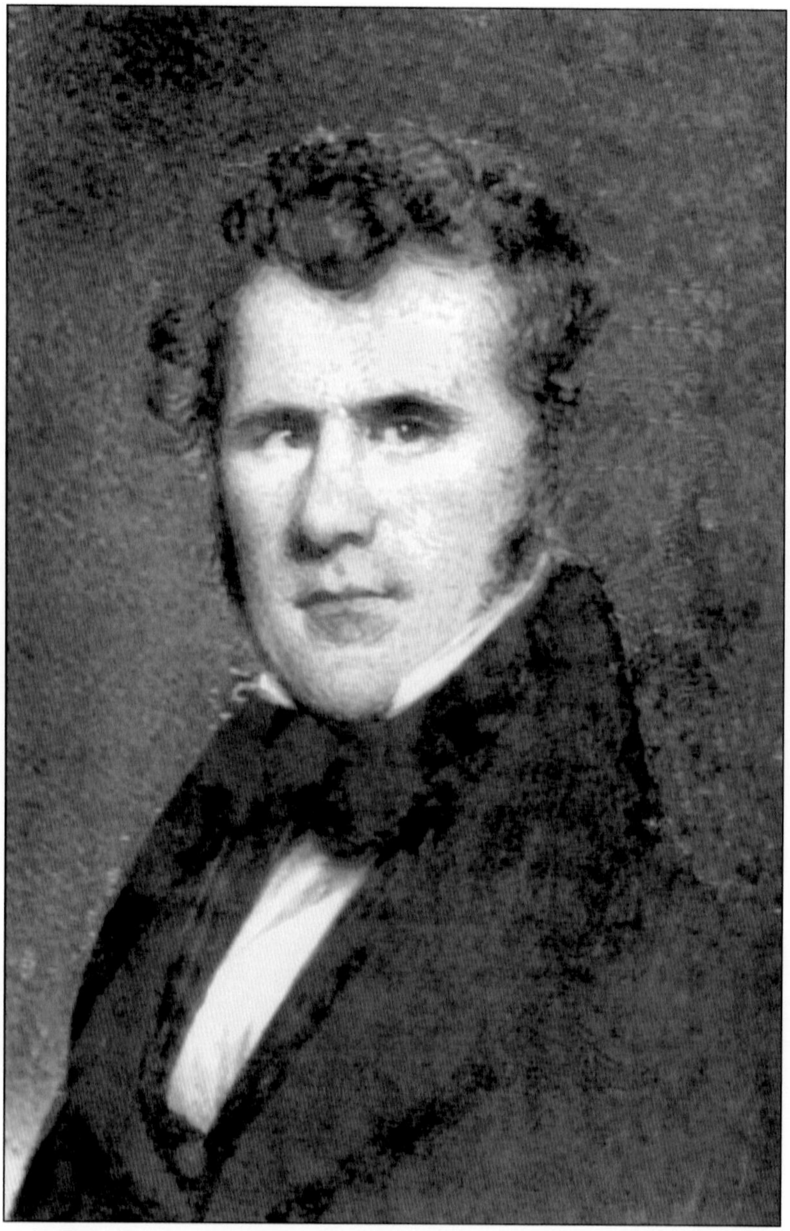

Archibald A. Ritchie, Early 1840s. The Gold Rush brought not only miners to California, but also shrewd businessmen like Captain Alexander Archibald Ritchie. After building the successful import and export business, Ritchie, Osgood & Company in San Francisco, he moved to Benicia in early August 1850 to expand his operations. Intrigued by the beauty and the potential of the vast lands in Solano County, he purchased the Rancho Suisun land grant from General Vallejo on August 26, 1850. Only months earlier in May, General Vallejo had bought this land grant back from Chief Solano for $1,000. A.A. Ritchie paid $10,000 cash and raised a mortgage of $40,000. Three days after his purchase, he sold an undivided one-third interest to Captain Robert Henry Waterman for $16,666. Captain Ritchie was killed in a carriage accident on July 9, 1856. Captain Waterman was named executor of the land grant together with Ritchie's widow, Martha Hamilton Ritchie.

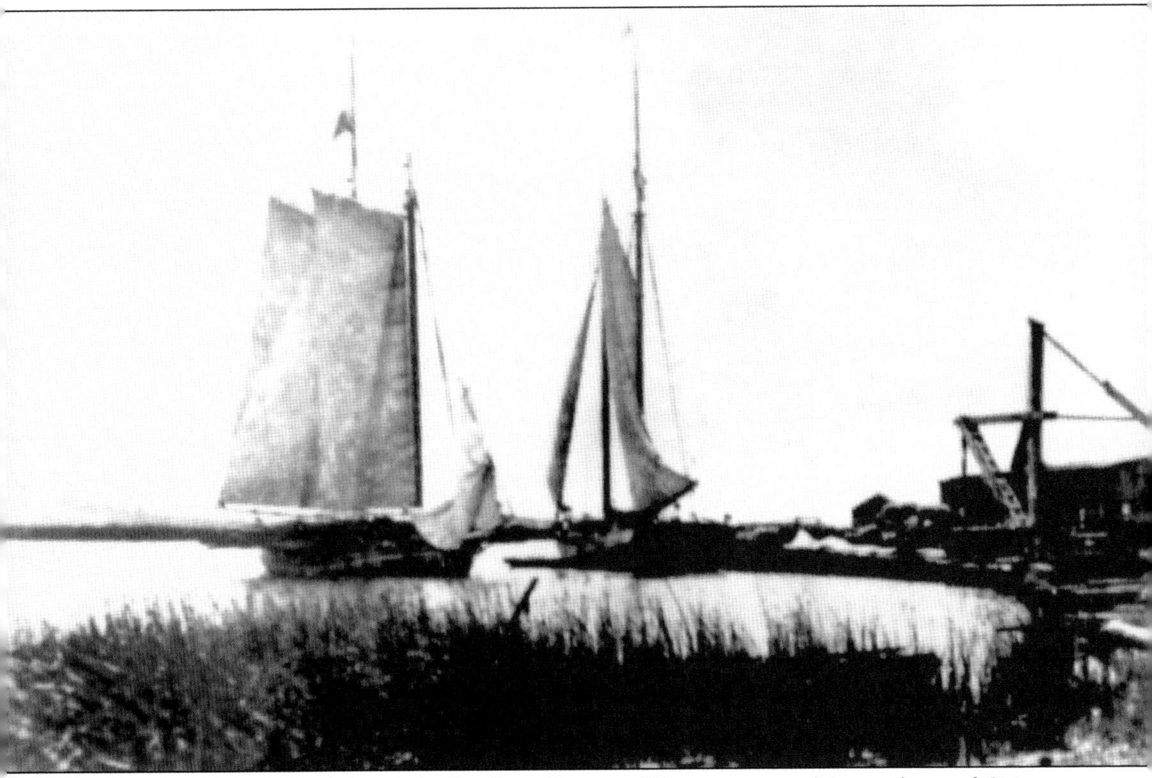

SUISUN WHARF, 1860. Like A.A. Ritchie, Captain Waterman saw his purchase of Suisun Rancho as a good investment opportunity. In June of the following year, Captain Ritchie cut 6,000 tons of hay, selling them for a profit greater than the purchase price of the ranch. Access to reliable transportation to markets in San Francisco was a main concern. In 1850, Captain Waterman set out to develop a harbor at a slough near the Benicia-Sacramento Road. He named the settlement Bridgeport—years later it would be renamed Cordelia after his wife. However, in 1851, Josiah Wing, another sea captain bent on making his fortune on land, recognized the potential of a small island in the marsh just outside Waterman's property. Here, Captain Wing founded a large "embarcadero," which grew into Suisun City by 1854. The new harbor was five miles closer to the growing farming centers in Lagoon and Vaca Valley than Cordelia. Waterman's attempt to establish a port town had failed.

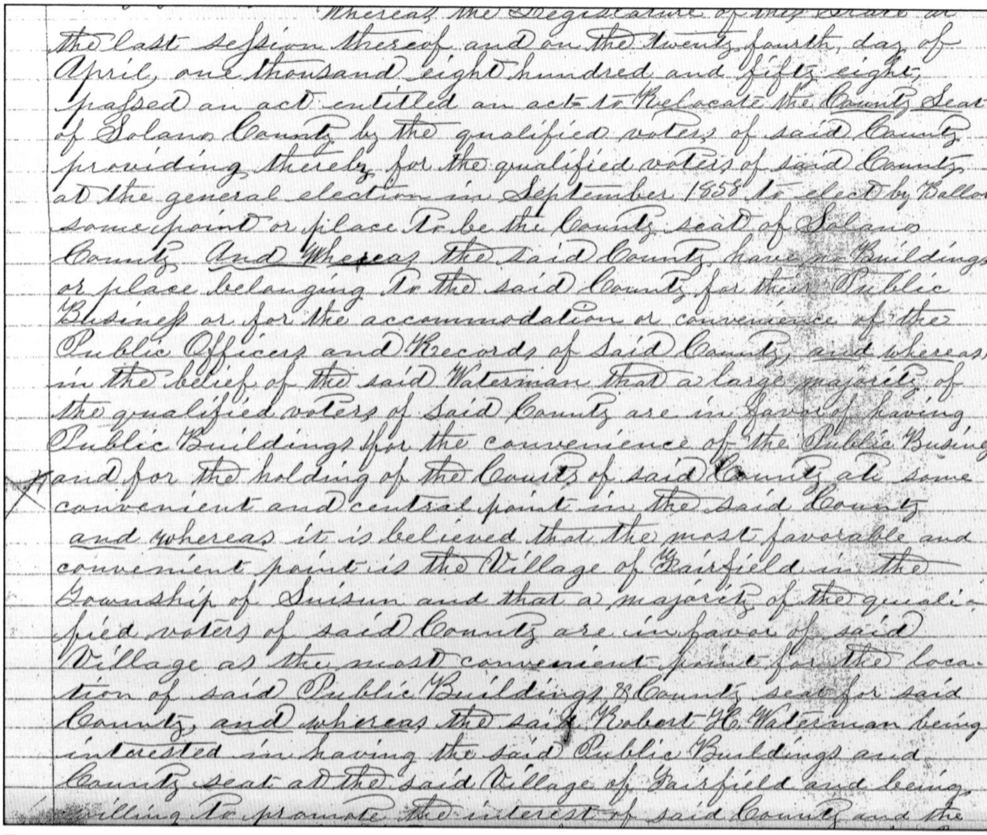

Whereas the Legislature of this State at
the last session thereof and on the twenty fourth day of
April one thousand eight hundred and fifty eight,
passed an act entitled an act to Relocate the County Seat
of Solano County by the qualified voters of said County
providing thereby for the qualified voters of said County
at the general election in September 1858 to elect by Ballot
some point or place to be the County seat of Solano
County And Whereas the said County have no Buildings
or place belonging to the said County for their Public
Business or for the accommodation or convenience of the
Public Officers and Records of Said County, and whereas,
in the belief of the said Waterman that a large majority of
the qualified voters of said County are in favor of having
Public Buildings for the convenience of the Public Business
and for the holding of the Courts of said County at some
convenient and central point in the said County
and whereas it is believed that the most favorable and
convenient point is the Village of Fairfield in the
Township of Suisun and that a majority of the quali-
fied voters of said County are in favor of said
Village as the most convenient point for the loca-
tion of said Public Buildings & County seat for said
County, and whereas the said Robert H. Waterman being
interested in having the said Public Buildings and
County seat at the said Village of Fairfield and being
willing to promote the interest of said County and the

EXCERPT OF THE DEED BETWEEN SOLANO COUNTY AND CAPTAIN WATERMAN. Despite his failure, Captain Waterman remained undaunted. In 1856, he laid out a new town, which he named Fairfield after a town in Connecticut. With upper Solano County's population growing, demand arose for a new, central county seat to replace Benicia at the southernmost edge of the county. In 1858, Fairfield, Vacaville, Suisun, and Denverton competed to become the new county seat. Captain Waterman, speaking on behalf of the town of Fairfield, offered 16 acres of free land for the county buildings, an area to be called Union Square, with the stipulation "that said Union Park is to be kept and used for public buildings." He also offered four adjacent blocks for the construction of a courthouse site and a personal bond of $10,000.

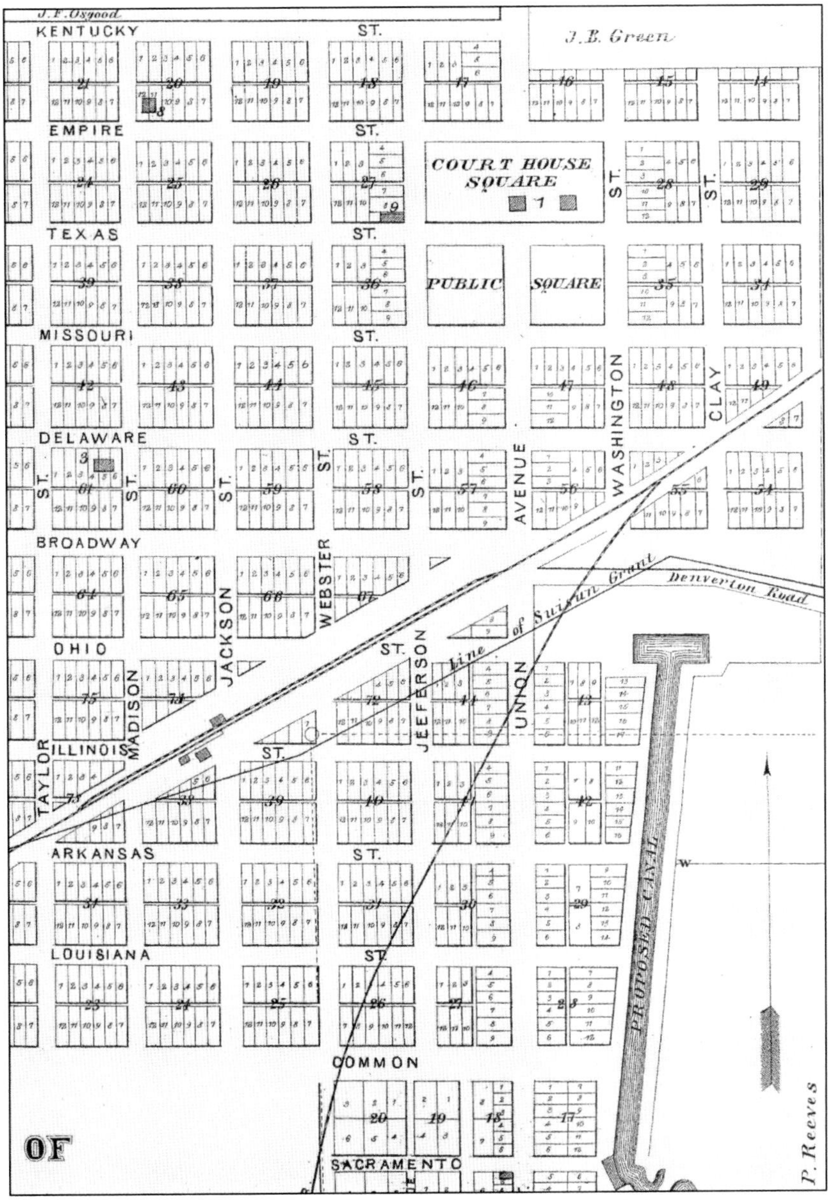

MAP OF FAIRFIELD, 1878. The voters determined the location of the county seat. After the September 2, 1858, election, Fairfield emerged as the winner with 1,029 votes. This victory was not just a result of Captain Waterman's generous offer, but came about in large part because of the rivalry between Benicia and Vallejo. Vallejo residents still smarted from having the county seat torn from their grasp by Benicia. They did not want to see Benicia win again, and instead cast their votes for a county seat in Fairfield. The *Solano Herald* commented a few days later: "In the list of killed and wounded of Wednesday's battle, our eye falls mournfully on the name of Benicia—Benicia! The long-suffering mortally wounded, if not dead—killed by Vallejo's unsparing hand! That the people of Suisun and the adjoining region should have desired a removal of the county seat was by no means surprising: but Vallejo! Et tu Brute?" This 1878 plat map of Fairfield shows the classic grid pattern of Fairfield, the courthouse and public square, and the borders of the Suisun Rancho grant.

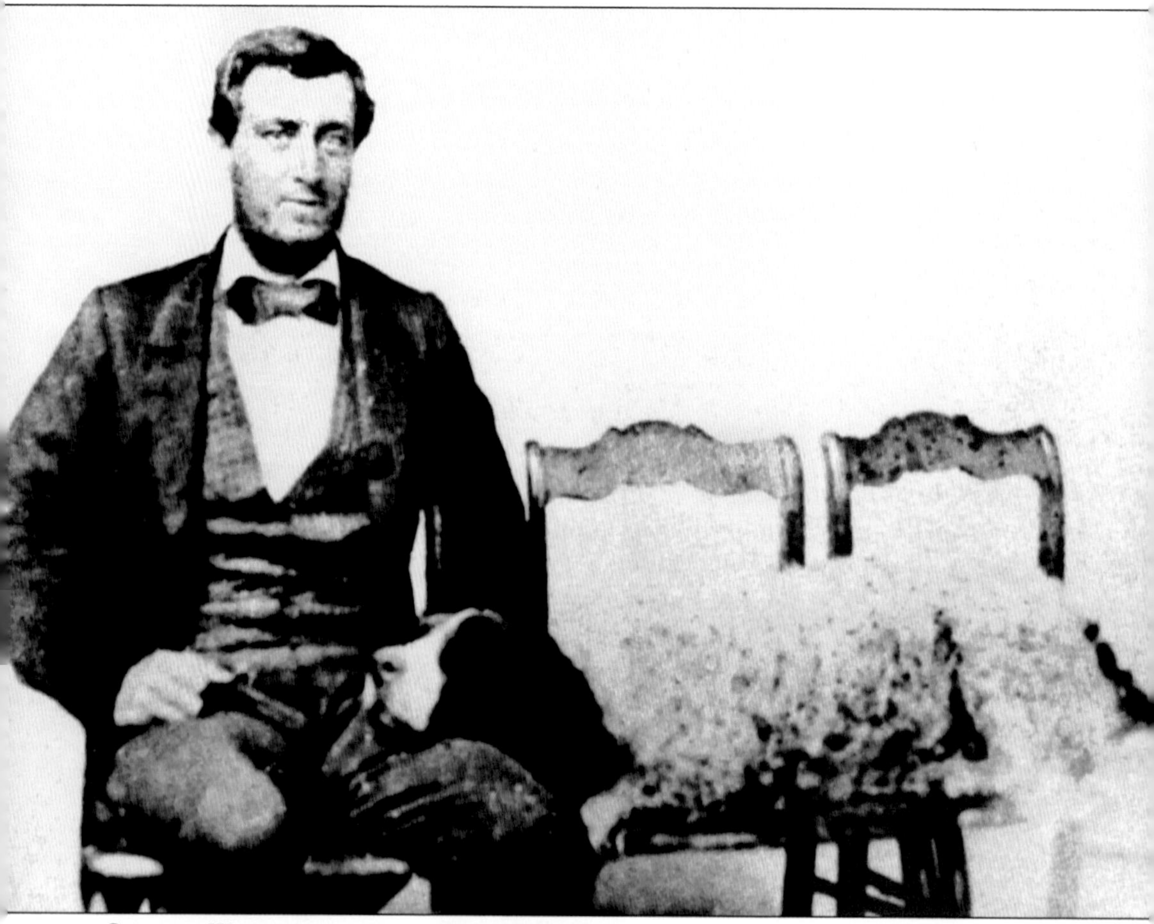

CAPTAIN WATERMAN AFTER 1859. With the question of the county seat settled, Captain Waterman finally began to concentrate on his own land holdings. Beginning in 1858, with more settlers coming to the area, he slowly began to sell land jointly owned with his deceased partner's widow, Martha Ritchie. Though designating land in the Suisun Valley for what would become his Ten Gates Ranch, Waterman resided in Fairfield throughout the Civil War period (possibly in a house located on the corner of Jackson and Illinois Streets). In 1866, Waterman moved to San Francisco to set up a business as a marine surveyor and serve as United States inspector of ship hulls for nearly a decade. He and his wife resided on Fillmore Street at the corner of Grove until his retirement, when they returned to Solano County to work his ranch. By 1883, Captain Waterman had increased his landholdings in the Fairfield area to over 1,200 acres. He died August 8, 1884.

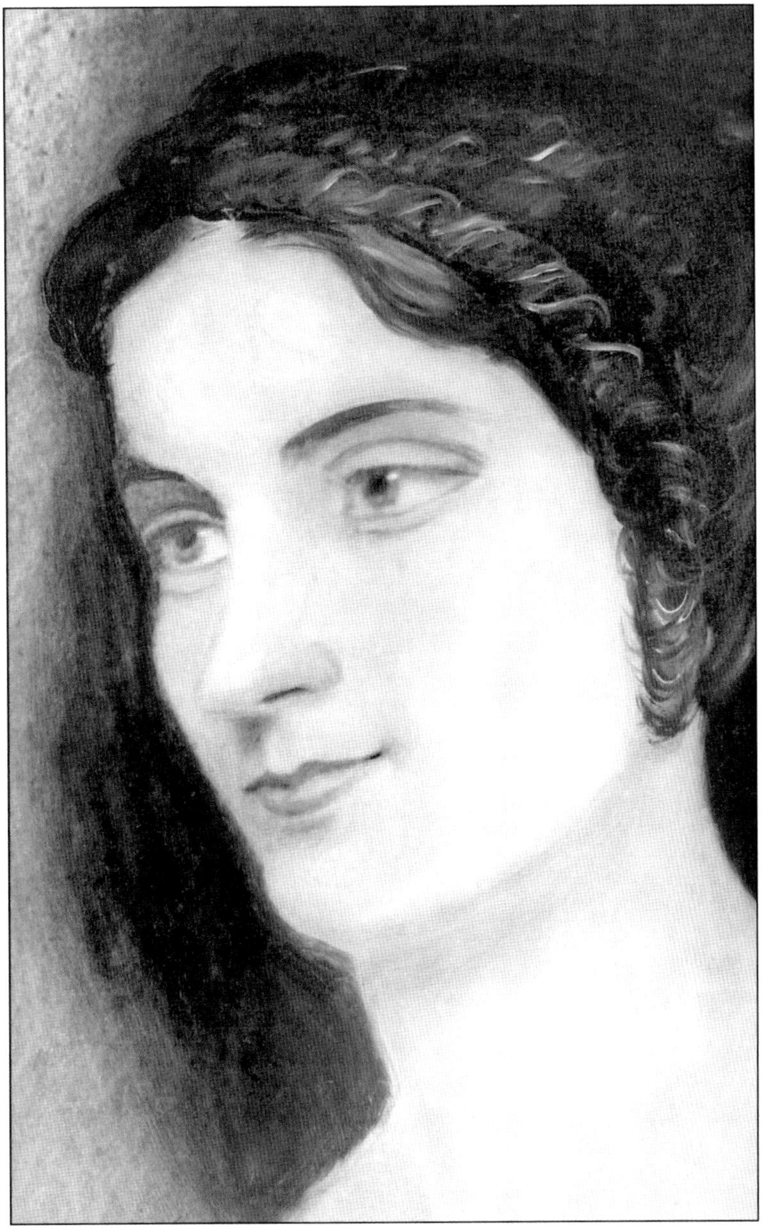

CORDELIA WATERMAN, C. 1848. Robert Waterman married Cordelia Sterling of Bridgeport, Connecticut, in 1846. Born in 1813, Cordelia followed her husband to California in 1852, experiencing the trials of crossing the Isthmus of Panama. The couple had no children. After 1875, the Watermans began to spend most of their time in Fairfield. His career at sea and business endeavors on land had made Captain Waterman quite affluent, allowing them to maintain an elegantly furnished home. Their home became one of the area's premier residences. On special occasions, Cordelia entertained family and friends at a table set with the elegant china and silver more typical of her San Francisco world. The Watermans were also quite visible in their community. Frank Whitby remembered that the couple visited his elementary school, observing a competition in reading and writing. As the winner, he was invited to take lunch with them.

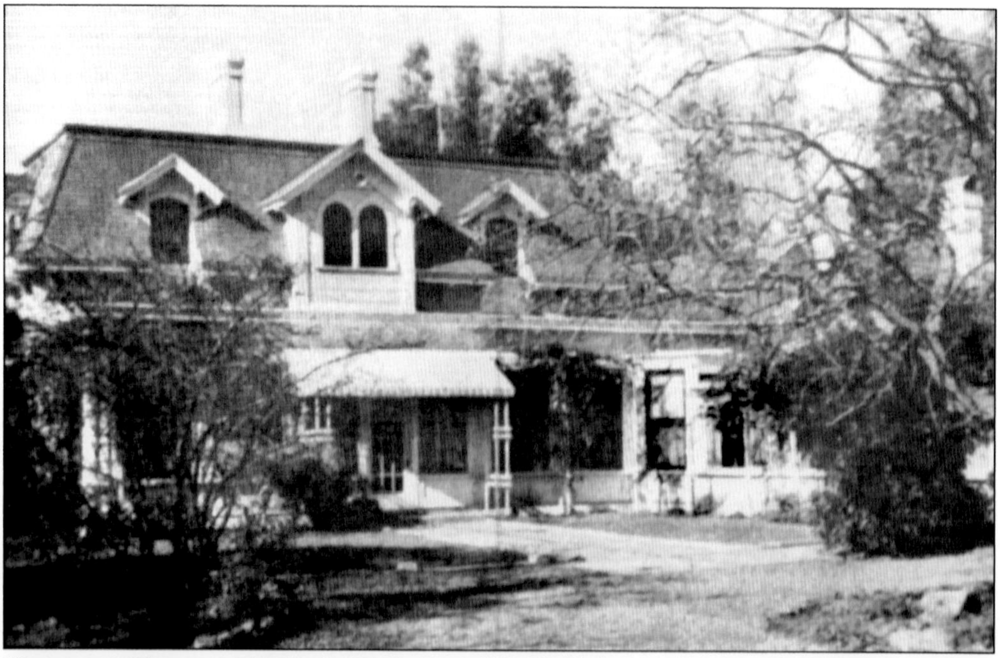

WATERMAN HOUSE, C. 1962. An early map of Fairfield shows a house at the corner of Jackson and Illinois Streets labeled, "Captain Waterman's House." This is the only visual clue of a possible site for the captain's first home in Fairfield. The *Solano Republican* noted in 1858 that Waterman "has contracted for an elegant mansion-house to be constructed to the design of a San Francisco Architect." Whether this is an earlier house or the house that Waterman constructed sometime before 1871 at Ten Gates Ranch remains unclear. Waterman House, as this house is still called today, is located on Ten Gate Road. It has undergone significant changes since Captain and Cordelia Waterman lived there. This photo, taken in 1962, shows the house before more recent remodeling.

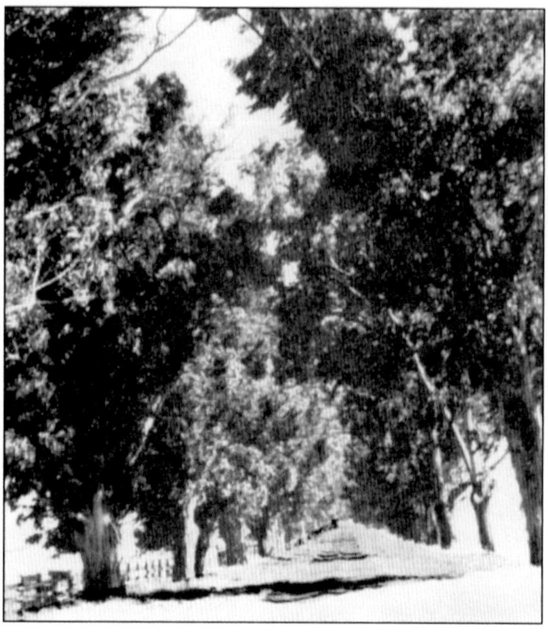

EUCALYPTUS AVENUE. Like many landowners at the time, Captain Waterman tried to improve his property by planting trees. Vacaville neighbor and friend Josiah Allison allegedly provided him with trees and advice. Besides Smyrna figs and white oak, he is credited with advising Waterman to plant eucalyptus trees imported from Australia to line the road to his house. A remnant of "Eucalyptus Avenue," leading to Waterman's home from the country road (now Waterman Boulevard), is still visible today.

Three

CREATING THE GOVERNMENT CENTER

COURTHOUSE SQUARE

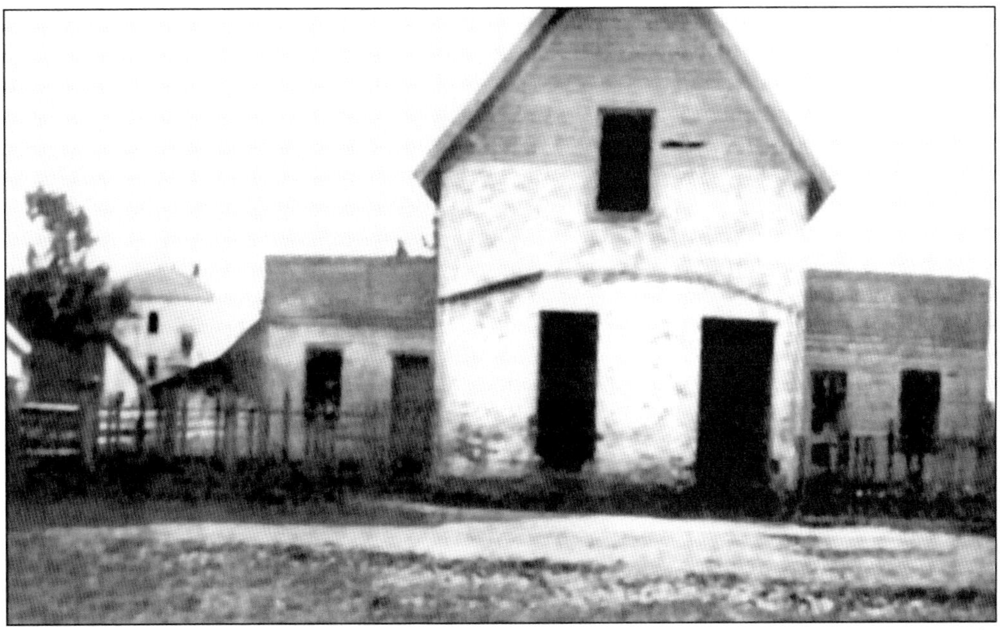

FAIRFIELD'S FIRST COURTHOUSE, 1858. After winning the vote on the county seat, Fairfield immediately went to work. The *Solano County Herald* announced on September 11, 1858, that Captain Waterman offered to build "a fine brick building" to house county offices and courtrooms. The building, constructed by builder A.P. Jackson, was to be finished in 30 days. This goal was reached even sooner. By October 2, the county clerk and county treasurer had already moved in. The county records were transported from Benicia. This is the only known photo of the first courthouse. Captain Waterman also rented additional buildings to the county. On October 1, 1858, the *Solano County Herald*, which until then had been published in Benicia, announced its move to Fairfield.

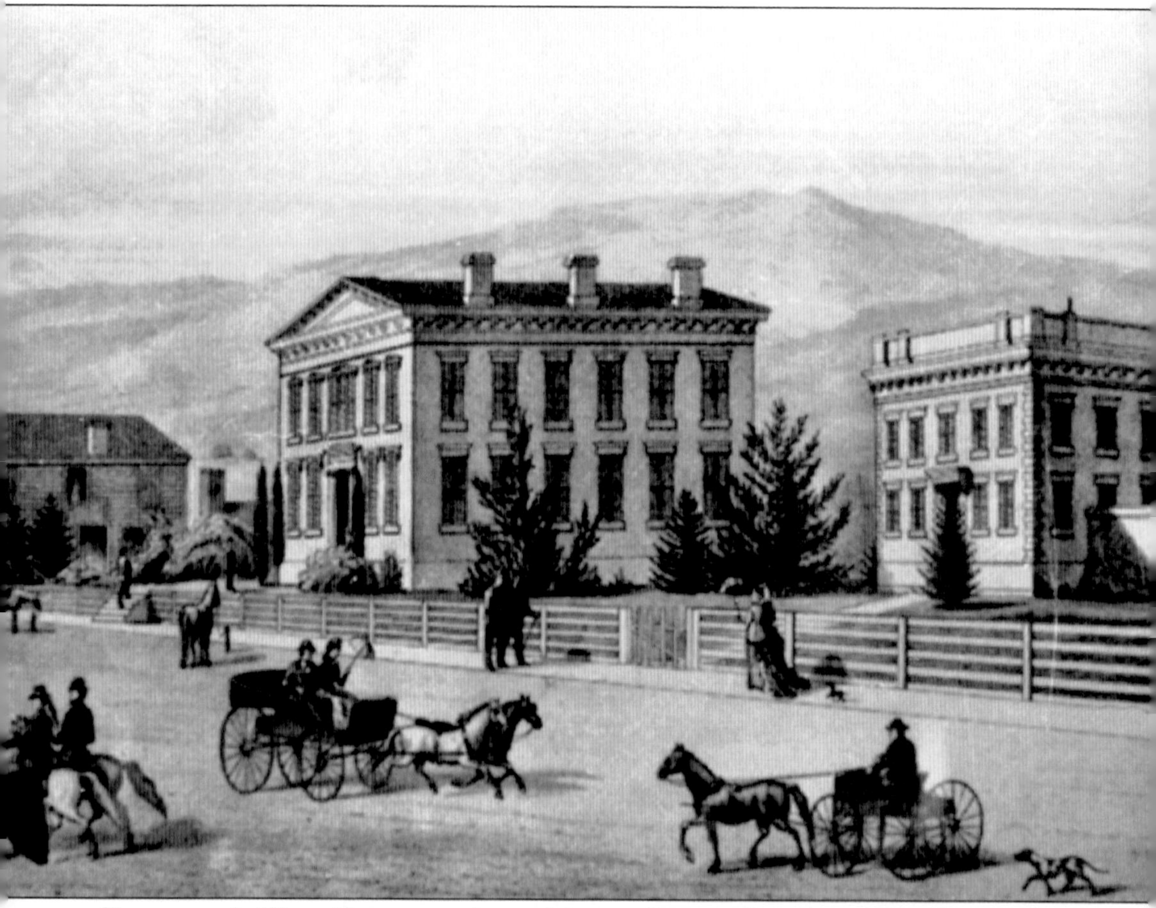

THOMPSON & WEST HISTORICAL ATLAS MAP OF SOLANO COUNTY, 1878. The courthouse quickly became too small for the county's business. The board of supervisors set aside $50 for architect's plans of a courthouse and jail. On January 21, 1859, a two-year tax of 50¢ on each $100 of assessed property was levied for the construction. On February 9, the board of supervisors accepted George Bordwell's plans for a courthouse and jail. On March 14 they reviewed the construction bids and accepted that of Larkin Richardson. At $24,400, it was the lowest bid by several thousand dollars. The new brick courthouse was completed by April 1860. Builders J.W. Pearce and Q.A. Hall were hired to move the old courthouse and place it in the new courthouse enclosure. The old building was repaired and re-plastered, and its offices were refitted and rented to lawyers at a monthly fee of $38.50. "Fairfield is a pretty little town of considerable promise, and possessing, as it does, the county buildings, there is considerable bustle to be observed during the sessions of the different courts," ran a description of the town in 1879. This spirit seems to be captured in this 1878 sketch of the new courthouse, with the relocated old courthouse on the left, and the county jail on the right.

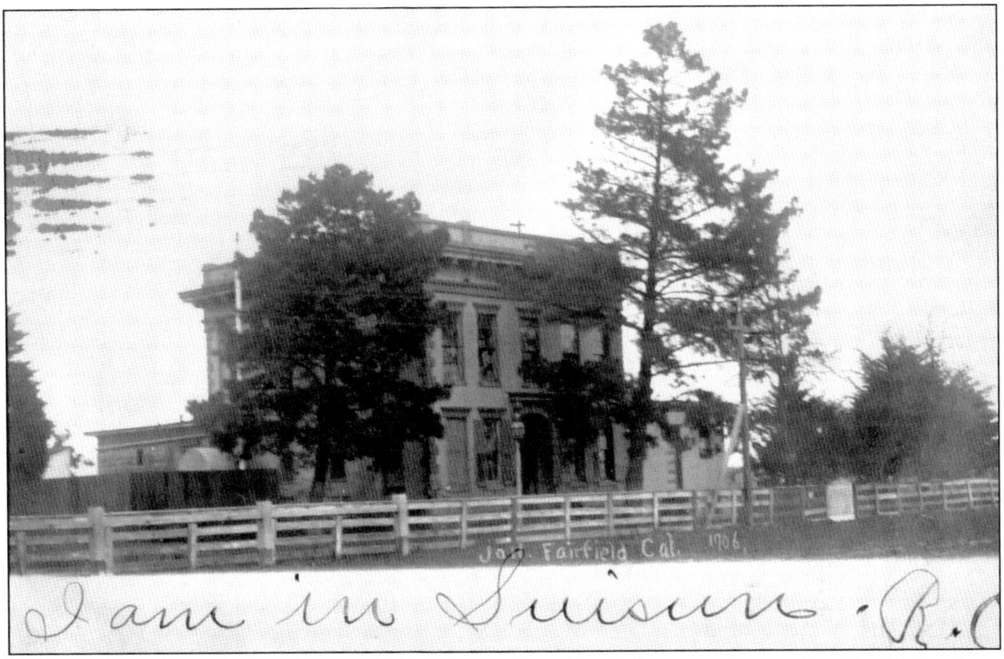

POSTCARD OF COURTHOUSE, 1906. On the right side of the courthouse, Larkin Richardson erected the county jail, which was finished in November 1859. With two stories, it was surrounded on the right side and the rear by a high wall. Immediately upon completion, prisoners were brought to Fairfield from their old detention facility in Benicia. Above, a 1906 postcard writer confuses this location with that of Suisun City.

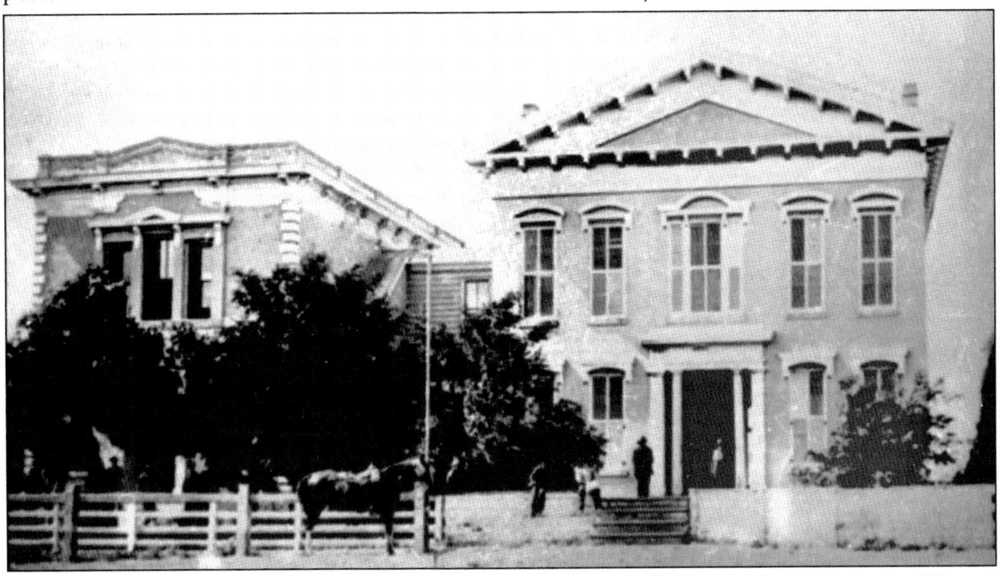

COURTHOUSE WITH BRIDGE. In 1878, the county issued a $15,000 bond to create the "Court-House Improvement Fund." This included construction of a hall of records, where county clerk and recorder's offices could be housed. Courthouse architect George Bordwell was once again selected and the building contract awarded to Richard and John McCann of San Francisco for the sum of $11,597. The building included a fireproof vault at the rear and was completed in November 1878. A steel bridge connected both buildings on the second floor.

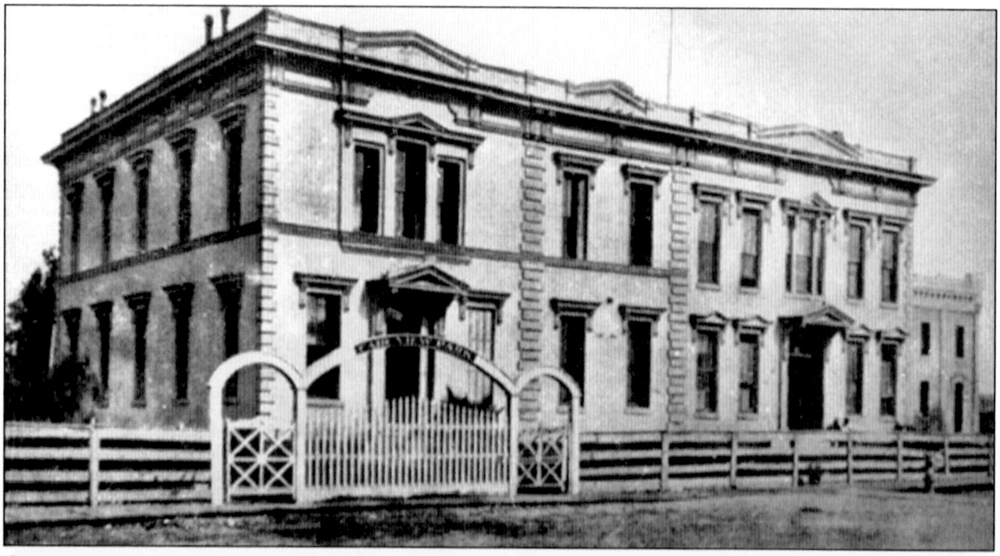

COURTHOUSE AND HALL OF RECORDS, 1887. Nine years later, in 1887, the space between the courthouse and hall of records was completely closed in. This created one continuous building, with the middle part echoing architectural features of the hall of records. The architect, J.M. Curtis, designed a brick addition costing $6,000. "While this will only make our courthouse a piece of patch work at best, it will be a great convenience to the officers, as some are so cramped in their present quarters that it is hardly possible for them to attend to their work." (*Solano Republican*, May 20, 1887). The perimeter fence remained, but the entrance gate, two gates framing a welcoming arch with the words "Fairfield Park," was moved to the left. The hitching posts for horses also remained in place.

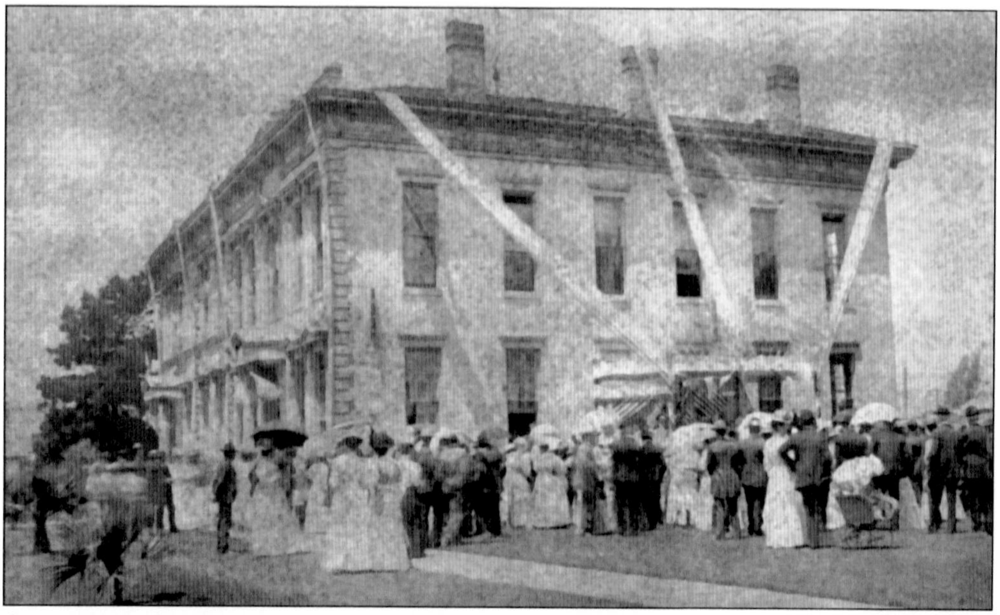

COURTHOUSE CELEBRATION, 1888. Fairfield citizens celebrated the new addition with a grand fete in the summer of 1888. Streamers from the roof to the ground decorated the building. Many of Fairfield's nearly 500 residents gathered to listen to speeches extolling the new government center.

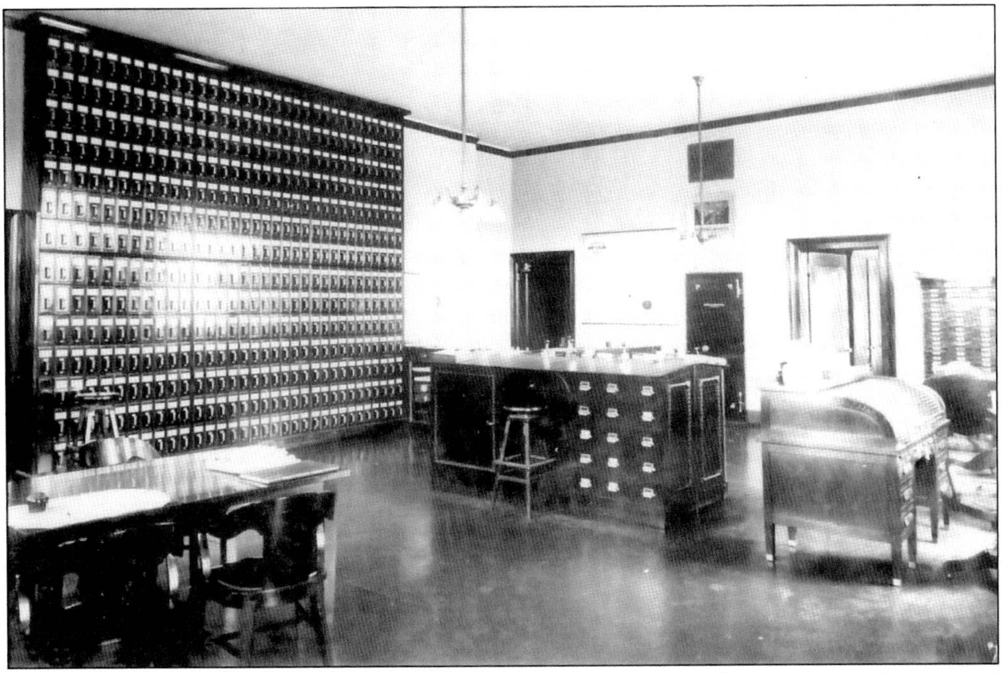

Recorder's Office. Solano County residents recorded their births, marriages, deaths, and property transactions at the recorder's office.

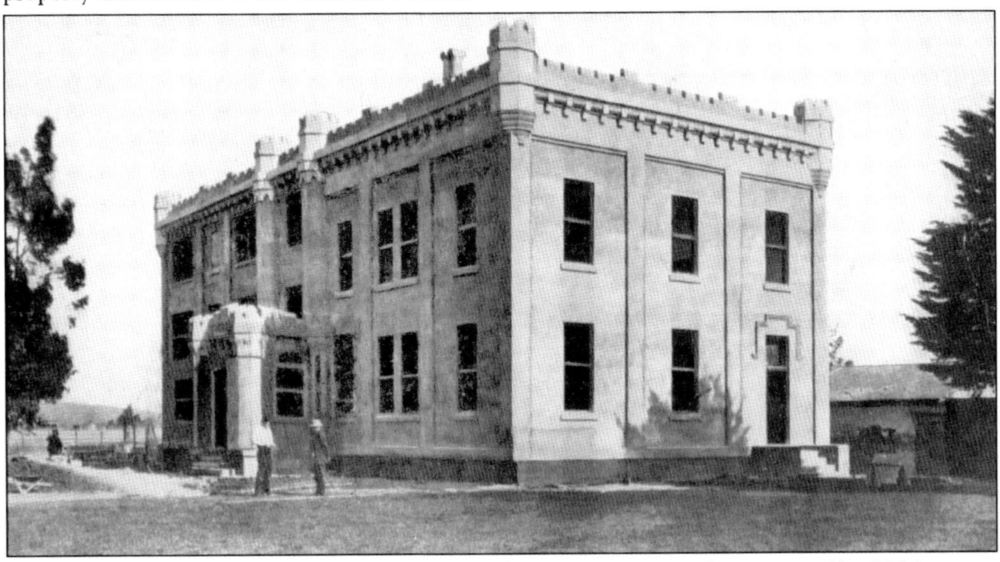

New County Jail, 1908. Growth also brought more crime to the county. By 1906, it was obvious that a larger jail was needed. On September 4, the board of supervisors awarded W.M. Concannon the contract for $35,136. The contract was later changed to describe a steel frame and concrete block structure, rather than a reinforced concrete building , which added another $10,984 to the cost. The Pauley Jail Company received a contract of $34,972 for the installation of steel cells. The new county jail was finished by February 1908. This Medieval-style jail reveled in a crenellated parapet and corbelled towers, made of galvanized iron, giving the appearance of a fortress—the original function of the castles of Europe. The following year, Concannon received an additional contract to install a jail kitchen and laundry for $5,774.

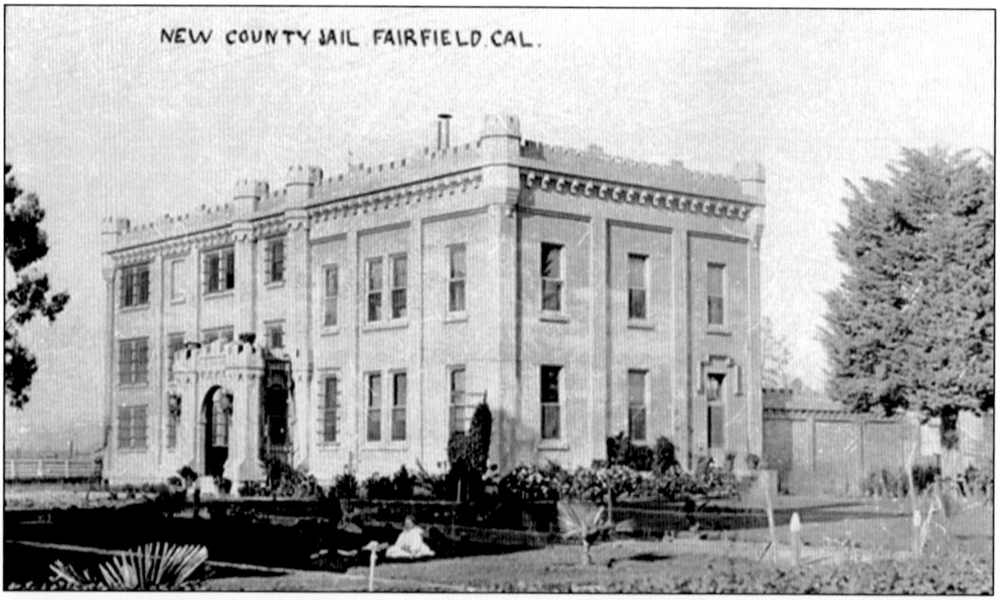

Flowers at the Jail. Within the next couple of years, a walled garden had been added. Formal landscaping followed. Around that time, the jail warden's young daughter posed for this formal photographic postcard. The jail's appearance would once again be altered at the end of World War II.

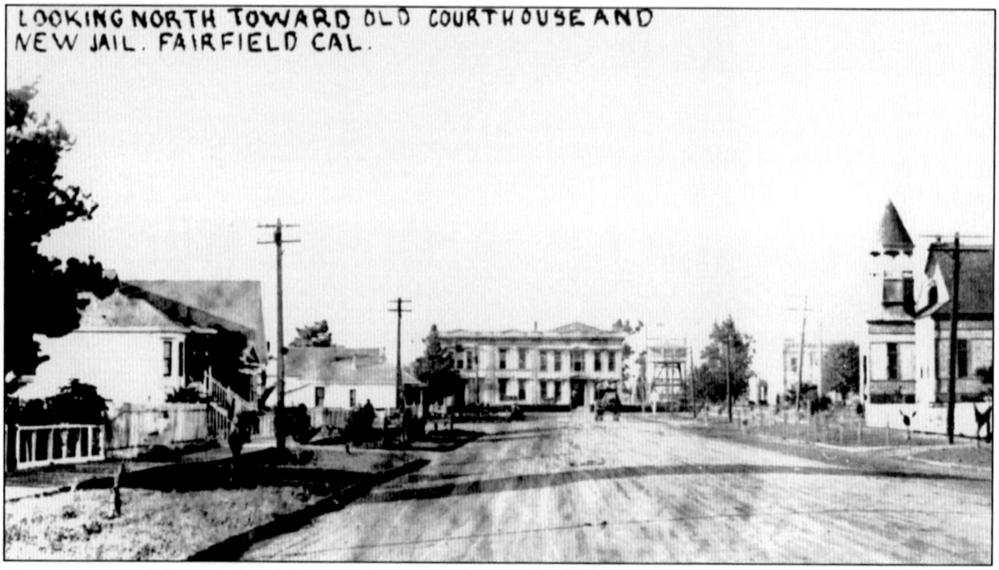

Courthouse View from Union Street. Around 1909, a visitor coming from Suisun down Union Street would have had this view of the courthouse complex. It included an elevated wooden water tank between the courthouse and jail. On the right side of Union Street is Armijo High School, built in 1894. Fairfield was incorporated as a city on December 12, 1903, which allowed the passage of bonds to grade streets and install sidewalks. The first improvements occurred mostly on Union and Texas Streets. The palm trees so characteristic of today's landscape have not yet appeared, but were planted a few years later. With its incorporation as a city, Fairfield moved into a new phase. In the following decades, the city would grow from a quiet, rural county seat to a bustling, expanding city.

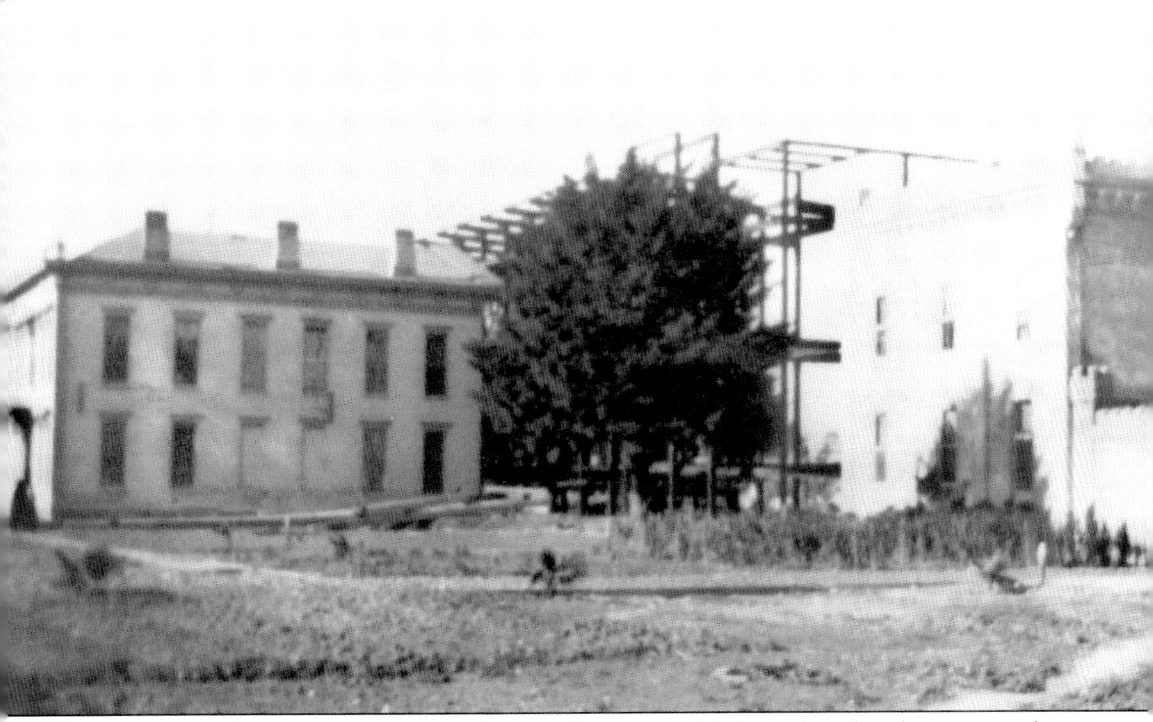

COURTHOUSE CONSTRUCTION, 1910–1911. The April 1892 earthquake damage to the courthouse had been quickly repaired, yet it became obvious by 1909 that the building had become dilapidated and unsafe. A $250,000 bond election was called in 1909. In April, supervisors visited several other county seats to study modern courthouse designs. County surveyor F.A. Steiger presented a preliminary sketch on May 18. In December, supervisors selected C. Hemmings and W.A. Jones as the architects. On June 10, 1910, they accepted the low bid of $209,000 by Thompson & Starret Company. Within weeks, construction began. The new building, a reinforced concrete structure faced with Raymond granite, was located just north of the old one. With the two buildings so close together, office furniture was moved across a wooden suspension bridge connecting the second stories of both buildings. The old building had to be razed before the steps of the new courthouse could be constructed. The wall on the right belongs to the jail and was constructed around 1910 or early 1911. The new courthouse was accepted as completed on December 4, 1911, although the supervisors acknowledged that the building had already been open to the public for over a month.

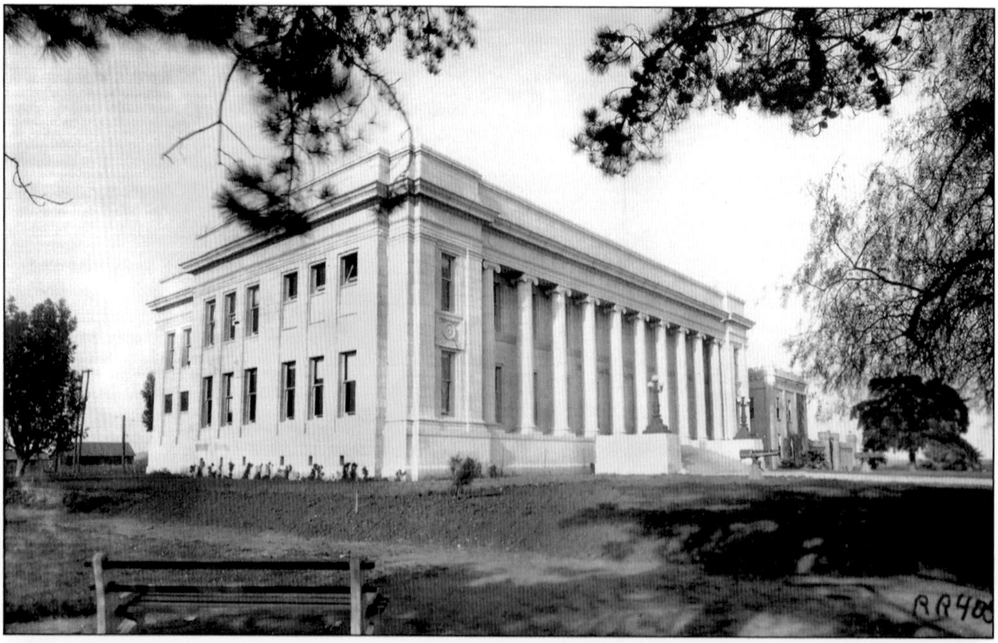

VIEW ALONG COURTHOUSE FACADES, 1911. This view of the courthouse dates to 1911. No landscaping has been installed yet. It shows the bare facades of the new building, with the new county jail at the far right.

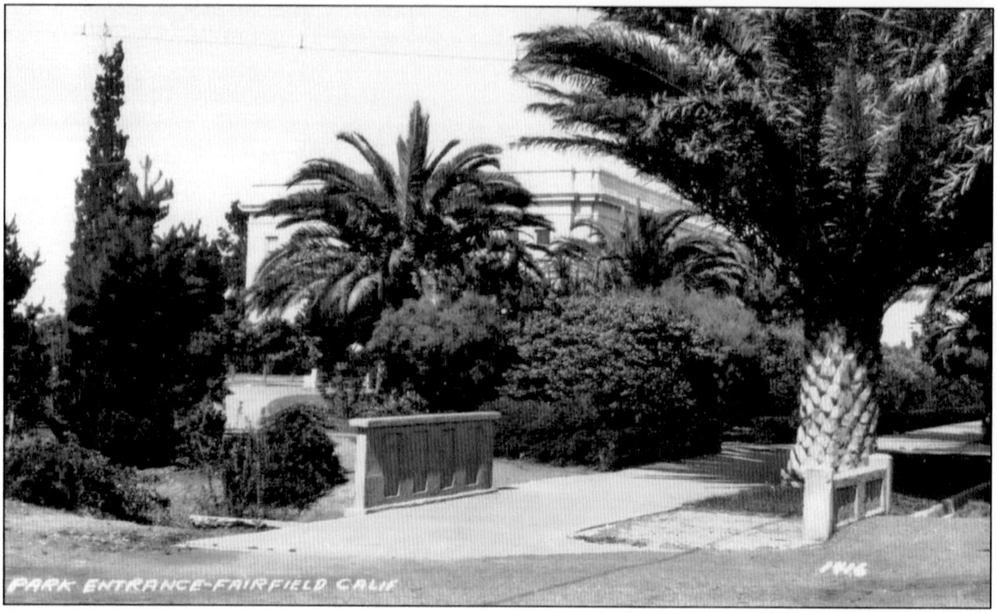

COURTHOUSE PARK ENTRANCE. In March 1912, P.B. Estrada was hired to lay out the courthouse grounds and create a small park on the west side. He received $150 per month. Finally on April 7, 1913, the supervisors directed that all the wooden fences be removed from the courthouse property, creating "a very presentable show place for the growing city of Fairfield." In 1924, the grounds were landscaped as planned by the McRorrie and Mclaren Company of San Francisco. Judging by the size of the palm trees, this photo shows the remodeled park in the late 1920s or early 1930s.

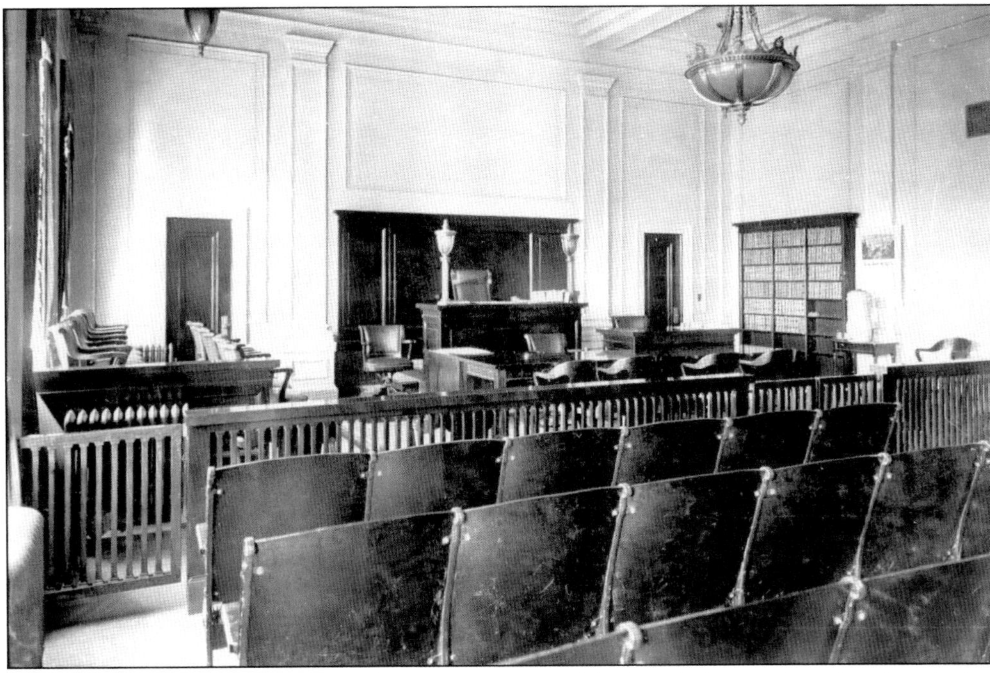

BOARD OF SUPERVISORS' CHAMBER. This is a rare shot of the board of supervisor chamber. Today, only the ornate ceiling and the door to the left of the stage remain in place.

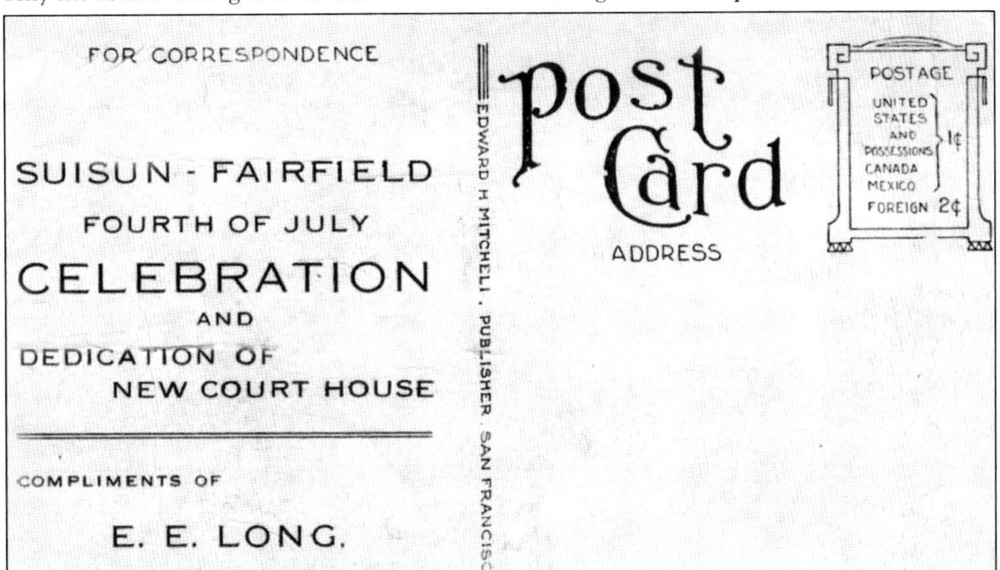

FOR CORRESPONDENCE

SUISUN - FAIRFIELD
FOURTH OF JULY
CELEBRATION
AND
DEDICATION OF
NEW COURT HOUSE

COMPLIMENTS OF
E. E. LONG.
ASSESSOR OF SOLANO COUNTY

EDWARD H MITCHELL . PUBLISHER . SAN FRANCISCO

Post Card

ADDRESS

POSTAGE
UNITED STATES AND POSSESSIONS CANADA MEXICO 1¢
FOREIGN 2¢

INVITATION TO DEDICATION CEREMONY, JULY 4, 1914. In December 1911, the *Solano Republican* wistfully remarked, "no ceremony of any kind marked the occupancy of the big building." Residents had to wait until July 4, 1914, when the grand dedication ceremony celebrating the new courthouse finally took place. Postcards were sent out inviting dignitaries and residents to participate in the event.

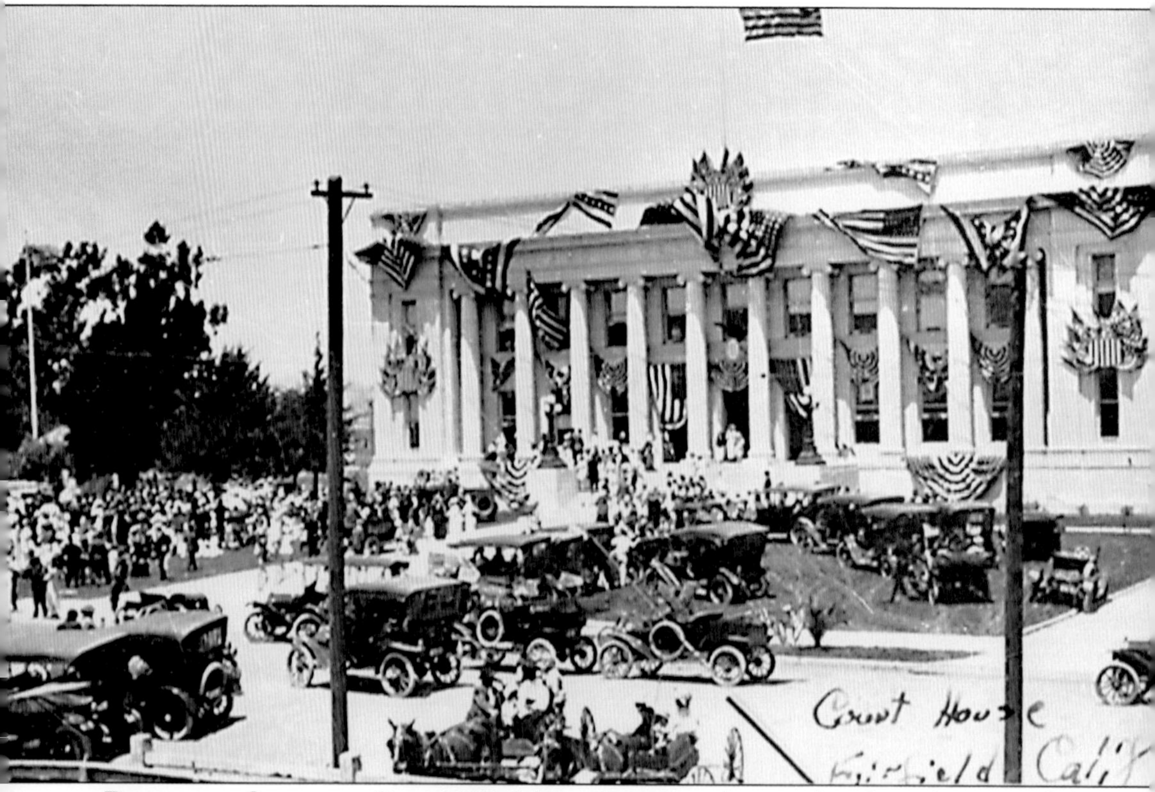

Dedication Ceremony. Over 6,000 Solano County residents gathered on the steps of the new courthouse on July 4, 1914, to celebrate the dedication of the courthouse with the biggest event the county had ever seen. California State Highway Commissioner Honorable C.F. Stern, was the featured orator, accompanied by Senator B.F. Rush, owner of Rush Ranch, and the Liberty Goddess, Miss Della Sherburne of the Wednesday Club. The day's events included a parade with floats, three local brass bands, and a fife and drum corps. A dance pavilion allowed afternoon dancing and hosted one of two formal evening balls. There was a "Horribles" contest, where townsfolk competed to have the most horrible costume, followed by a band concert and Japanese fireworks. Sports events included track and field and a motor boat race in Suisun's new deep harbor. The highlight was a two-day rodeo organized by Lewis Pierce. The whole dedication ceremony, sponsored by Fairfield and Suisun residents, businesses, and the board of supervisors, cost nearly $6,000.

VICTORIA. The winged statue of the goddess Victoria was added in on January 5, 1920, to commemorate Solano County's fallen soldiers of World War 1. Their names are listed on the pedestal. In recent years, large granite panels have been added next to the courthouse staircase, listing the names of those fallen in all recent wars.

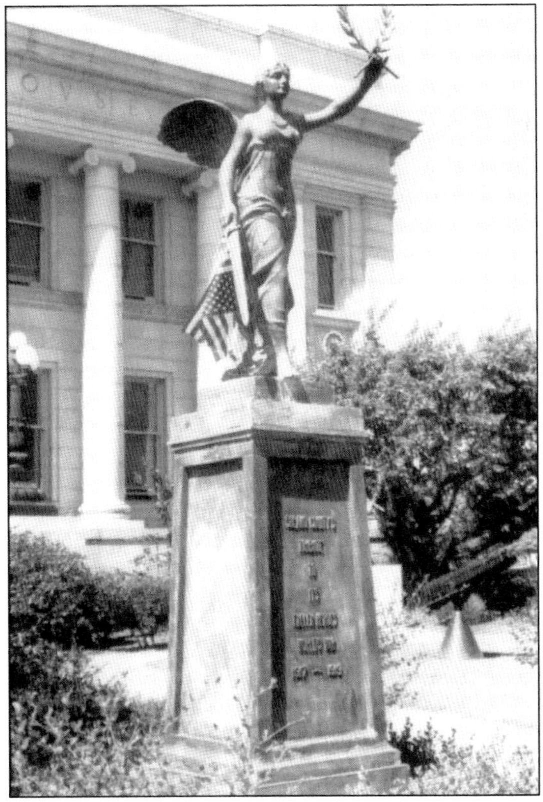

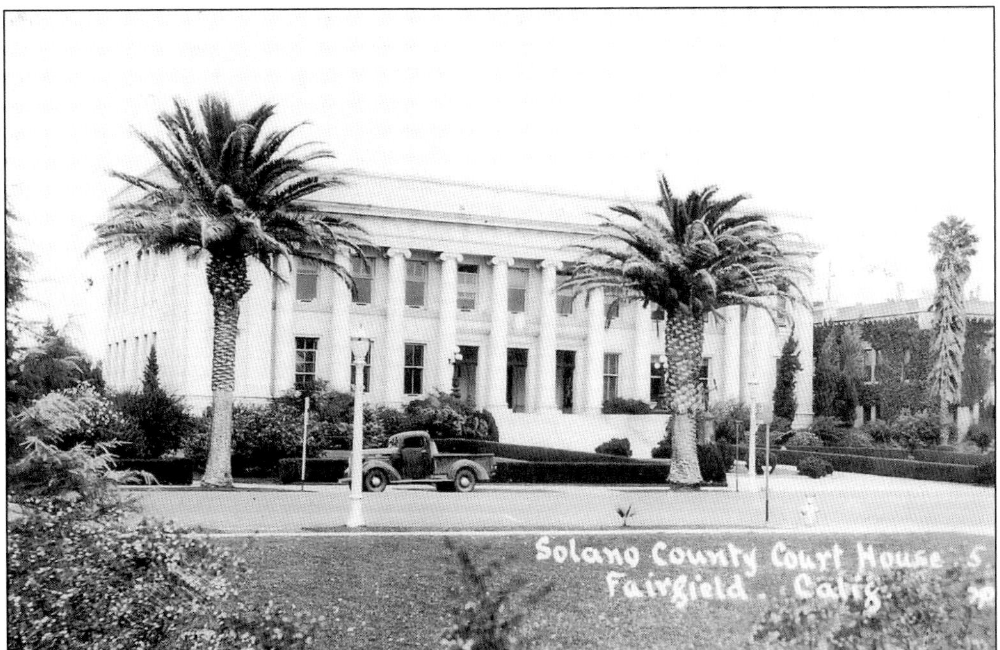

COURTHOUSE, 1930S. This postcard shows the courthouse and county jail complex in the 1930s. By then, the signature palm trees had been planted along Union and Texas Street.

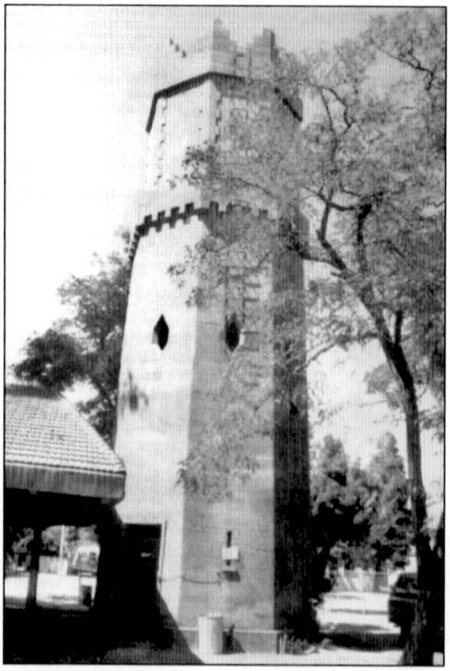

Water Tower. Both courthouse and county jail had to rely on well water and a water tank until 1932. The construction of the new courthouse in 1911 forced the tank's relocation nearby, likely on Empire Street. In February 1919, the board of supervisors accepted plans by county surveyor Frank Alexander Steiger for a 50-foot octagonal county water tower. Steiger's bridges and building plans throughout the county, including the courthouse, are testimony to his confidence in reinforced concrete as a building material. Olof Olson built the reinforced concrete tower for the sum of $2,264. Its crenellated parapet copied similar architectural elements on the county jail. After a successful bond measure in 1931, the City of Fairfield overhauled its water system, including a new, deep well and a stainless steel water tank, which provided water for the county civic complex. Today, the water tower is the beloved last reminder of Fairfield's first jail complex.

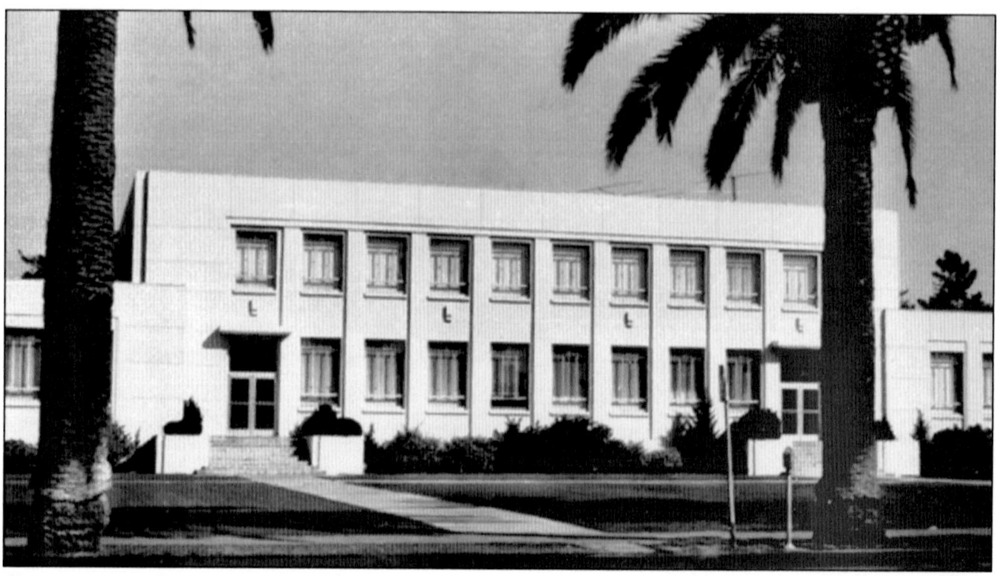

Courthouse Annex, 1948. The growing number of county businesses needed more room, resulting in this 1948 annex. It housed the recorder's office, auditors, and other county offices.

Four

Completing the Government Center

High School and Library

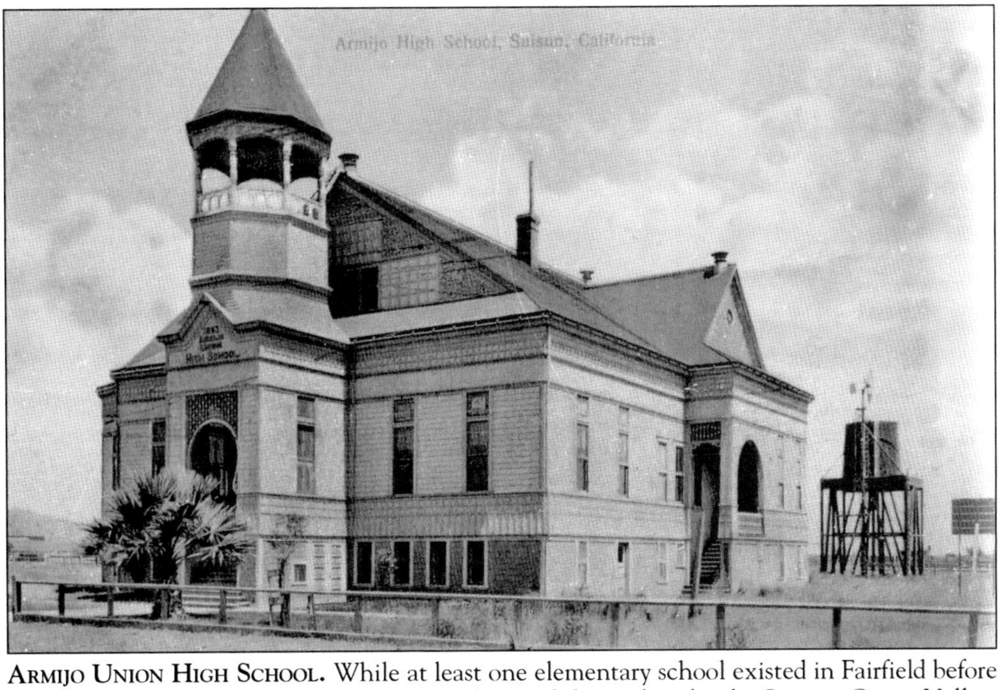

Armijo Union High School. While at least one elementary school existed in Fairfield before 1866, no photograph has been preserved of any of the early schools. Suisun, Green Valley, and other surrounding settlements all had their own schools. Pioneer residents also sent their children to excellent private schools in Benicia and Vacaville. By the 1890s, resident numbers had grown enough to create the need for a local high school. The first Armijo Union High School was installed on the second floor of Crystal School in Suisun in 1891. New construction began on the east side of Union Avenue during the school year of 1893–1894. It was a rambling Queen Anne–style, wooden structure. A wooden tank supplied the school with water. This school served Fairfield, Suisun, and the surrounding valleys until 1913–1914, when the new Armijo High School was built. Although by then the high school was clearly situated within Fairfield's limits, this postcard still cites Suisun as its location.

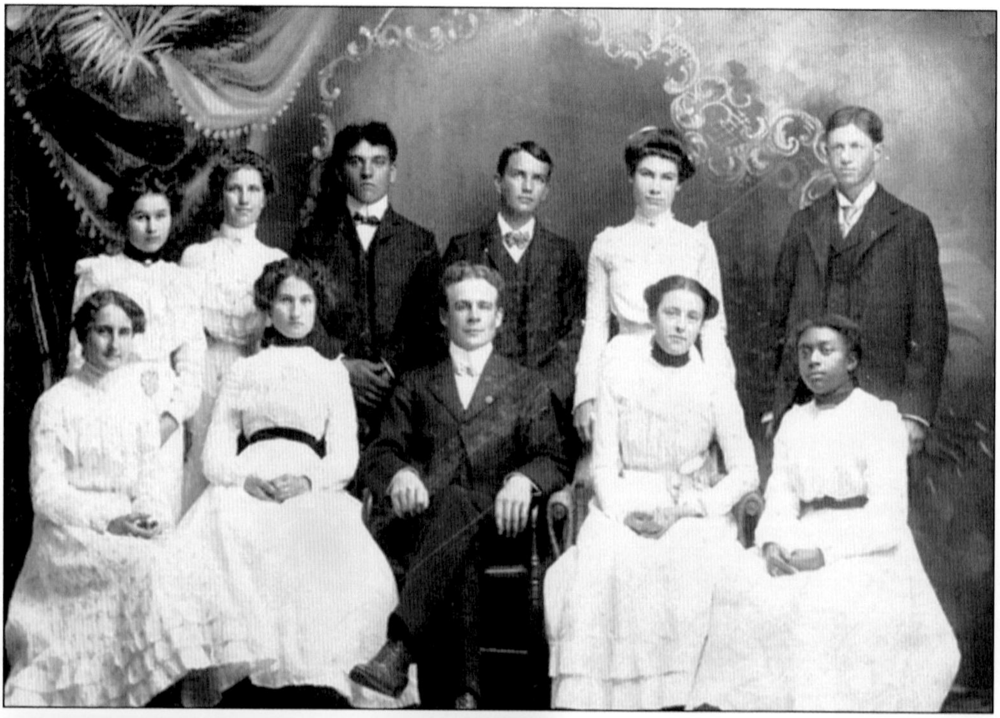

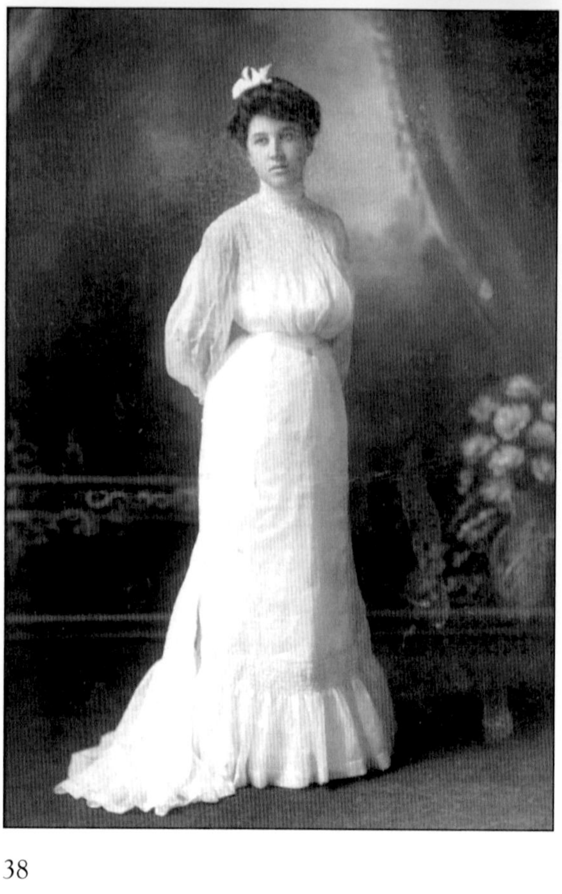

ARMIJO HIGH CLASS OF 1901. This photo shows the first high school graduating class of the 20th century. In the front row, from left to right, are Della Carpenter, Guy Carpenter Bennett, Will C. Wood, Lola Gray Stewart, and Elizabeth Scott. Standing in the back, from left to right, are Elizabeth Eager, Agnes Kerr, Joe Serpas, William Battersby, Lena Henderson, and John Lambert. World War II brought the first real influx of African-American families to Fairfield.

CLARA ARMSTRONG. Graduation photos were as important then as they are now. Here, Clara Armstrong poses for her graduation portrait in 1901.

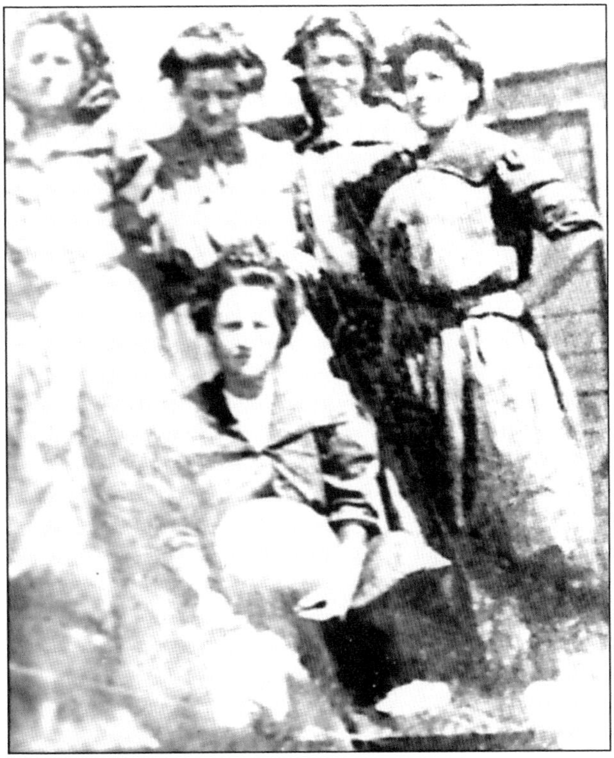

WOMEN'S BASKETBALL TEAM. At the turn of the 20th century, women began to revolt against tight corsets and confining clothing. One of the results was a strong emphasis on sports. Here, Armijo's women basketball team poses in the early 1900s.

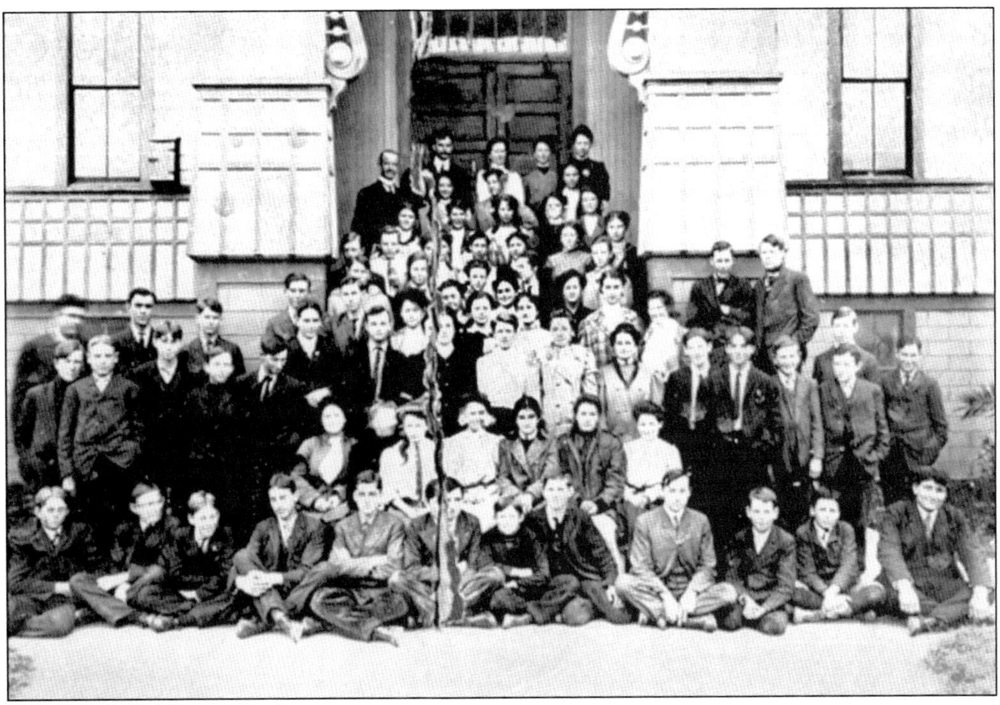

ARMIJO HIGH CLASS OF 1907. Most of the students in this class photograph remain unidentified. The top row, from left to right, includes "Oh Boy" Firehammer, Professor Sheldon, Mary Stewart, and Elsie Wood Hall.

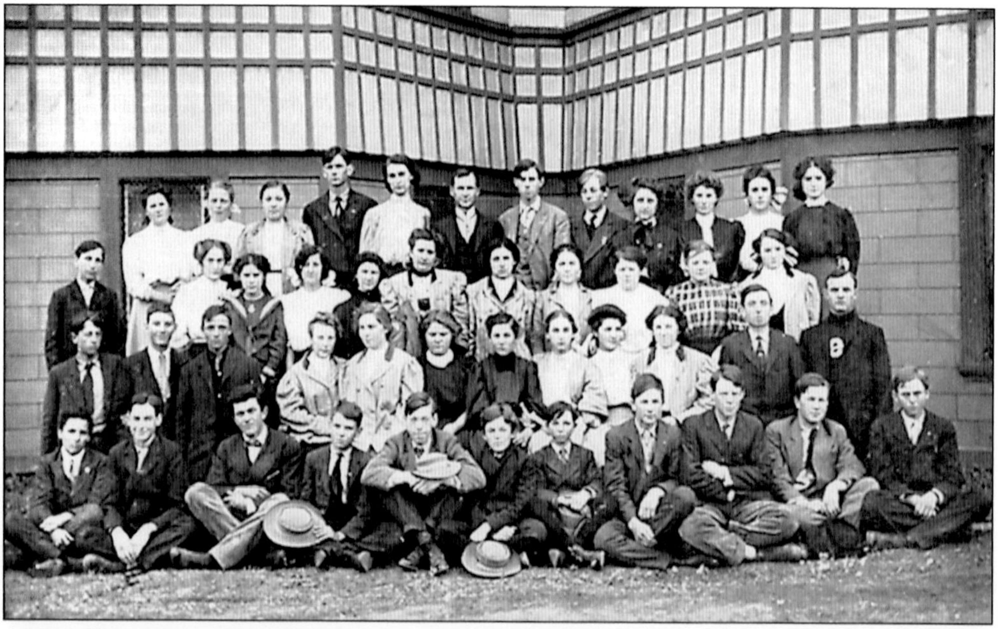

ARMIJO HIGH CLASS OF 1908. These graduates, from left to right, are (front row) Mark Haines, Walter Woods, Harry Mortinsen, Hiram Rush, Phil Saunders, Gilmer Whitby, Ralph Mason, Lester Dickson, Bob Wood, Al Gregory, and Harry Nelson; (second row) Elmer Burrell, Walter Peabody, Andrew Smith, Blanche Glashoff, Audrey Cooper, Janet Smith, Mabel Morrill McDermitt, Carrie Joys ?, Anita Joys ?, Amelia Glashoff, Jack Lynch, and Bob Peabody; (third row) Walter Parker, Esther Eager, Pearl Lambert Wright, Sylvia King, Marie Hyatt, Mary Silverman, Clara Joyce Hopkins, Grace ?, Clementine Lenahav ?, Hazel Fields, and unidentified; (back row) Madge Service Jackson, Delia Taylor, Marcia Smith, Lewis Morrell, Carol Davisson, Professor Dyer, Asa Scarlett, Frank Rutherford, Mary Williams Taylor, Marie Glashoff, Peabody ?, and Ruth Manager.

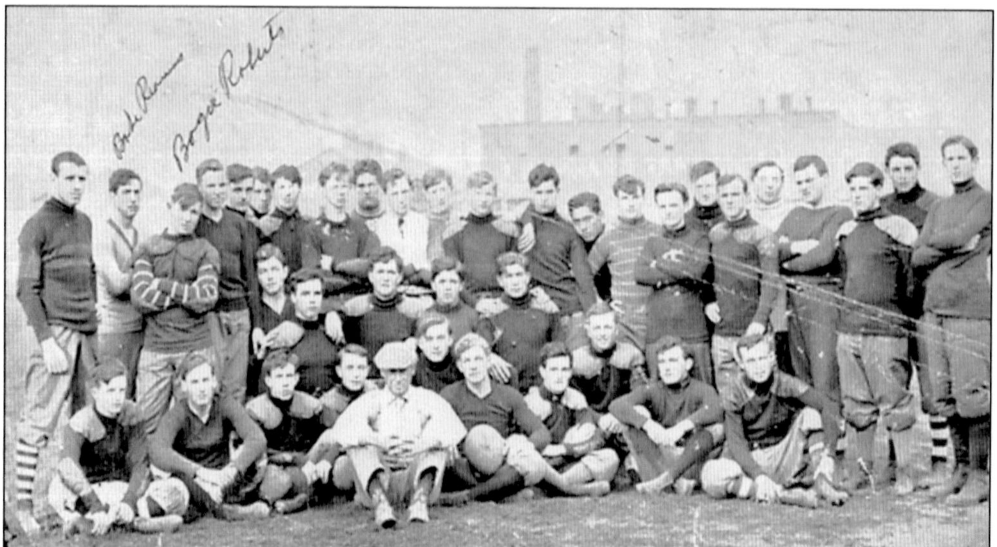

VARSITY RUGBY TEAM, 1936. Only two of the rugby players are identified: Babe Reams and Bogie Roberts.

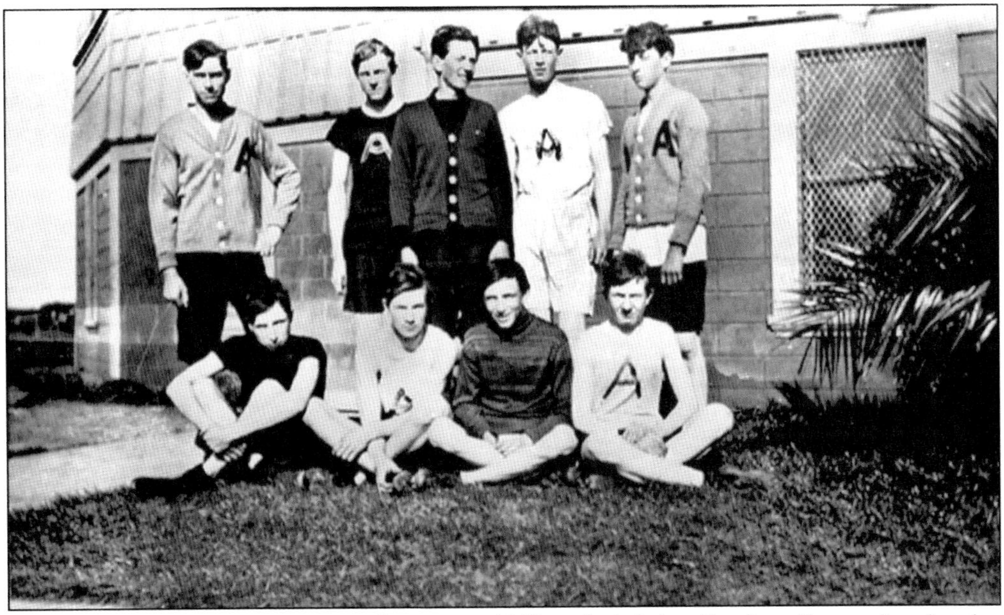

Track Team, 1908. Armijo's track team in 1908 included Asa Scarlett, Everett Lambrecht, Oswald Glynn, Elmer Burrell, John Lynch, Lester Dickson, Walter Parker, and Don Schulds.

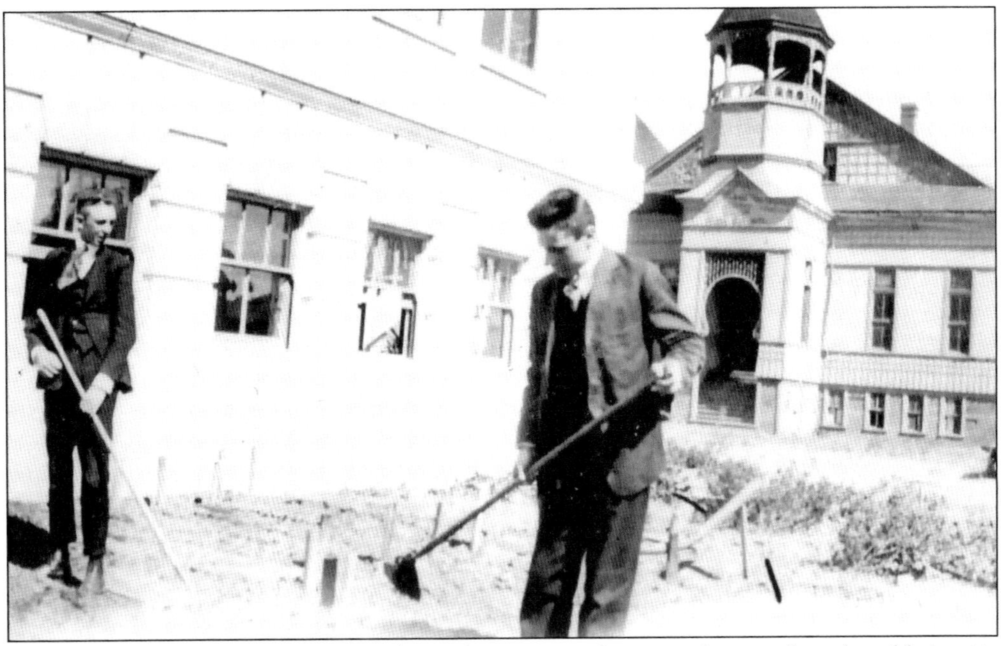

Old and New Armijo High. By the early 1900s, it became obvious that the old Armijo High School was too small to accommodate the growing number of students. In 1913, after a successful bond election raised $70,000, San Francisco architect Henry C. Smith began with the construction of the new school building directly in front and to the left side of the old Queen Anne–style structure. The new Armijo High School was officially finished in August of 1914. These two young students are cleaning up around the new school in preparation for the installation of landscaping. The old Armijo High School was eventually torn down.

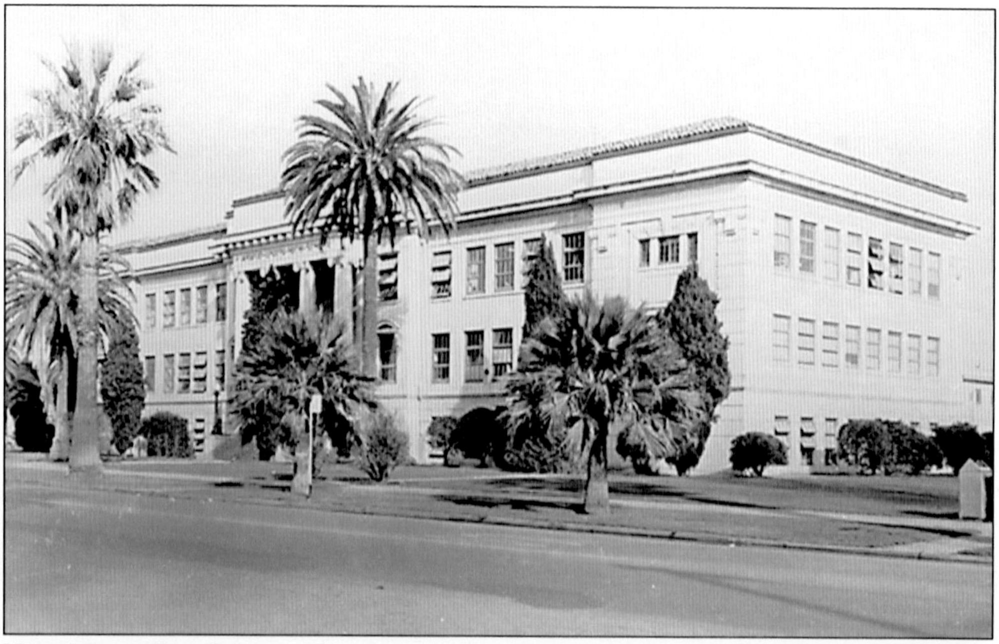

New Armijo High School. This imposing neoclassical building quotes architectural elements of the courthouse, tying the two buildings together visually and creating a strong, unified look. Armijo High School boasted 16,000 square feet over two floors with classrooms, an auditorium in the basement, a gymnasium, study hall, physics and chemistry laboratories, and other modern amenities. Construction ran to $85,000. For a few years after it opened, the marbled entrance steps posed quite a problem for fashion conscious female students in their tight hobble skirts. The building was extensively remodeled in the 1970s and serves today as the Solano County Hall of Justice.

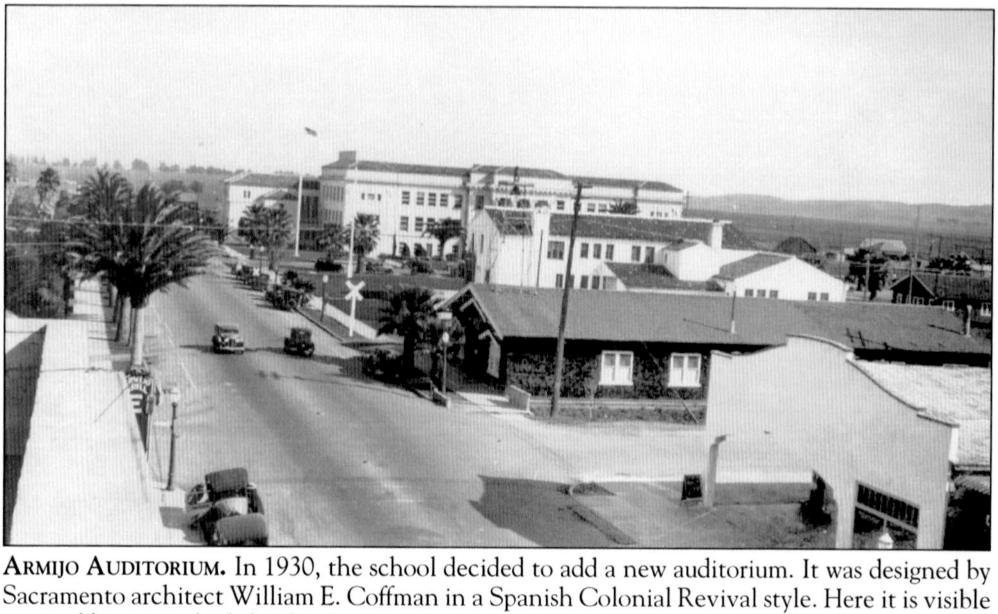

Armijo Auditorium. In 1930, the school decided to add a new auditorium. It was designed by Sacramento architect William E. Coffman in a Spanish Colonial Revival style. Here it is visible as an addition on the left side of Armijo High School, fronting Texas Street. By the late 1970s, its condition had so deteriorated that it was torn down, despite much public opposition.

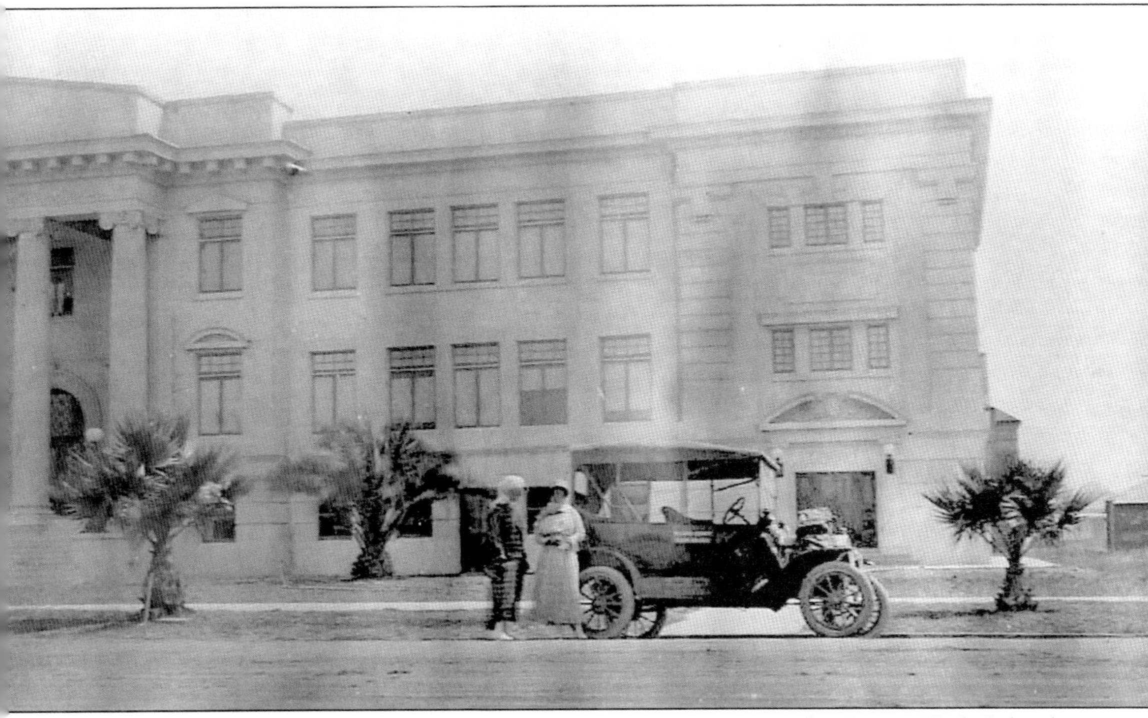

SOLANO COUNTY FREE LIBRARY IN ARMIJO HIGH SCHOOL, C. 1914. The Armijo High School also housed the Solano County Free Library. Founded in 1914 in response to the California Free Library Law of 1911, the Solano County Free Library offered residents the opportunity to obtain books. Its facility was housed in the county superintendent's office until January 1915, when the move into the new facility was accomplished with wheelbarrows. The library functioned as the county headquarters, the Fairfield Library branch, and the Armijo High School library. Until 1929, librarian Clara Dills directed its operations. Independent from the school, with its own entrance, the library had to reimburse the school for electricity. Heat, on the other hand, was provided by the school—but not on Saturdays, after school hours, or during vacation. This 1914 photo shows the right side of the school where the library was located on the second floor. The palm trees along Union and Texas Street had just been planted. The first Armijo High School building is still visible in the rear.

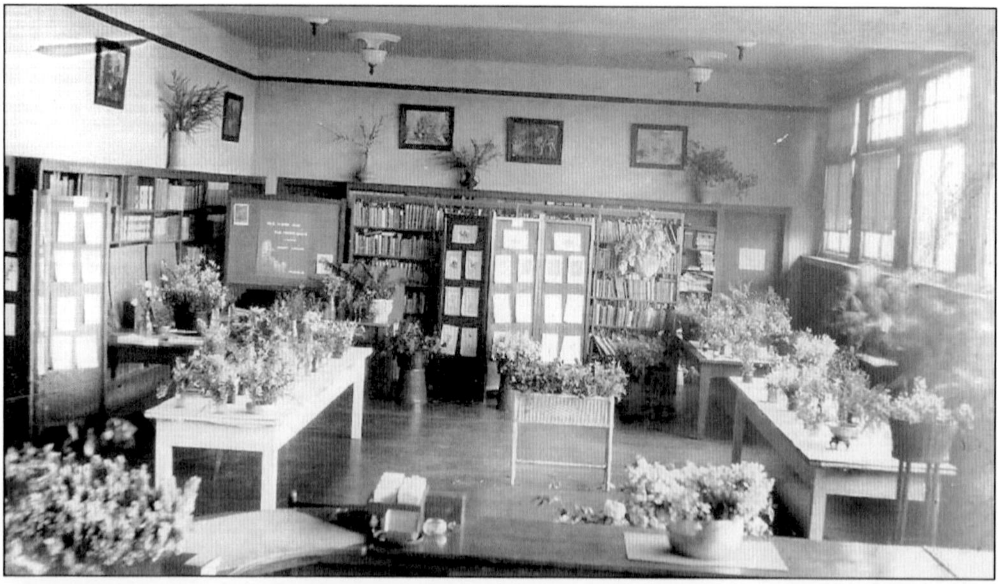

First Annual Wildflower Show at Library. The annual Wildflower Show, shown here for the first time in March 1925, took place under the guidance of Professor Willis Jepson, the well-known California botanist and Vacaville native. It became a popular annual event. Schoolchildren collected local wild flowers, classified them, and then had their work judged, photographed, painted, and exhibited at the library.

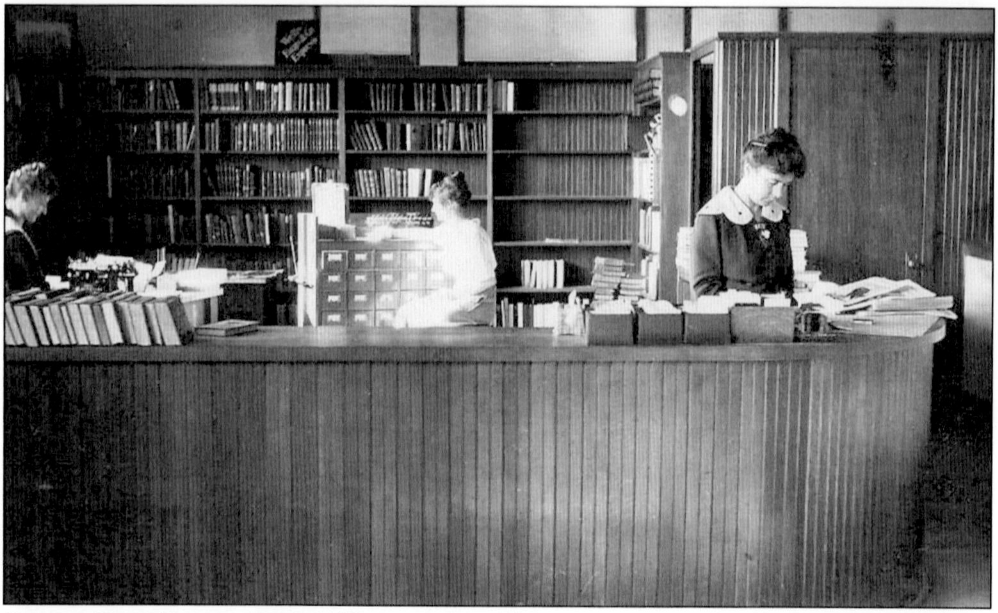

County Fair, Dixon, 1916. Public awareness of the importance of local agriculture increased with the Panama Pacific International Exposition in San Francisco in 1915. Clara Dills and her staff had prepared and exhibited a cabinet full of agricultural books for Solano County's booth. While visitors learned about Solano's agriculture, they also discovered the new county library. Buoyed by that exposure, staff installed a complete mini-library display the following year at the Dixon May Fair.

ANNA KYLE. In 1921, the county appointed music teacher Anna Kyle as the rural music supervisor. The library already housed and collaborated with the University of California at Davis farm advisor and the county home demonstration agent. Now the "Solano County Triplets," as the three representatives were nicknamed, together with Clara Dills, traveled throughout the county visiting schools, clubs, and other organizations.

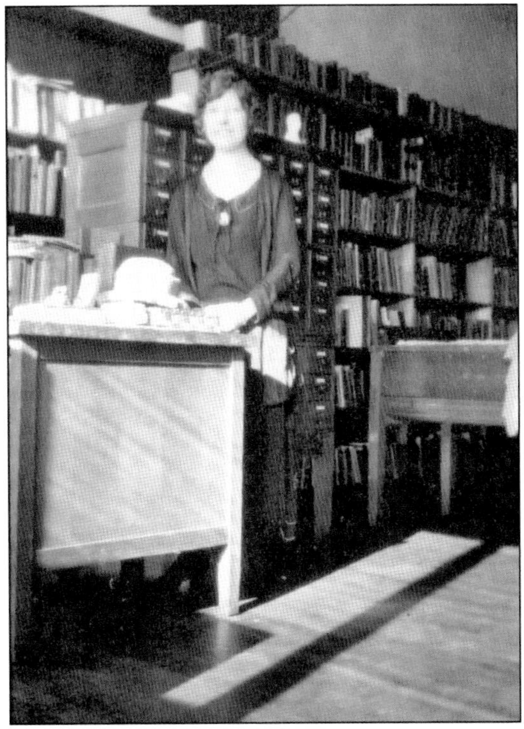

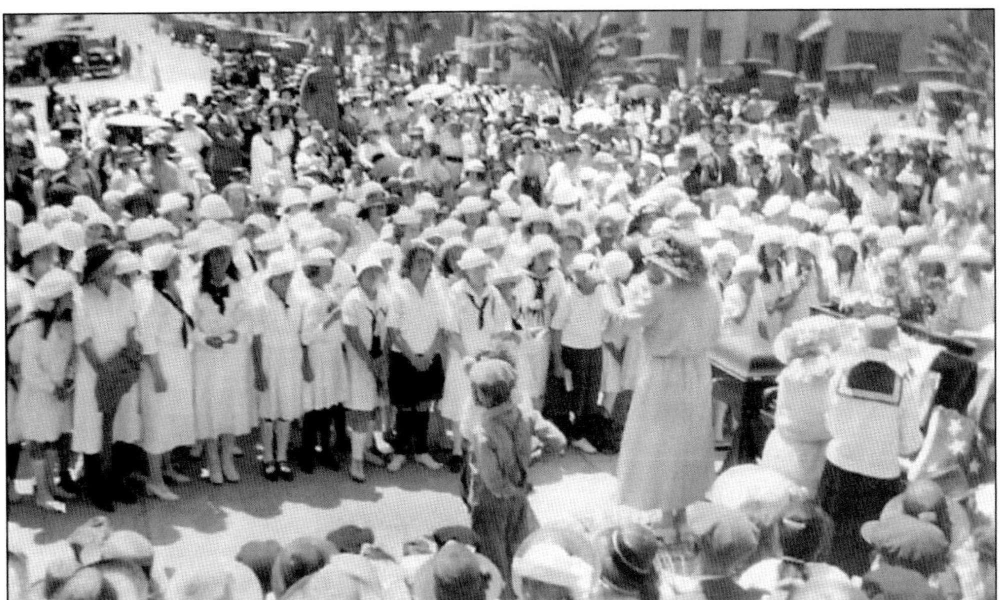

FAIRFIELD PLAY DAY. On May 5, 1922, Solano County supervisor of music Anna Kyle organized the first children's play day in Fairfield. Called the "County School Day," it involved children from all grammar schools throughout the county. Over 2,000 children, parents, and teachers assembled in front of the courthouse. In the morning, the children gathered in a chorus to sing songs, accompanied by three pianos. They danced folk dances, performed calisthenics in the afternoon, watched a health play, and played competitive games, one school against the other.

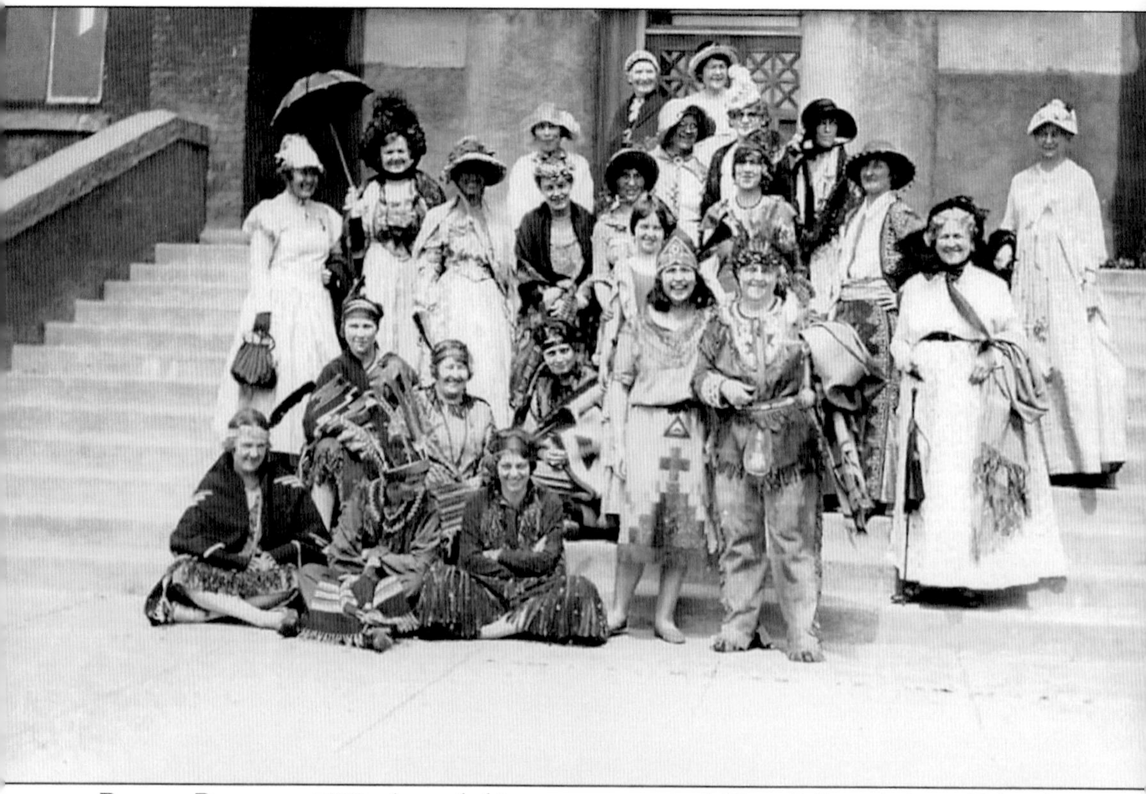

Benicia Pageant, 1923. A much bigger event awaited Clara Dills and Anna Kyle when, backed by Suisun's Wednesday Club, they chaired the 1923 Solano County Historical Pageant. This historical extravaganza in Benicia involved many actors, including hundreds of school children. Together they staged nine scripted scenes from the county's history. Each city in the county presented one of these scenes. Preparations occupied school clubs and women's clubs throughout the county for months. Jean Davis of the Armijo High School Department wrote the text for the pageant. Douglas Wright composed appropriate music. Members of the Wednesday Club reenacted native Patwin stories and a tule dance. The Wednesday Club, an important local women's service organization, was founded in 1911 and is still in existence today. More than 10,000 visitors attended the spectacle. This photo shows some Wednesday Club members posing in colorful costumes on the steps of the Benicia Capitol.

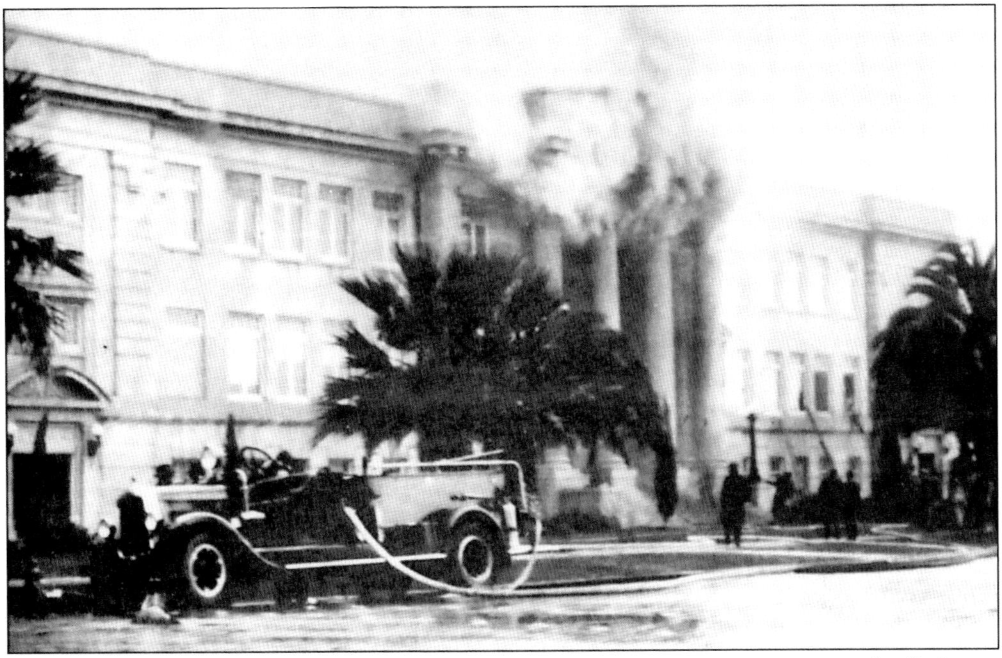

The Library Burns. By 1929, the library was outgrowing its one-room operation and talks began about construction of a new home. On Sunday afternoon, December 8, 1929, a fire broke out in the school. Student athletes and their teachers, practicing for a marathon, discovered the fire. Within 40 seconds of sounding the alarm, Fire Chief Matt Knolty and his men were on the scene. Unfortunately the fire already was burning too hot for them to bring it under control. In addition their ladders proved too short to reach the upper story. Despite additional help from the Napa and Vacaville fire departments, the interior of the building was completely destroyed.

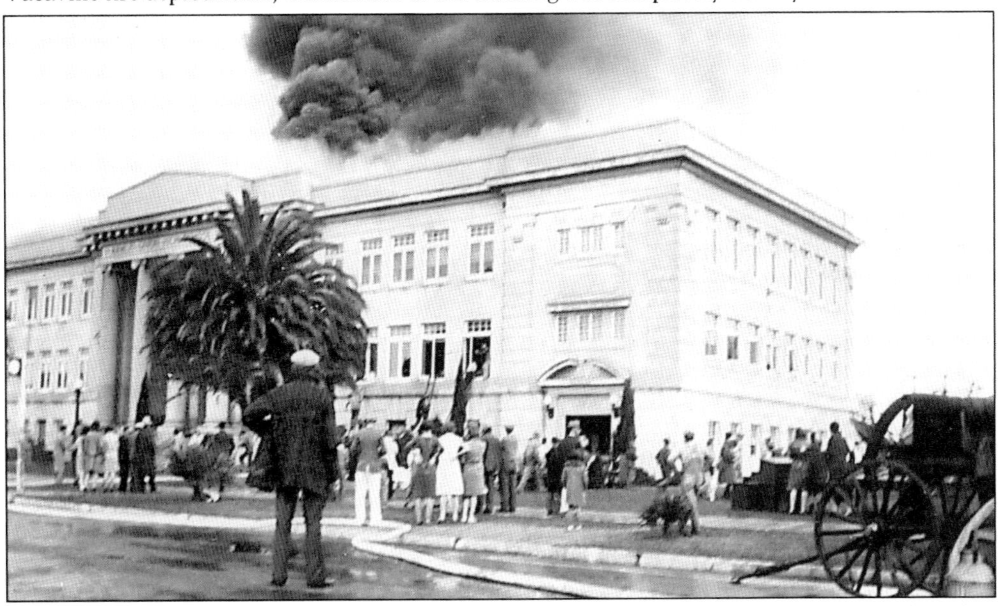

Burning Library. Word spread quickly throughout the community and people gathered to help. Books and catalog drawers were handed through the windows. Police cars with blaring sirens escorted librarian Clara Dills from her home in Oakland to Fairfield.

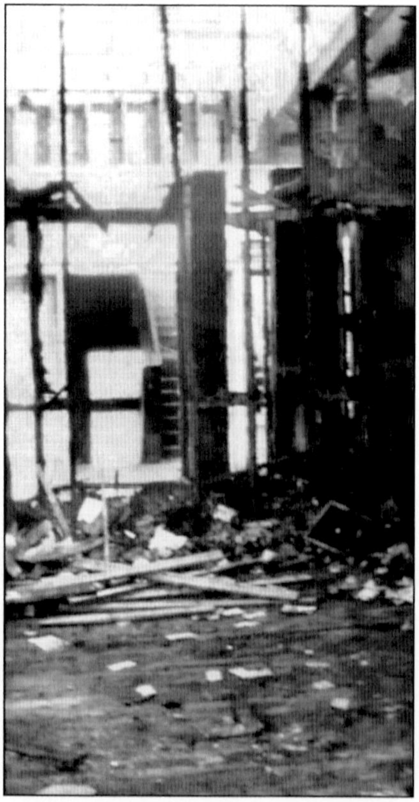

INTERIOR VIEW OF BURNT LIBRARY. Damage to Armijo High School was estimated at more than $200,000. The library loss totaled more than $150,00, of which the insurance only carried $15,000. In all, 22,047 books were destroyed. "The days of salvaging that followed are sad ones," Clara Dills wrote later. "Jagged walls, charred openings where doors had been, cracked ceilings, sagging book shelves, muddy pools . . . and everything dripped, dripped, dripped in the softly falling rain."

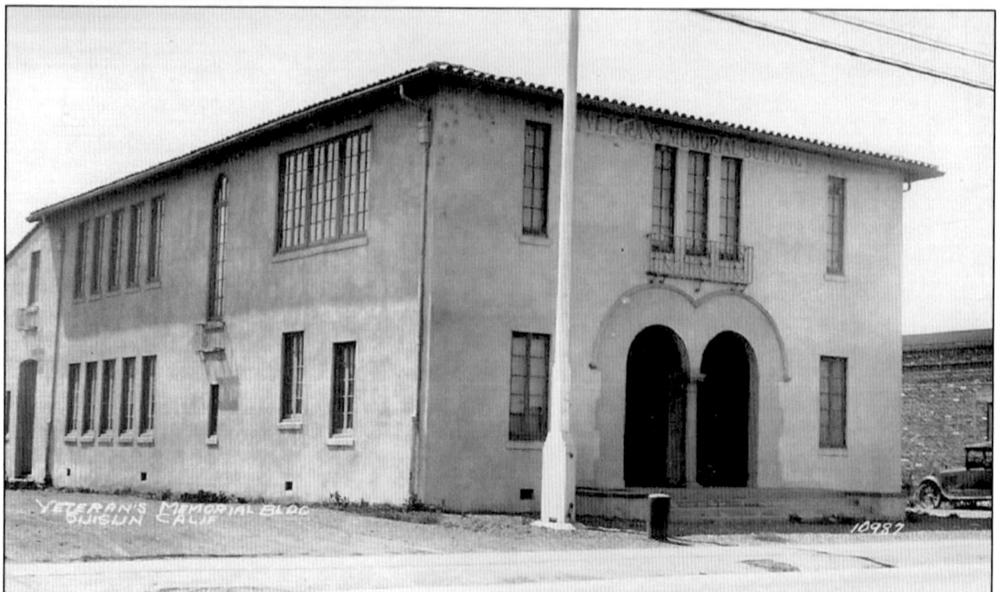

AMERICAN LEGION BUILDING, SUISUN. After the library burned, the most important task was to find a new home for the books. The American Legion in Suisun offered its building. Here, the Solano County Free library would remain until its new, permanent home was finished in 1931.

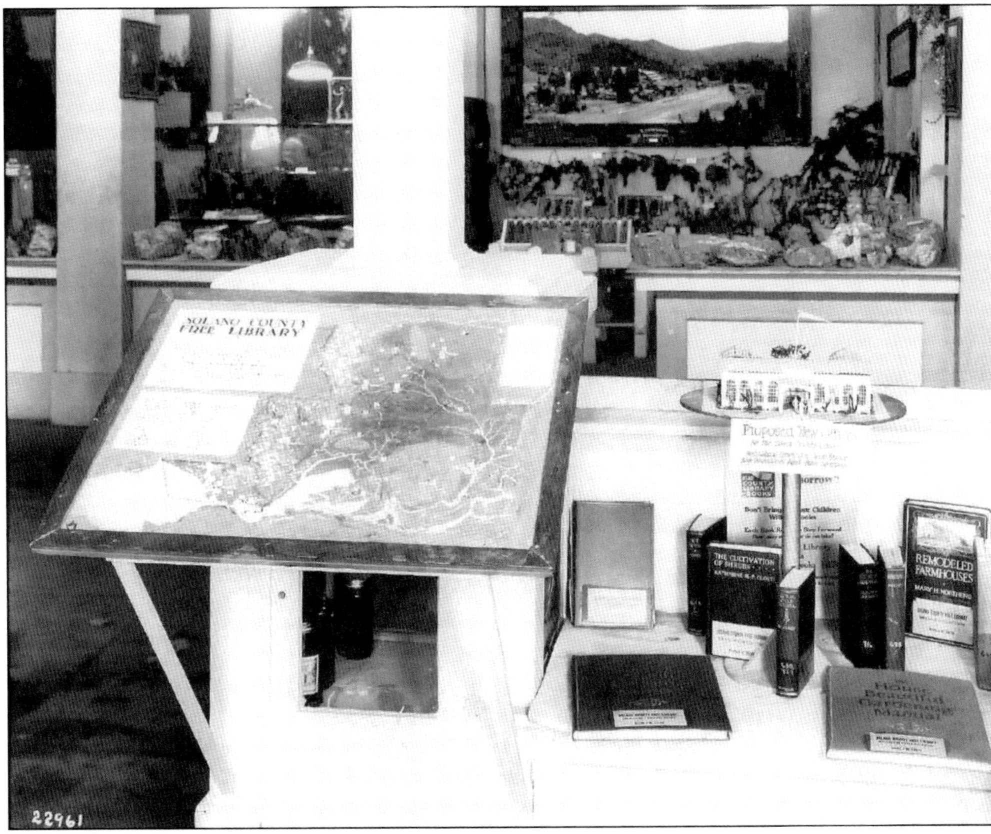

State Fair Exhibit, 1928. Discussion about a new, separate library had started a few years earlier. Clara Dills had even hired a San Francisco artist to create a model of a proposed library. The model, complete with electricity and showing visitors inside reading books, debuted amidst the Solano County library exhibit at the California State Fair of 1928.

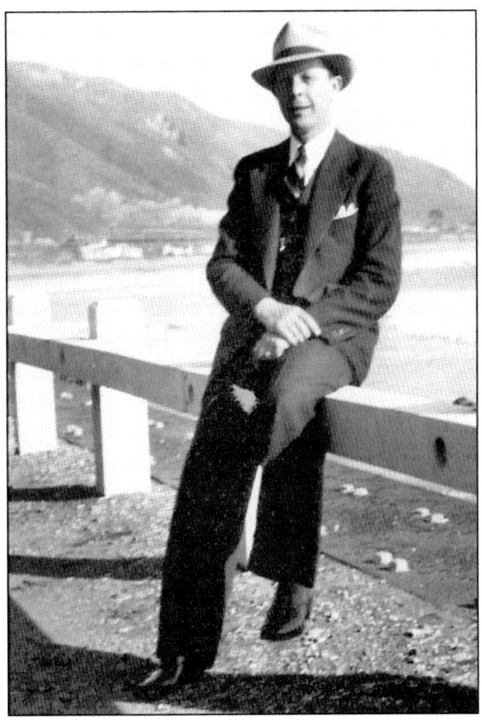

William E. Coffman. After much deliberation, the board of supervisors finally decided in October 1930 to hire Sacramento architect William E. Coffman of Coffman, Sahlberg, and Stafford. The 1930–1931 budget allocated $40,000 for the project. W. Coffman was already employed in adding the auditorium to the newly rebuilt Armijo High School. A gifted architect, who also designed the Veteran's Memorial building in Vallejo, he was killed in an automobile accident in December 1937.

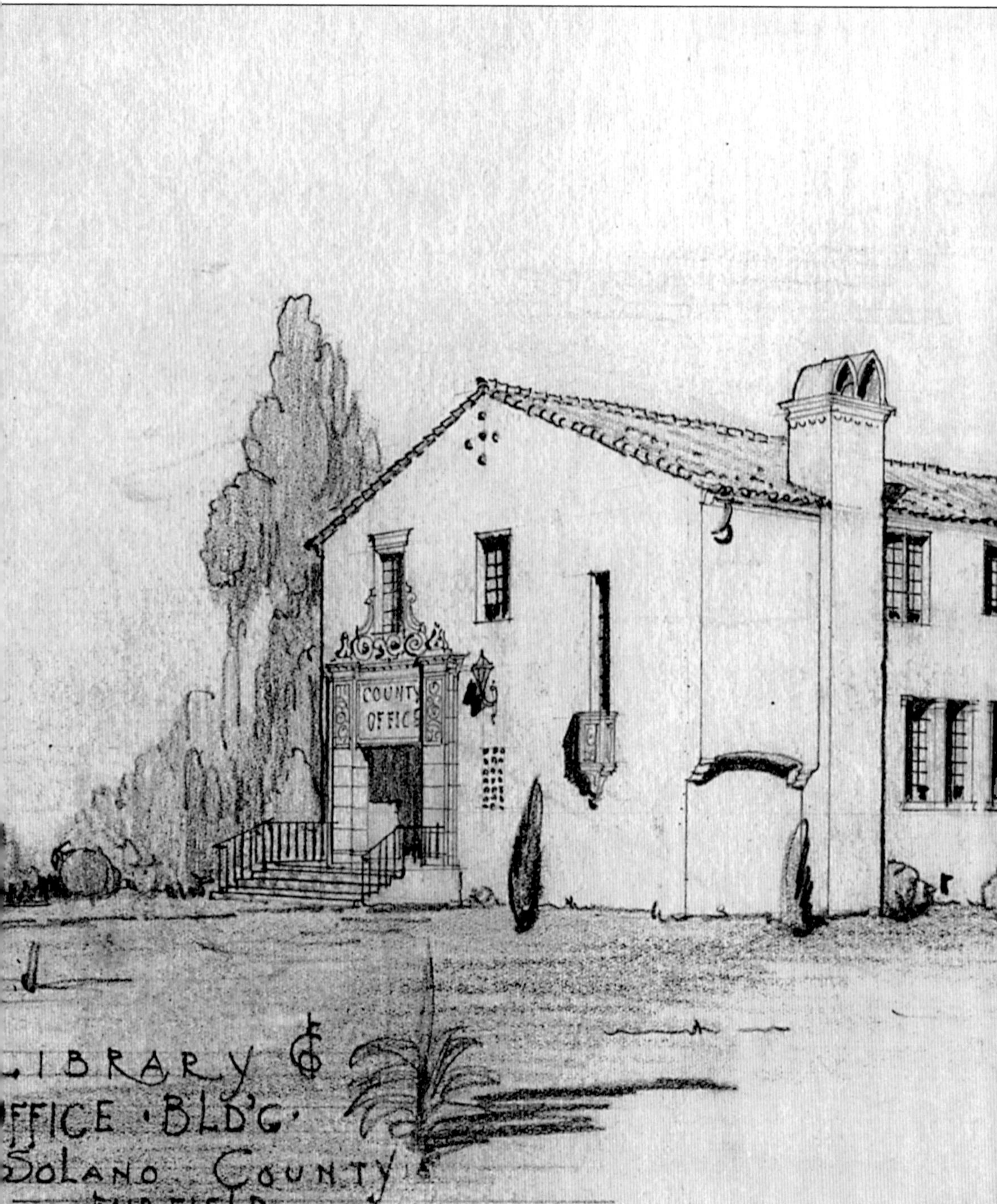

COFFMAN'S LIBRARY DRAWING. The original floor plan for the new library building consisted of a number of small rooms. Clara Dills worked with William Coffman to design this building in the Spanish Colonial Revival style. The L-shape could accommodate the Fairfield Library branch and the Solano County Free Library, as well as the offices of the library staff. The second floor was designated to house the office of the horticultural commissioner, the farm advisor,

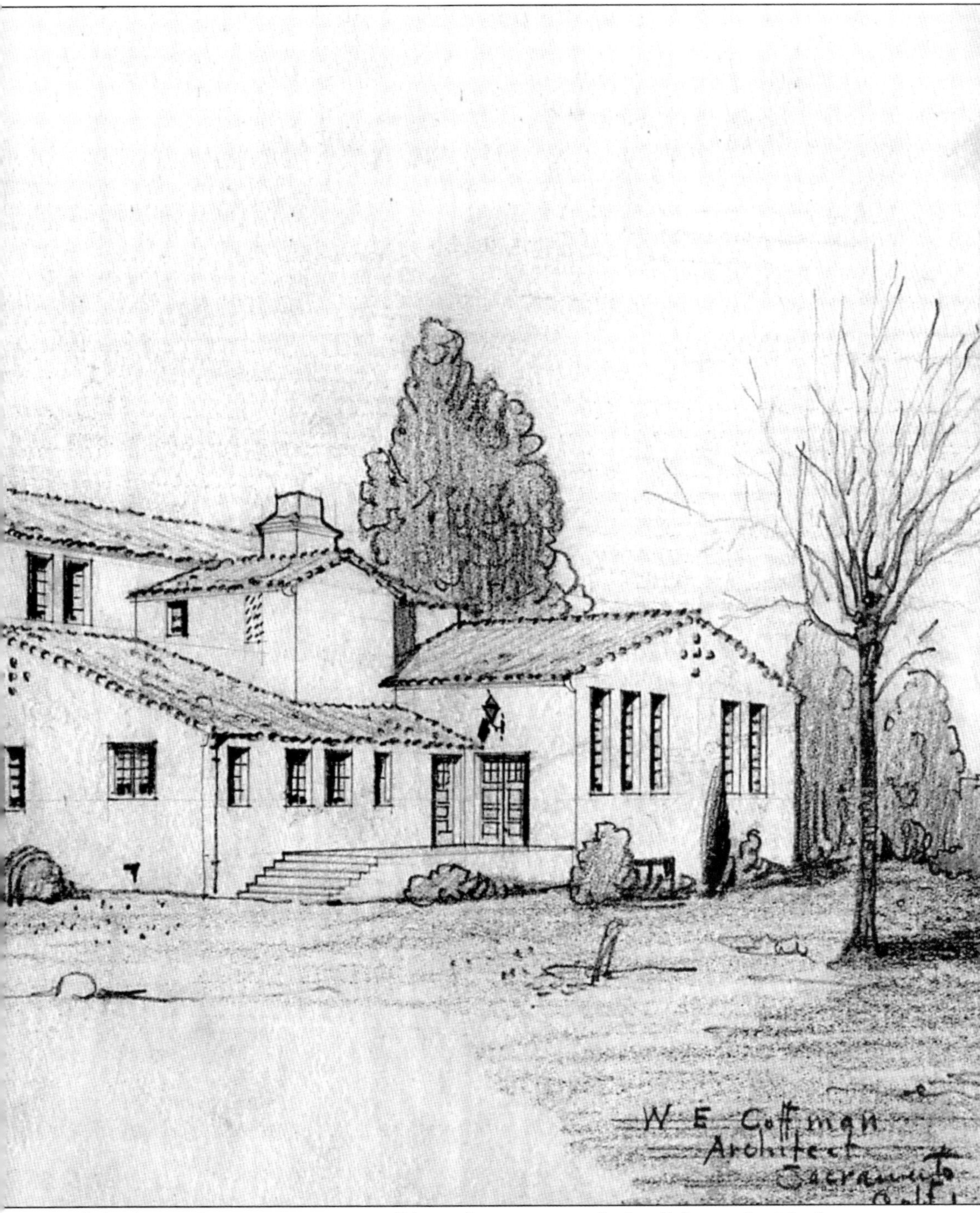

and the home demonstration agent. These three agencies had collaborated with the county library since its inception. They also worked hard to help raise funding for the new library. The community at large mounted numerous fundraising events as well, raising large sums to purchase new books.

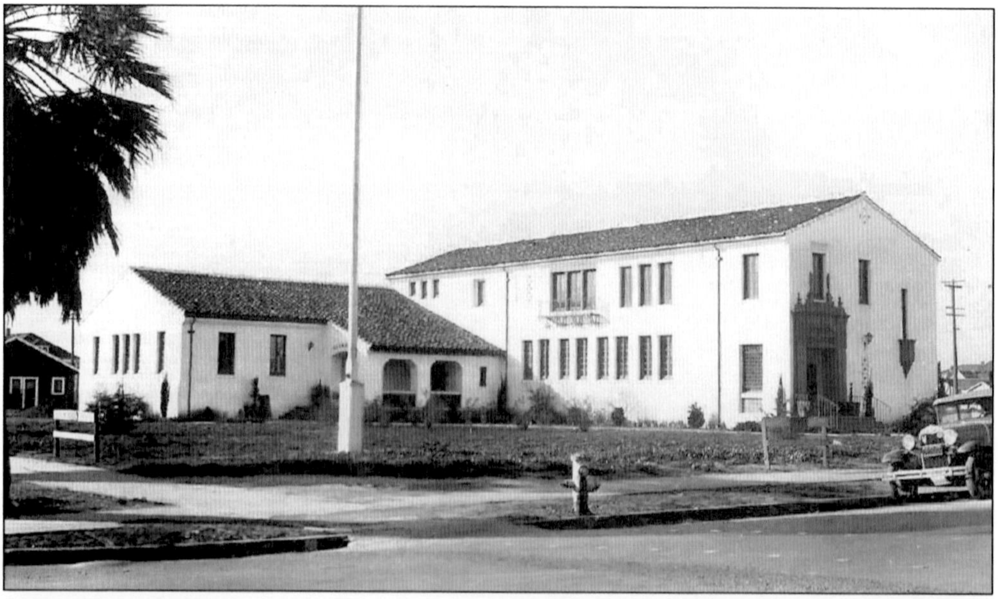

Solano County Free Library Building. The new library was dedicated on October 5, 1931. Hundreds of Solano residents, as well as dignitaries from throughout California, attended the ceremony. This early shot shows the new building before the landscaping had been installed. The inscription over the door reads "County Building."

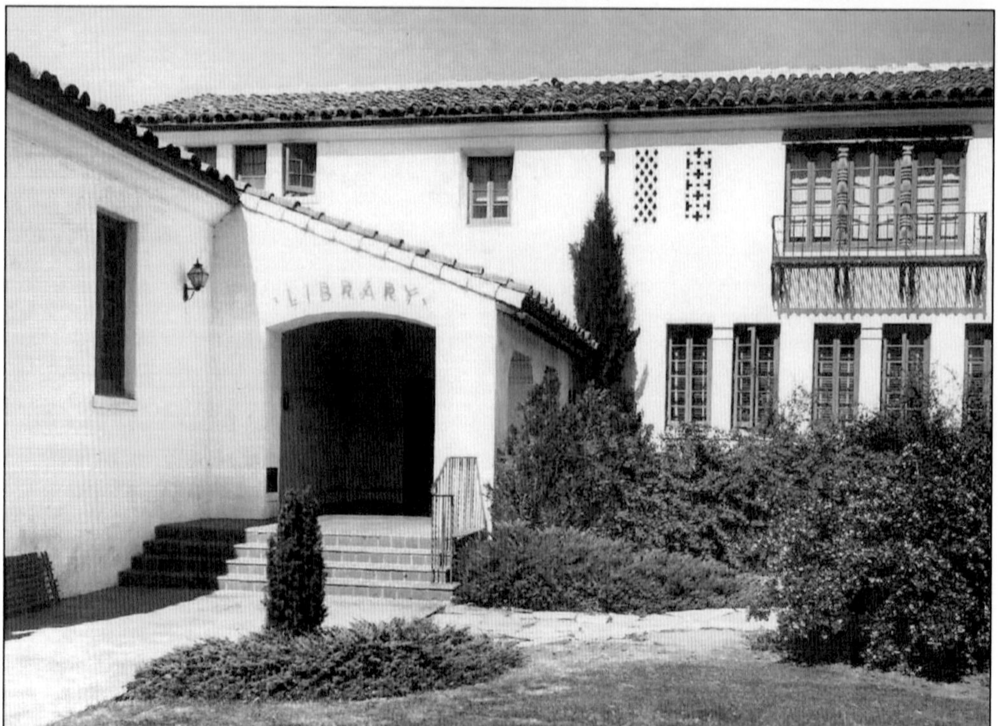

Entrance Detail. The main entrance to the library fronted Union Street. This view shows some of the architectural detail, as well as original landscaping that has since been replaced with a rose garden.

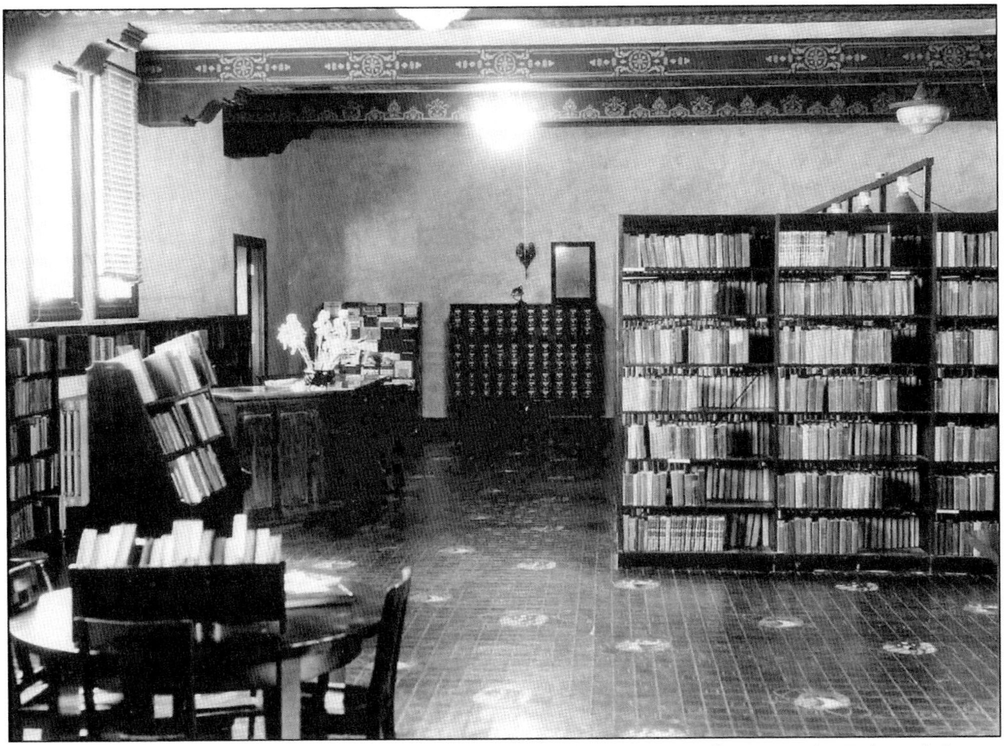

READING ROOM. This photo shows one of the two reading rooms. The Spanish-Colonial theme continues throughout the building. Here, massive wooden beams with delicate floral paintings and tile floor continue the theme.

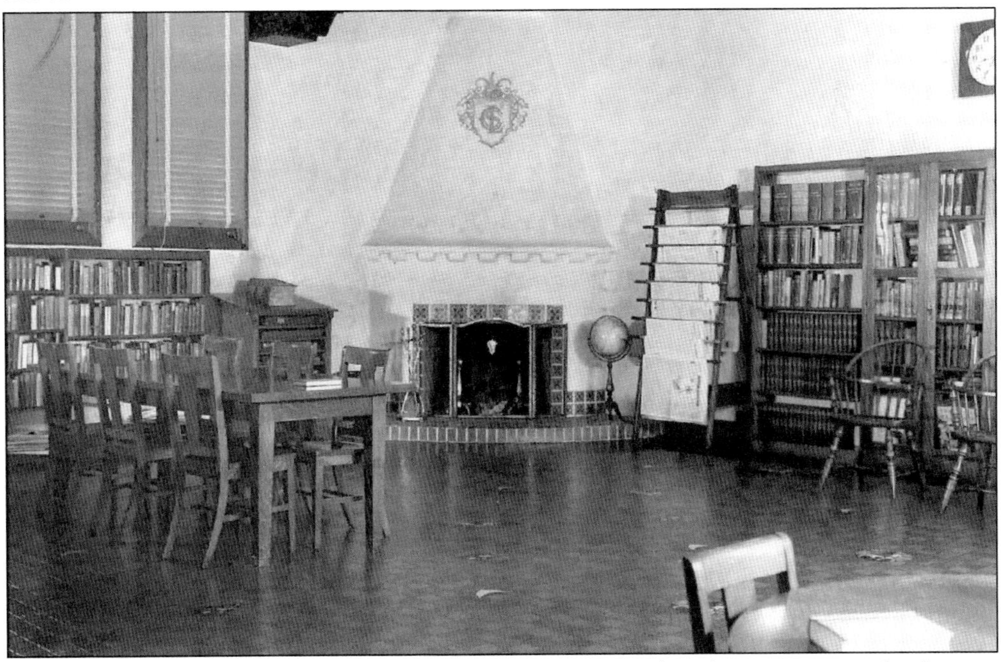

FIREPLACE ROOM. When visitors entered from Texas Street, they first came upon this homey, rustic scene with wooden beams and a fireplace with lovely stucco molding and Spanish tiles.

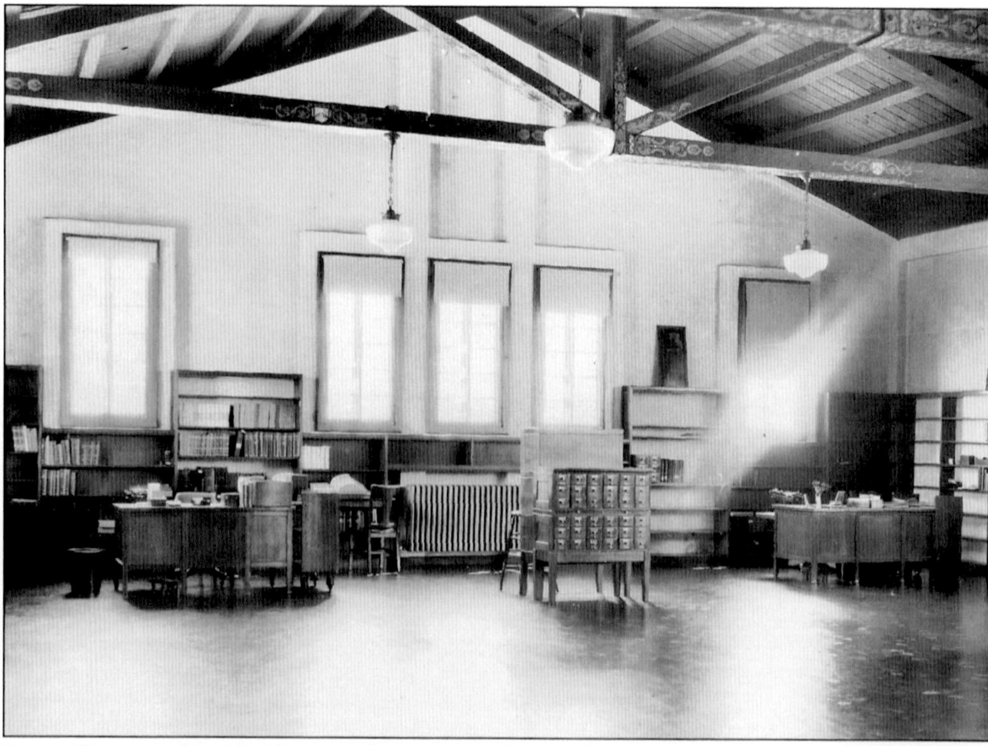

LARGE READING ROOM. Many residents remember the large, sun-lit reading room to this day and have fond memories of spending long summer afternoons there.

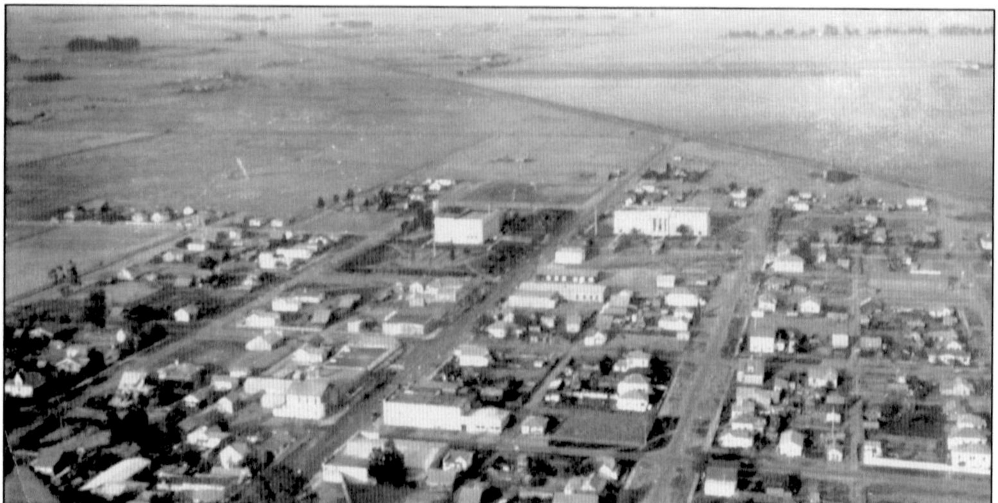

AERIAL VIEW OF GOVERNMENT CENTER. This *c.* 1930 view, shows the government complex at Texas and Union Avenues. On the left is the courthouse and jail, on the right Armijo High School, and below, the beginnings of the new county library construction. At the library dedication, the *Dixon Tribune* concluded on October 9, 1931, "This county building is unsurpassed in appearance and equipment by any other county library in northern California and with the imposing courthouse and the new Armijo high school, completes a mighty fine center."

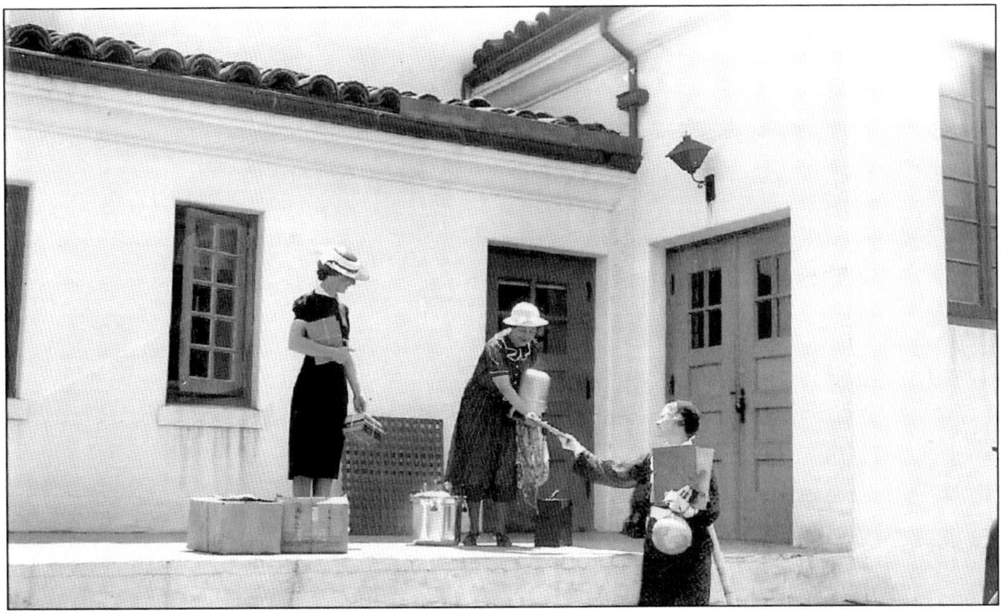

Loading Dock, c. 1942. By 1929, the library served 56 school districts with a school department that served a population of 50,000. Many school districts were quite remote and had no easy access to educational materials. Schools such as Blue Ridge Mountain, Pitts, Cement, Currey, Flosden, Gomer, Maine, Prairie, Mountain Junction, Pitts, Rhine, Wolfskill, and others are now only remembered in street names. All were guided by Solano County librarian Edith Gantt, librarians Helen Luce, (on the left), and Maryalice Maxwell (at right), shown here at the library's loading dock, where books were sent to these remote locations.

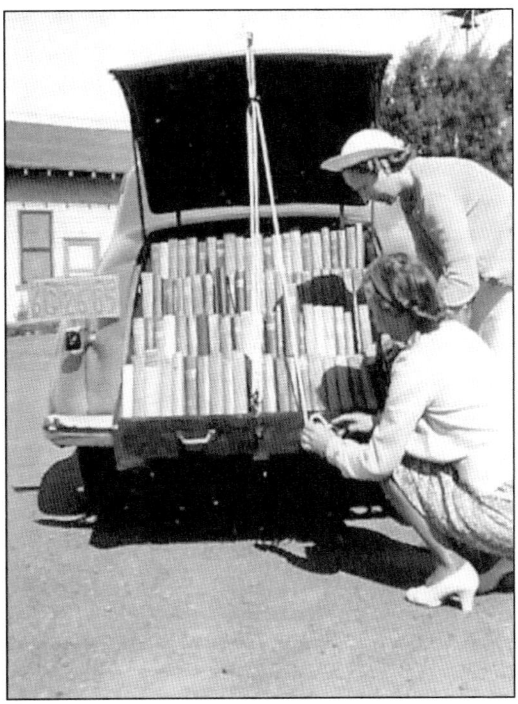

Loading the First Bookmobile. Without a precedent, staff decided to convert Edith Gantt's car into a bookmobile. Shelves were installed in the back and filled with books. Shown here in 1942 are Helen Luce and Maryalice Maxwell securing books for the trip. Besides books, the librarians, music advisor, nurse, and other staff would often take fruit, fresh vegetables, and other commodities to outlying areas. In return, they would be plied with cakes and other treats.

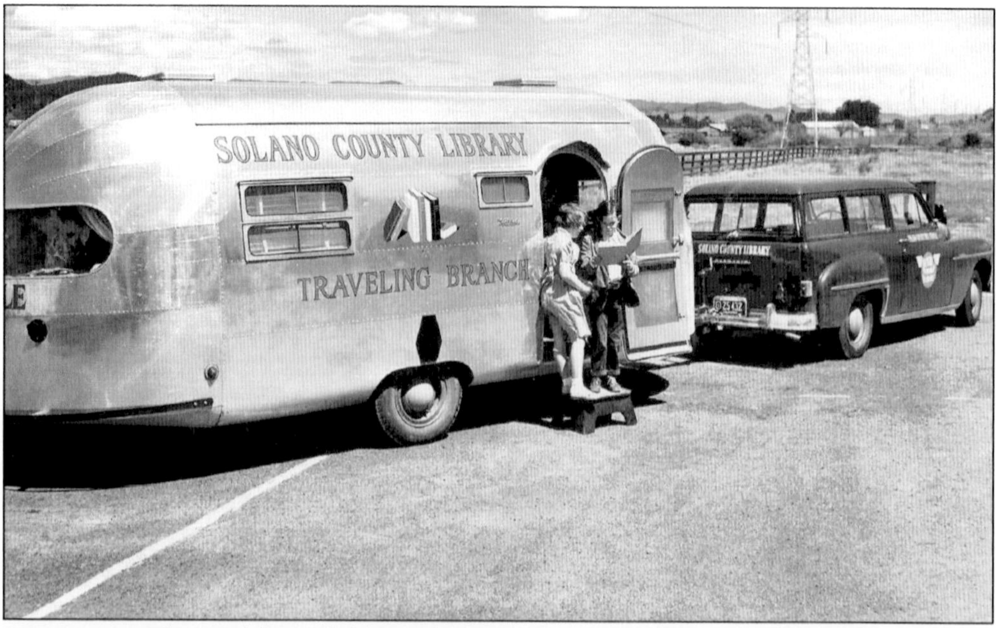

Bookmobile. The need for a circulating library eventually outgrew the librarian's car. By the 1950s, the county library owned its own bookmobile for visiting remote areas of the county.

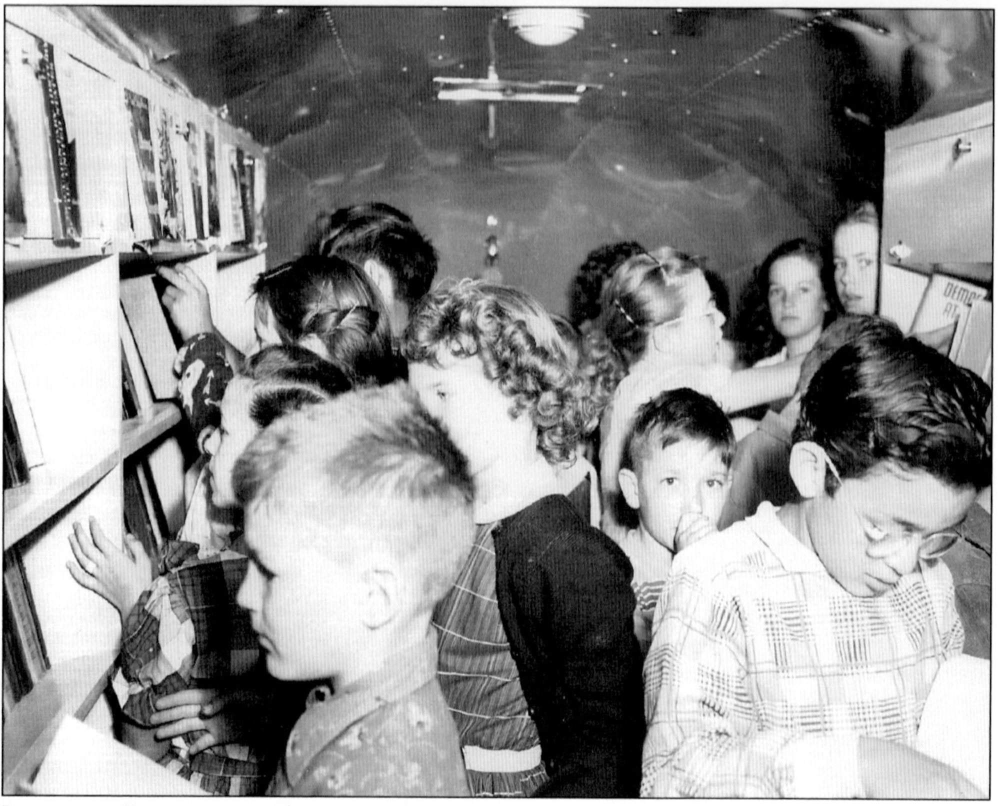

Inside the Bookmobile. This image shows a group of children trying to squeeze through the interior of the bookmobile with hope of finding a new book by a favorite author.

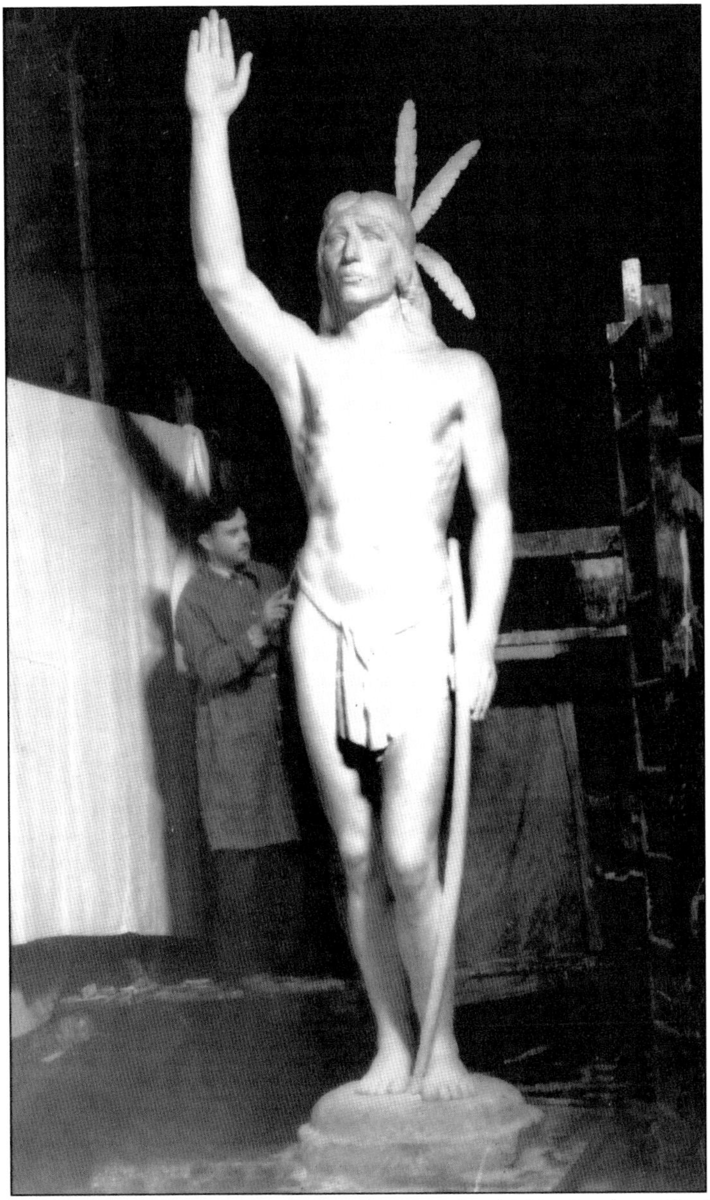

WILLIAM HUFF CREATING STATUE OF CHIEF SOLANO. In 1931, the local Red Men's lodge lobbied Senator Tom McCormack to present a bill in the senate to erect a monument honoring Chief Solano. That Chief Solano's burial site was unknown, they argued, was not important, but "all who pass through Solano County should be able to look upon a monument erected in his honor in the county that bears his name." It was proposed that the monument be erected alongside Highway 40, close to his original rancho. In 1932, John Nolan, the owner of the *Oakland Tribune*, sponsored a statewide competition to select an artist. Sculptor William Huff was selected with his proposal for a 12-foot-high bronze statue representing Chief Solano. Typical for the time, the artist represents the chief as a romanticized Plains Indian in native garb, offering his open hand to new settlers in friendship. Recent research paints a much different image of Chief Solano and his role in aiding and abetting General Vallejo's brutal suppression of all Indian uprisings.

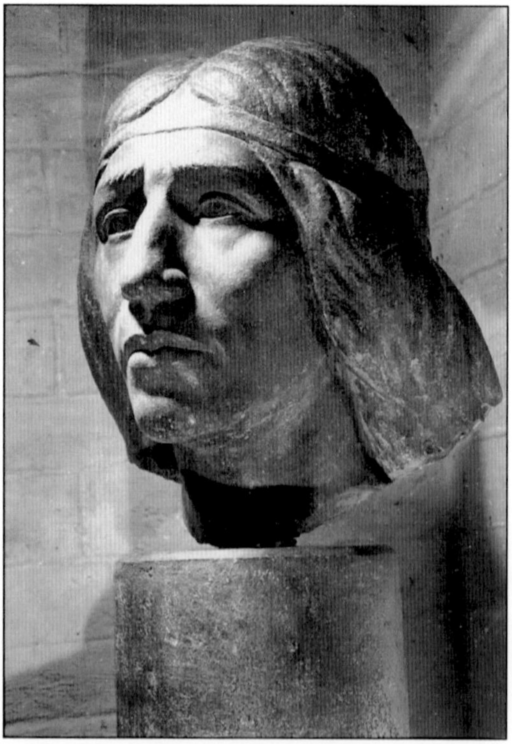

CHIEF SOLANO'S HEAD. William Huff's model for the head of the statue of Chief Solano currently graces the meeting chamber of the board of supervisors at the courthouse.

STATUE OF CHIEF SOLANO. This statue was originally installed with much fanfare on a hill near Rockville in the summer of 1934. Unfortunately vandals soon damaged the statue, and it was decided that it should be relocated to downtown Fairfield. After considering several different locations, Armijo High's shop crew created a life-size model. On a Monday in late April 1938, the statue was "spotted" here and there on the courthouse and library grounds to determine where the real statue should be placed. Most residents thought that placing the giant statue on the library grounds "would simply ruin the beauty of the library." Yet this is exactly where the statue ended up, and it has become one of the iconic images of Solano County.

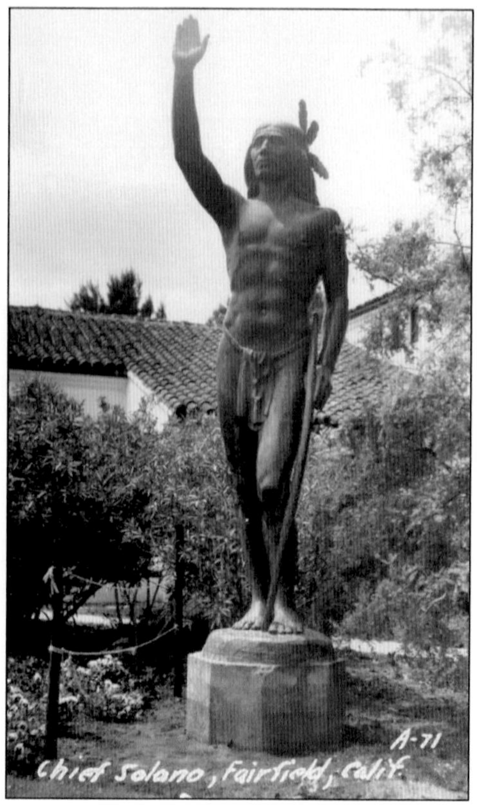

Five

Business Growth along Texas Street

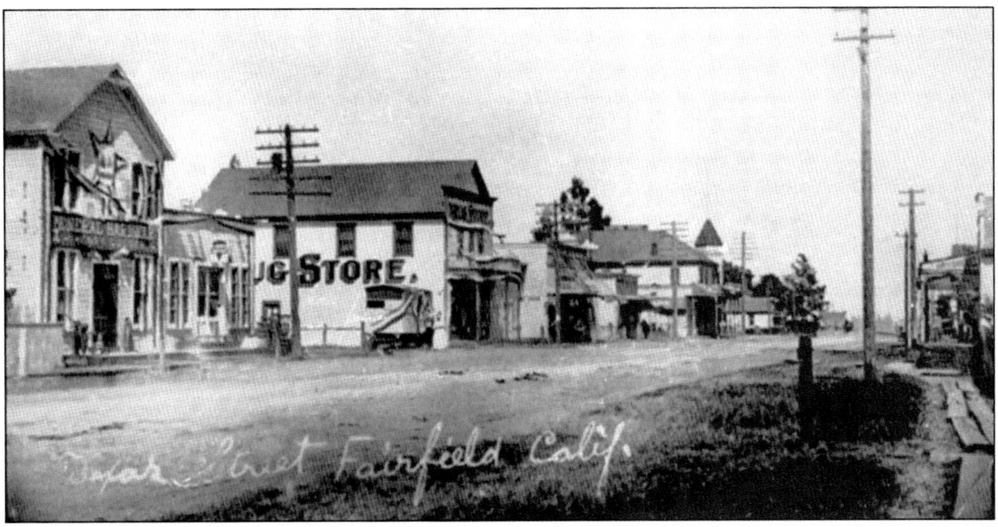

Texas Street, c. 1904. This is the oldest known photo of Texas Street, looking towards Courthouse Square, sometime after 1904. The City of Fairfield had been incorporated on December 12, 1903 with a population of about 700. While the street seems to have been graded, no sidewalks have as yet been installed. Planks serve as an improvised sidewalk instead. Businesses from left to right are: Henry Goosen's General Hardware Store (established in 1904), Parr's Repair Shop, A.H. Munroe's Drug Store (across Webster Street), Silverstine's Store, Mrs. Mean's Store and residence, and Mayfield's cottage, which is not visible. This is followed by the Capitol Hotel, recognizable by its tower, located on the corner of Texas and Jefferson Street next to the government center. Originally known as the Plants Hotel, it was Fairfield's first hotel, built in 1858. On the other side of Jefferson Street, situated on Courthouse Square, is the small white post office building. The first postmaster was William Losh, who operated in a little white shack as early as 1856. Harry Miller followed him in 1868, serving until 1880.

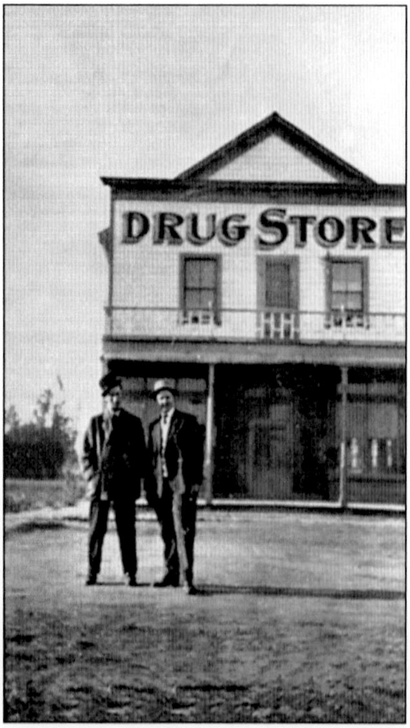

A.H. Munroe's Drug Store. Photographed before 1909, these two gentlemen are captured in front of A.H. Munroe's Drug Store.

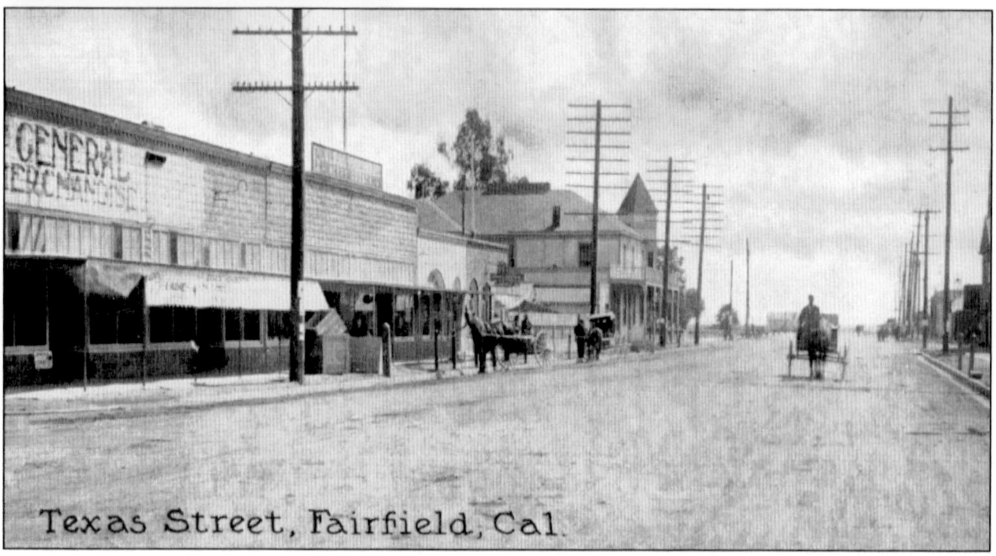

Texas Street, 1911. In 1909, a large fire devastated the 744–750 block of Texas Street. Most of the businesses had to completely rebuild. By 1911, when this photo was taken, the city had finally raised enough bond money to have the street graded and sidewalks installed. During those final years of horse and buggy, hitching posts were still a necessity. The building on the left is the newly constructed Goosen Hardware Store. With fire destruction on his mind, Henry Goosen elected to use modern reinforced concrete material for his building. Though its facade has been remodeled, the building still stands today. The Capitol Hotel and its tower are clearly visible. By order of the board of supervisors on May 1, 1911, the post office was moved from the square to make room for the new courthouse.

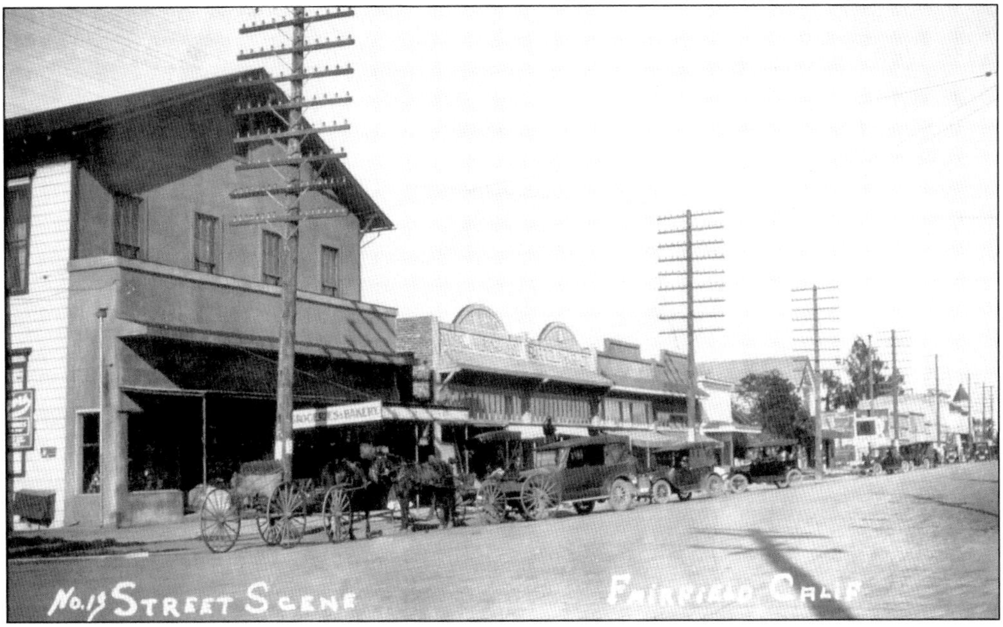

TEXAS STREET LOOKING TOWARDS THE COURTHOUSE, 1920S. By the early 1920s, much of the 700 and 800 block of Texas Street had recovered from the fire and had been rebuilt. The rerouting of U.S. Highway 40 through downtown Fairfield along Texas Street in 1915 brought an economic upswing to the area. Businesses moved into downtown, finally making it an economic center equal to, and soon even surpassing Suisun. The building on the left was Jensen's Grocery and Bakery.

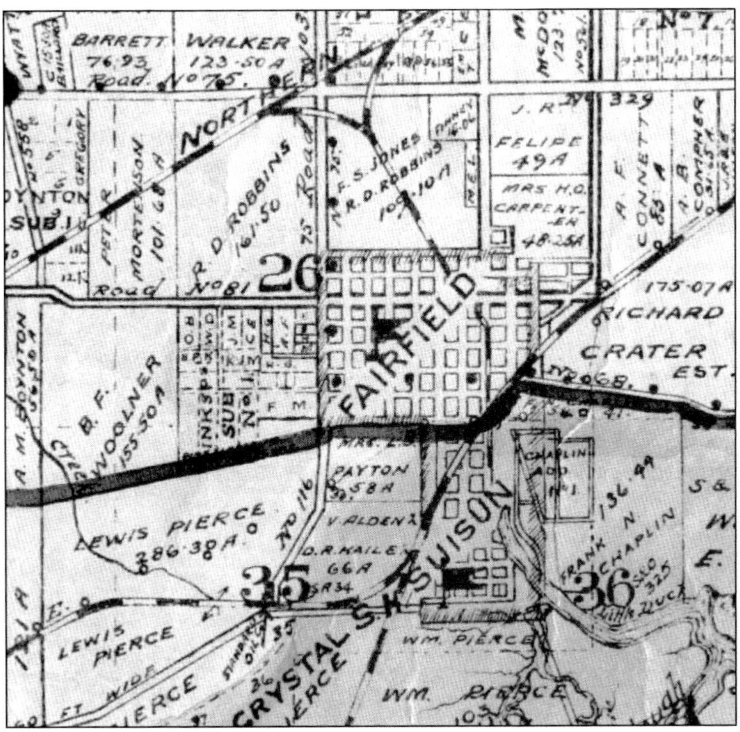

DETAIL FROM 1915 MAP. This portion of a 1915 map shows a smaller Fairfield and Suisun than we now know. Road No. 81 is Texas Street; Road No. 75/116 is the future Pennsylvania Avenue. Also visible is the branch linking the Southern Pacific railroad tracks to the Northern Electric Railroad, which connected Sacramento and Vallejo. Today, Webster Street and Linear Park preserve the memory of these local public transportation media.

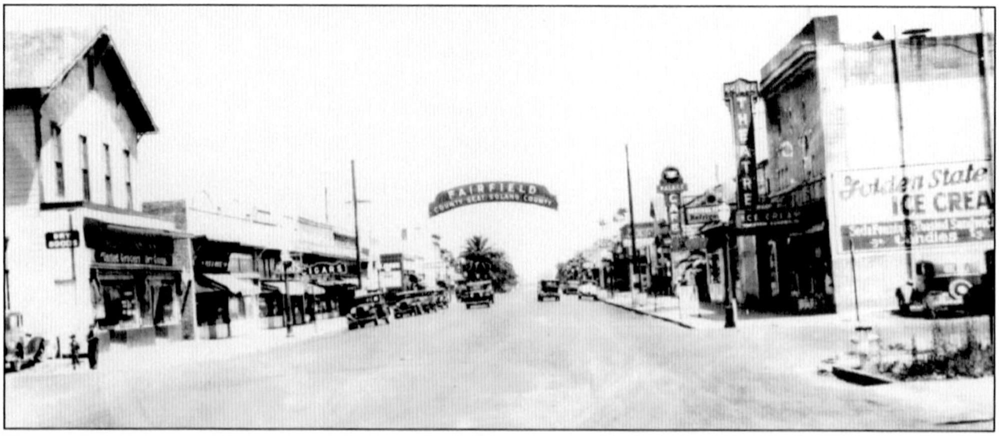

TEXAS STREET, C. 1925. Texas Street acquired another important feature in 1925—the arched Fairfield sign. Fairfield Community Club members merged into the Fairfield Lions Club on July 30, 1925. Their first chosen task was the creation of "tentative plans and specifications for a concrete or steel sign to be placed at the outskirts of Fairfield" to make certain that passing motorists could identify the town. The Lion's Club organized a public raffle, with a $135 washing machine as the main prize, raising $700. They then commissioned the National Electric Sign Company of Oakland to build the sign at a cost of $924. On October 22, 1925, the Company delivered the finished sign on a flatbed truck. Employees of the Great Western Power Company installed it between two poles. The community was invited to an unveiling ceremony on October 23, at 7:30 p.m., "when the new street sign will blaze forth the illuminated fact that this is the Town of Fairfield, County Seat of Solano County" (*Solano Republican* newspaper). This shot also shows the theater at the corner of Texas and Jackson Streets, which opened its doors on July 21, 1921, with Charlie Chaplin's *The Kid*.

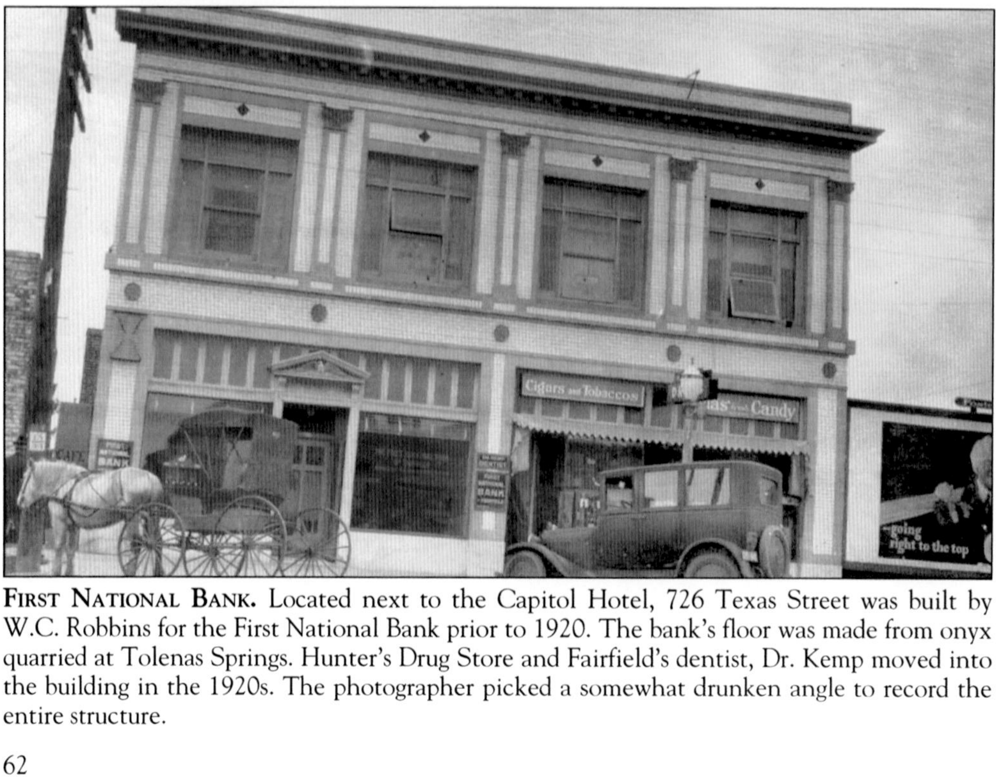

FIRST NATIONAL BANK. Located next to the Capitol Hotel, 726 Texas Street was built by W.C. Robbins for the First National Bank prior to 1920. The bank's floor was made from onyx quarried at Tolenas Springs. Hunter's Drug Store and Fairfield's dentist, Dr. Kemp moved into the building in the 1920s. The photographer picked a somewhat drunken angle to record the entire structure.

Dr. Kemp's Office. One of Dr. Kemp's patients took a series of interior shots of the dental office. Note the high-tech chair with foot pedal. From this perch, patients could enjoy a view across Texas Street.

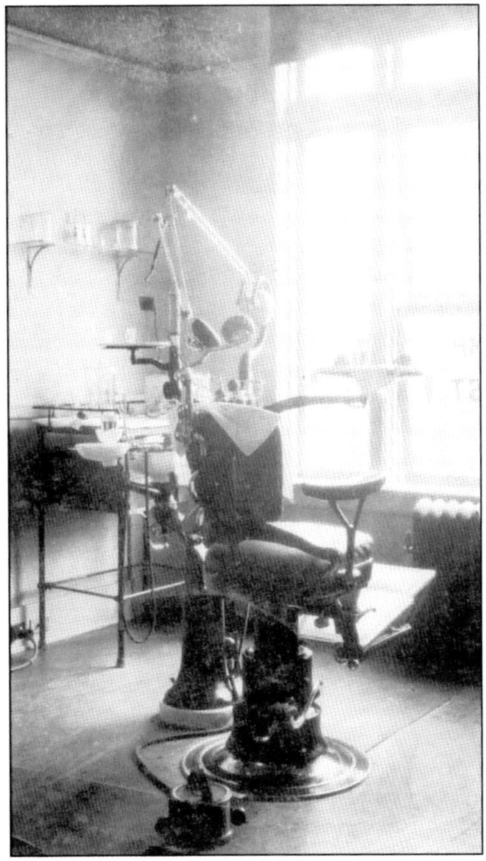

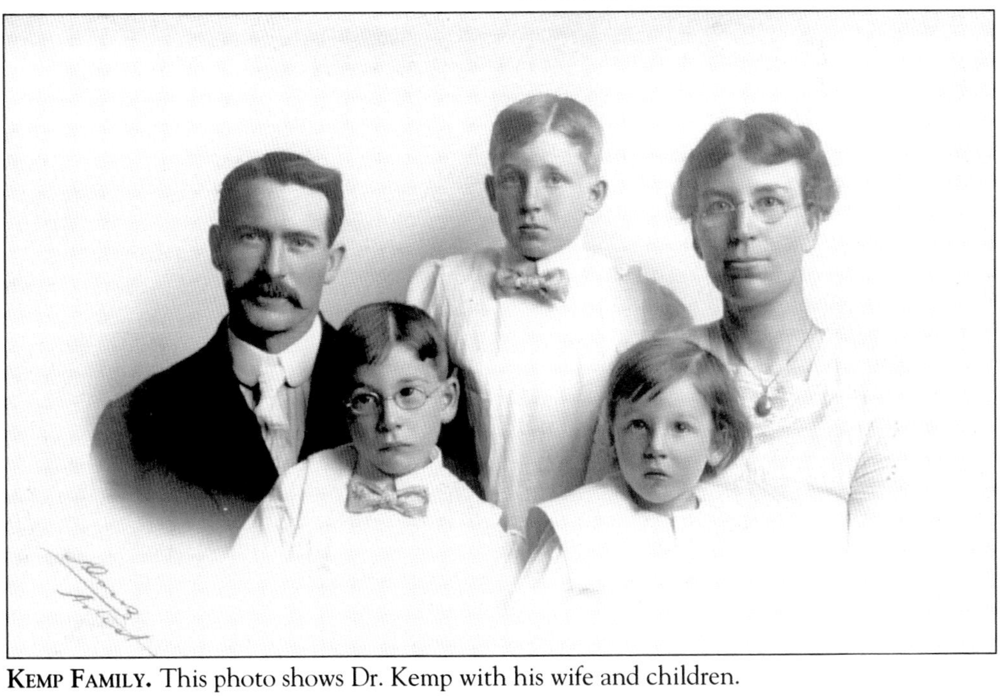

Kemp Family. This photo shows Dr. Kemp with his wife and children.

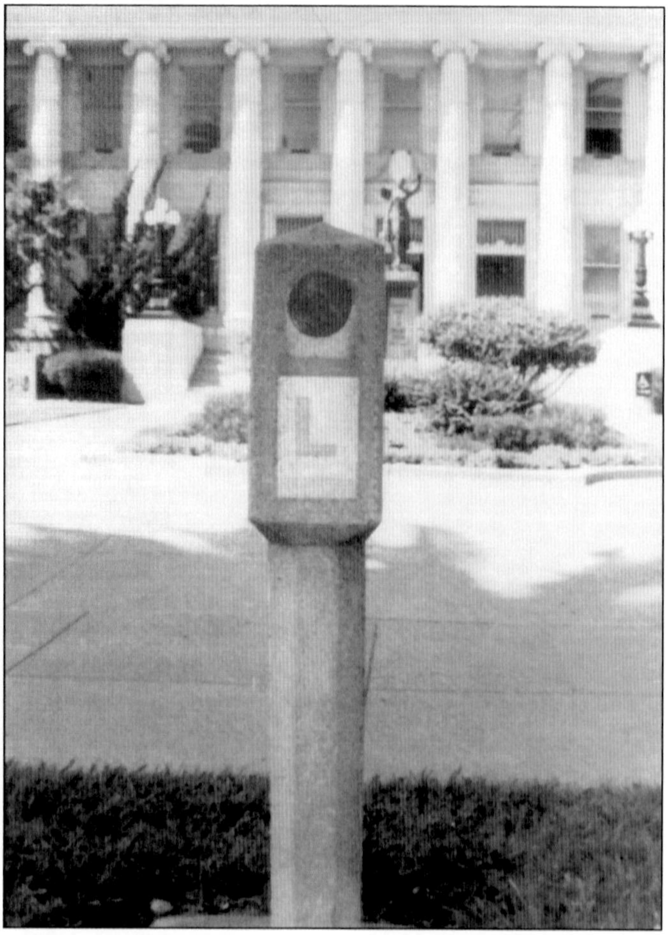

LINCOLN HIGHWAY MARKER. The opening of the Carquinez Bridge in 1927 established a new route between the Bay Area and Sacramento—right through downtown Fairfield. In 1928, parts of U.S. State Highway 40 were designated as the Lincoln Highway, connecting East and West Coasts. That same year, the Boy Scouts erected this Lincoln Highway marker in front of the courthouse.

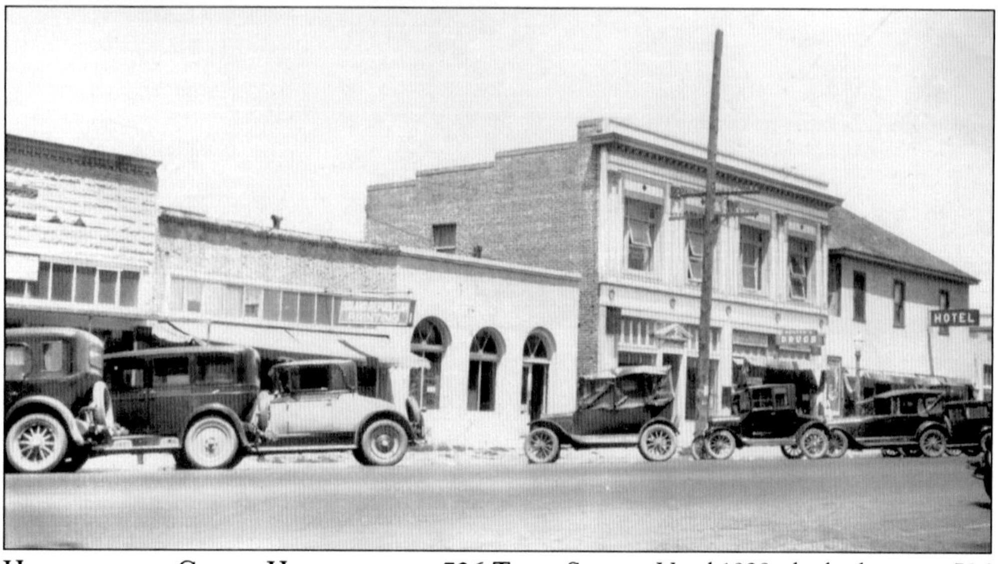

HOUSE BETWEEN GOOSEN HARDWARE AND 726 TEXAS STREET. Until 1929, the lot between 726 Texas Street, at right, and Goosen Hardware Store, at left, was occupied by two businesses.

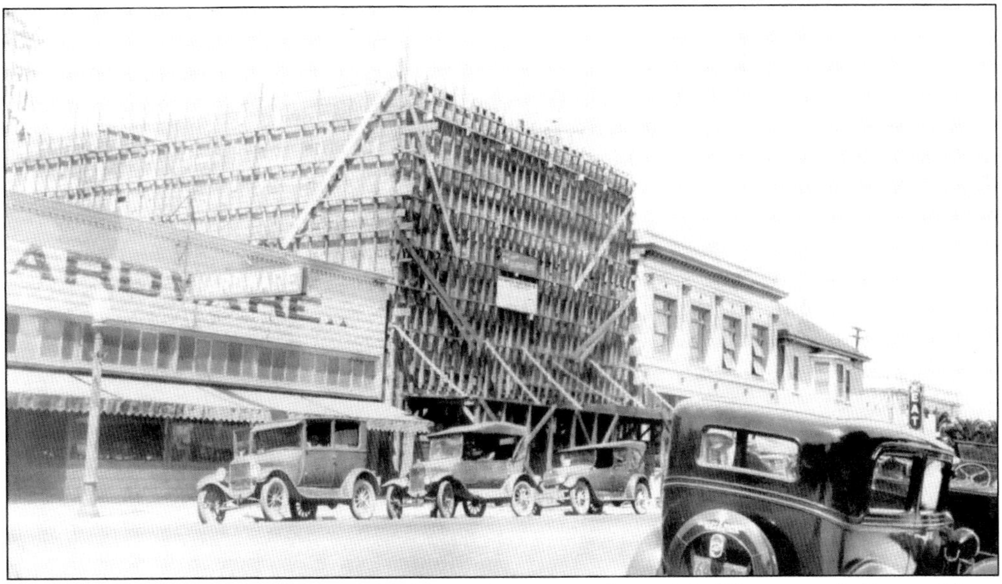

Construction of Solano County Title Company. James N. Watson and George Hope established the Solano County Title Company on November 6, 1900. Incorporated by 1907, the office moved to the old law building opposite Armijo High School. E.L. Dearborn bought out the previous owners in 1917 and changed the name to Solano County Title Company. He purchased the lot, had both buildings torn down, and began construction of the three-story Solano Title Company in August 1930.

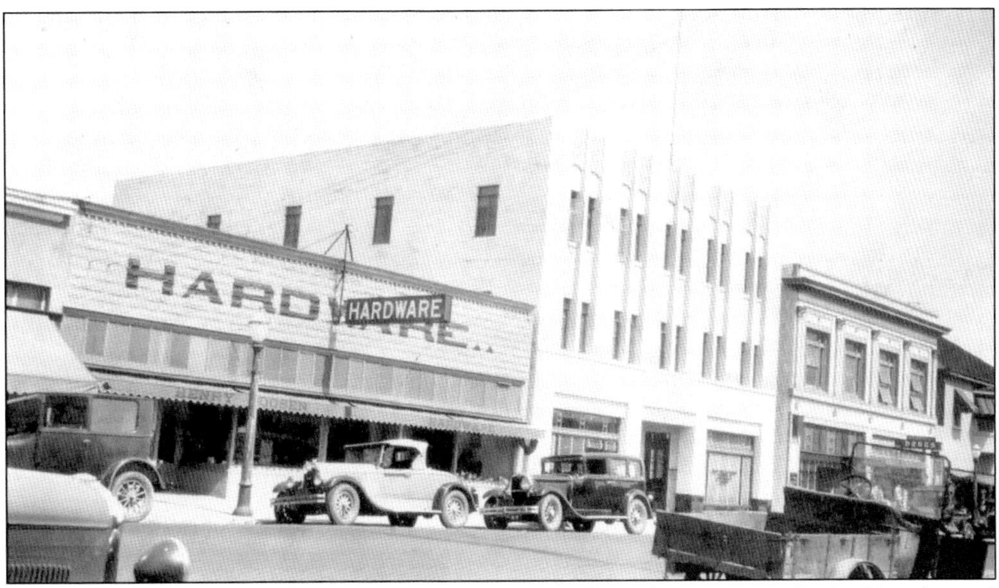

Solano County Title Company Building. Besides the title company, the building housed dentists Dr. Webster and Dr. Howe, attorney K.I. Jones, accountant Malcolm Gordon, and Dr. Felix Rossi. The building also held Fairfield's first elevator, a special treat for children invited to ride. In addition, the post office was relocated here. To this day, the Solano County Title Company is one of the most elegant buildings on this part of Texas Street.

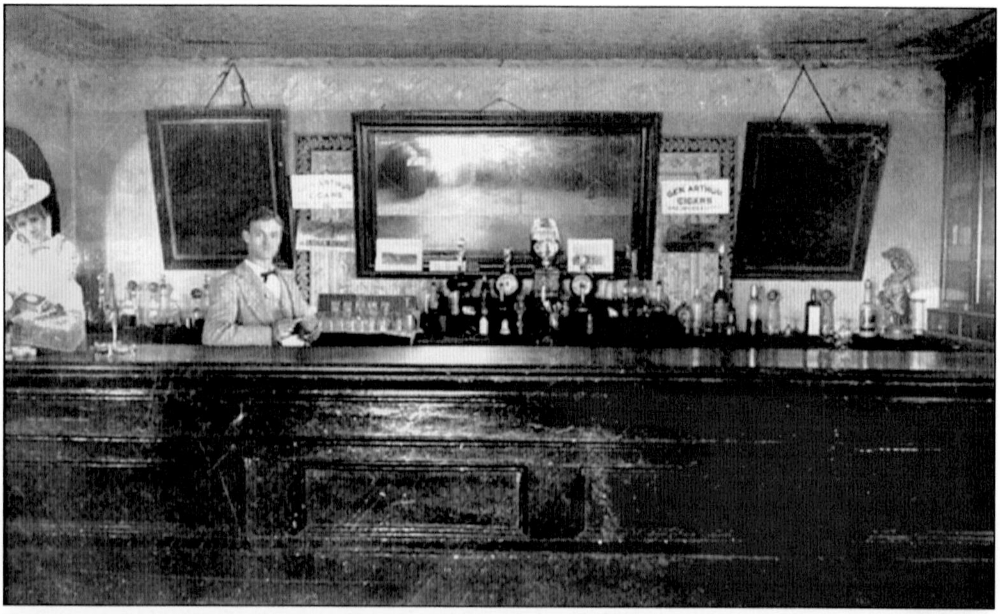

Barroom of Fairfield Hotel Before 1895. The Fairfield Hotel was one of several hotels established in the vicinity of the government center. Located on Union Avenue, it advertised that, "In connection with the house is a bar, where you will always find Wines, Liquors and Cigars, of the best brand." This is a view of its barroom taken prior to 1895, with W.B. Fields behind the counter.

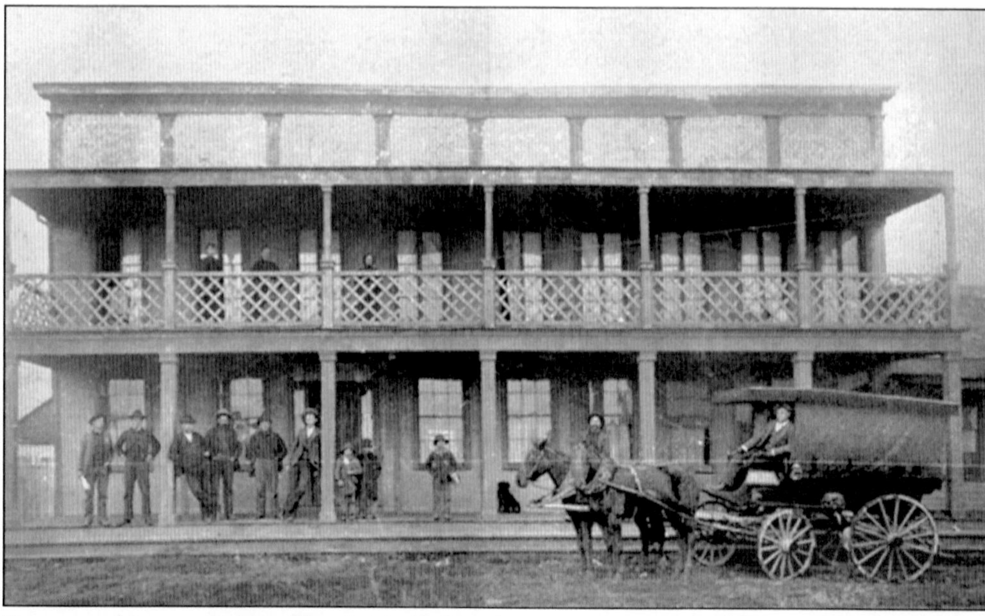

Fairfield Hotel, 1890s. The Fairfield Hotel was a two-story building and each room on the upper floor had its own private balcony. By 1877, it advertised that, "This house has just been refitted, and thoroughly renovated by the proprietor, who is now prepared to provide anything for his guest that can be asked." The proprietor at the time was T. Joyce. The hotel was completely destroyed in a fire in 1897, but was immediately rebuilt. The driver in this photograph is W.B. Fields.

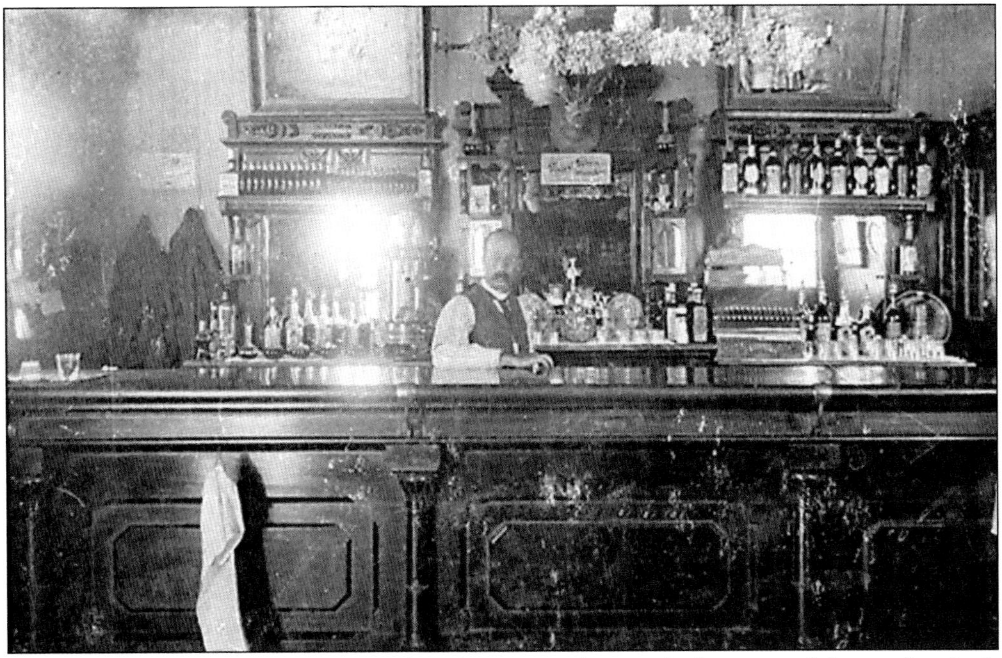

FAIRFIELD HOTEL'S NEW BARROOM. This photo was taken in the barroom of the newly rebuilt Fairfield Hotel. It seems to be much more elaborate than its predecessor.

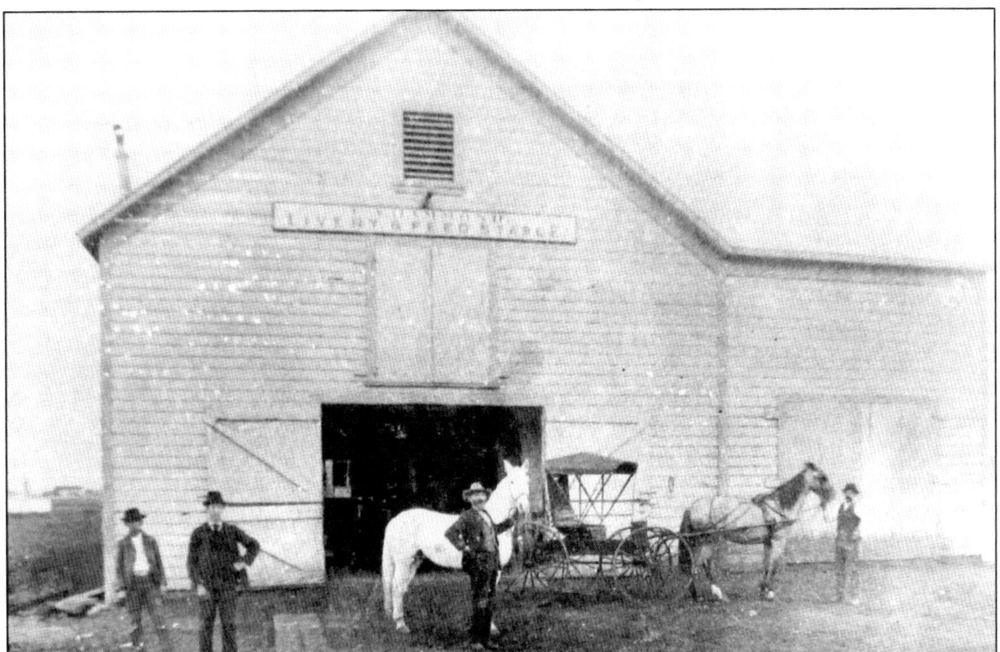

HAMMOND LIVERY STABLES. Livery stables offered food and stabling for customers' horses. They also repaired buggies and sold equipment. In 1863, N.C. Butler operated the Monitor Feed Stable. E.K. Yost and Mr. Markwood operated the Fairfield Livery Stable, advertised as the "Fashion Stable," during the Civil War years. This c. 1900 photo shows the Hammond Livery & Feed Stable.

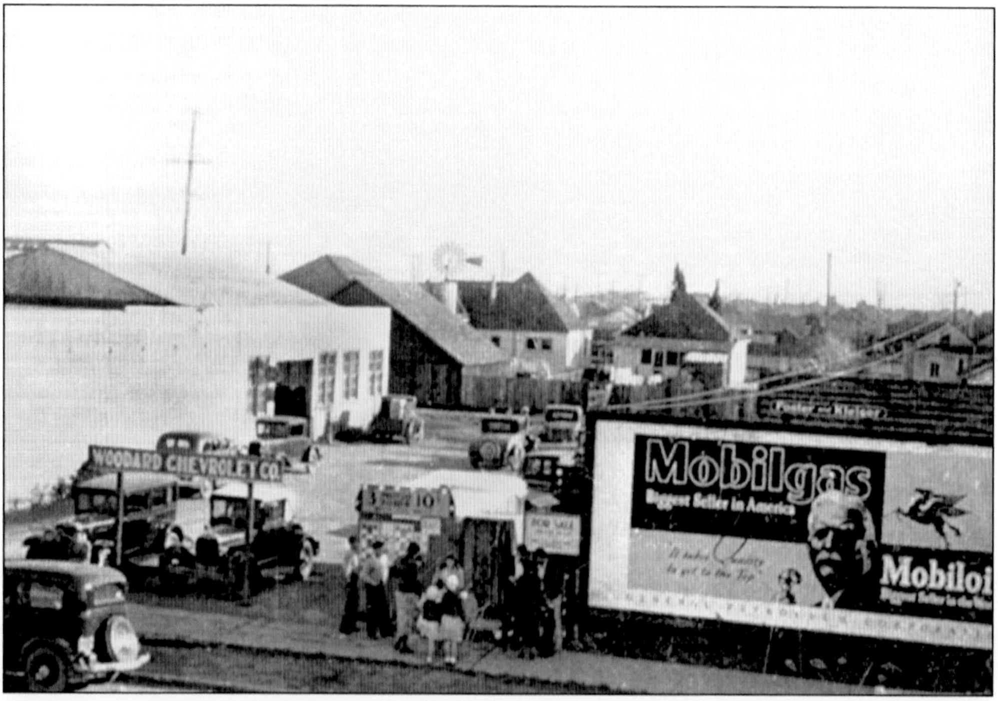

WOODARD CHEVROLET. Cars began to replace horses and buggies by the mid 1910s. One of the earliest car dealerships in Fairfield was Woodard Chevrolet, which opened as a car lot on the 700 block of Texas near Jefferson Street. This photo was taken in the early 1930s, after the installation of their sign.

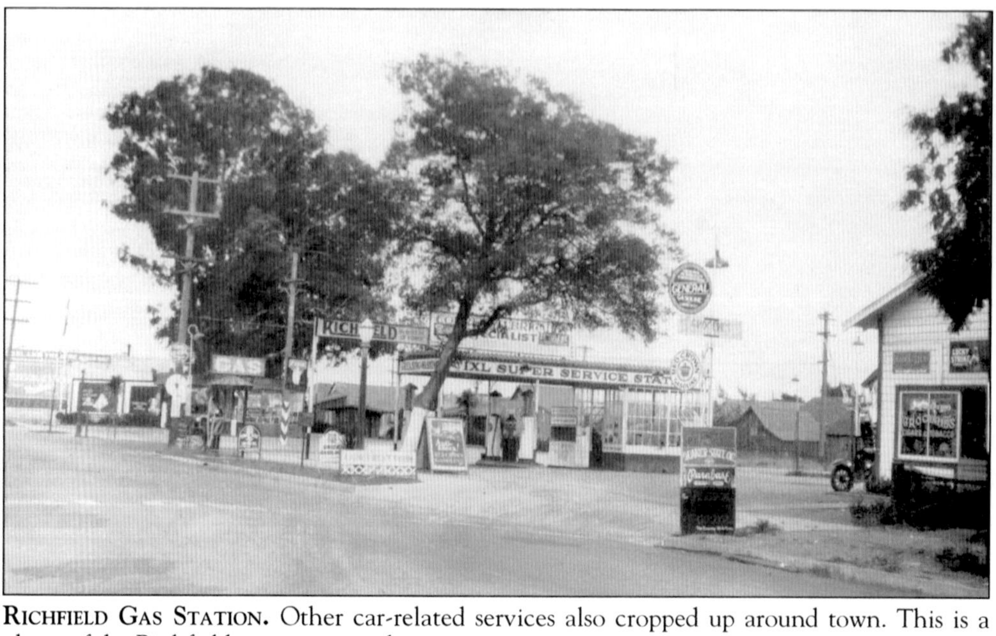

RICHFIELD GAS STATION. Other car-related services also cropped up around town. This is a photo of the Richfield gas station and grocery store.

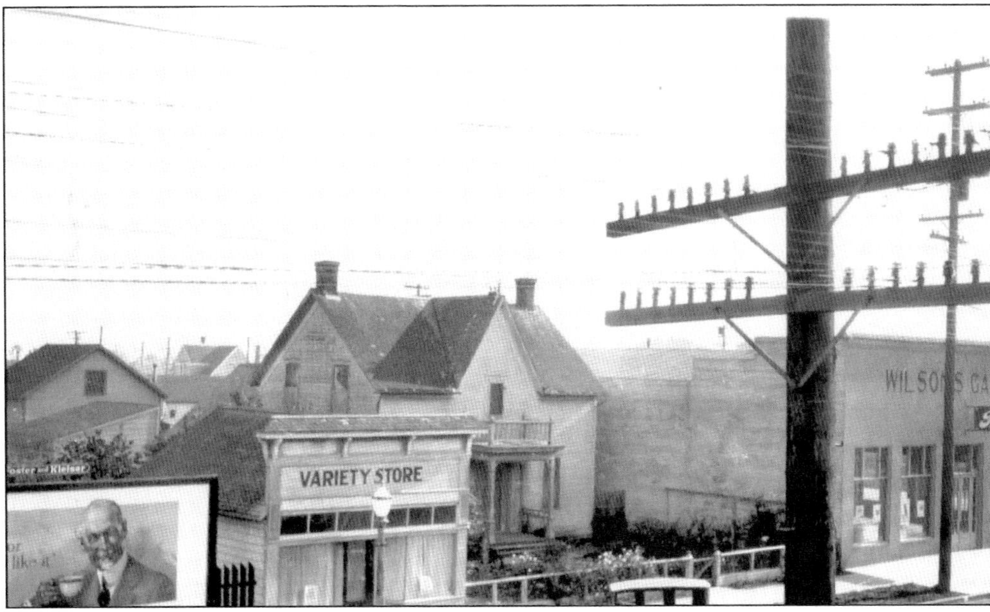

WILSON'S GARAGE, 1928. In 1928, the Wilson Garage could be found two lots to the right of Woodard Chevrolet, next to the variety store.

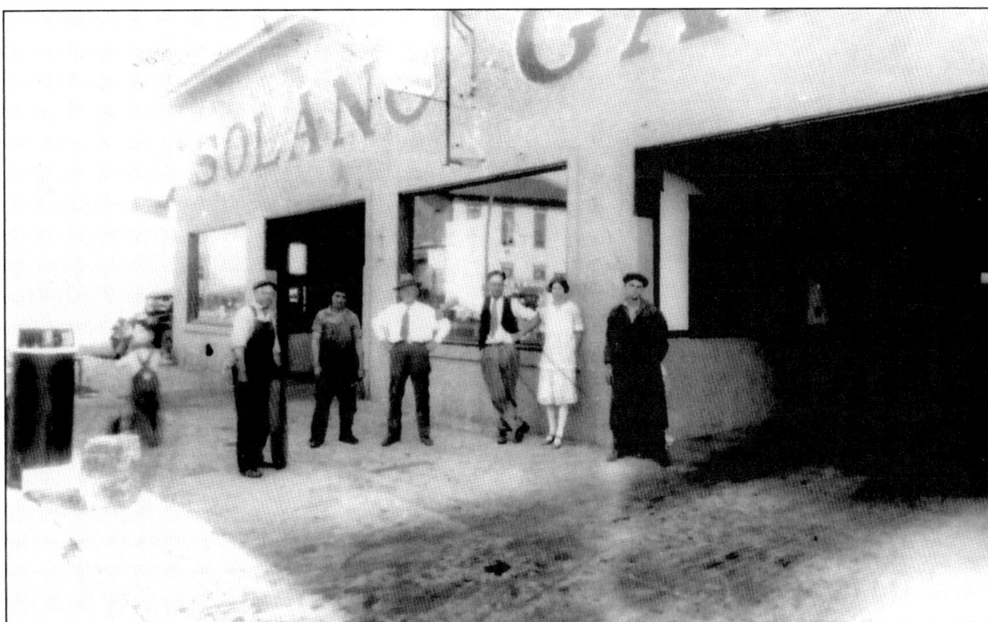

SOLANO GARAGE. This *c.* 1928 image shows another popular garage of the time, with employee William Braker Sr. and customers standing in front.

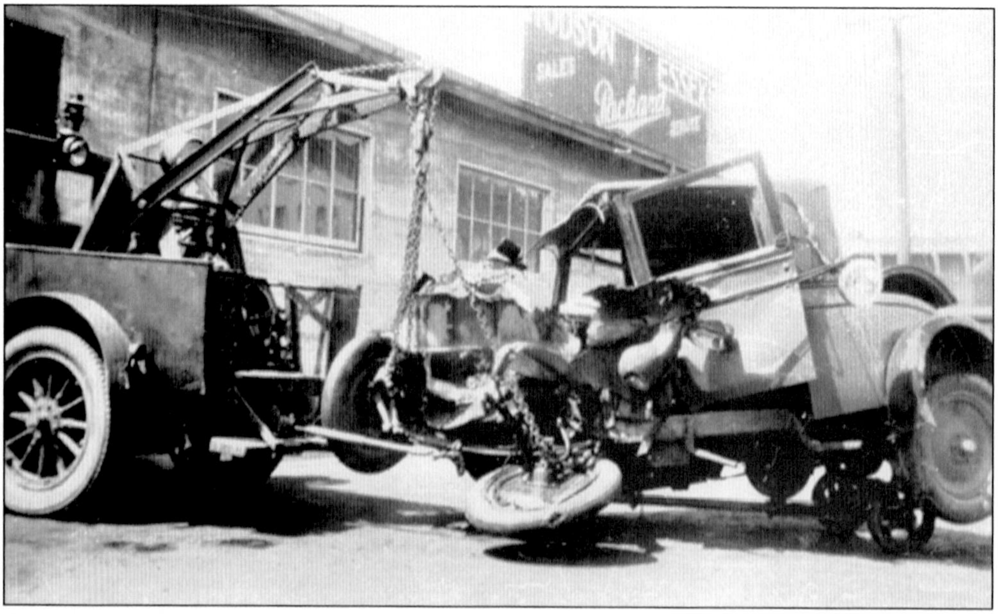

Car Wreck. This impressively mangled auto was towed to the Solano garage in 1928.

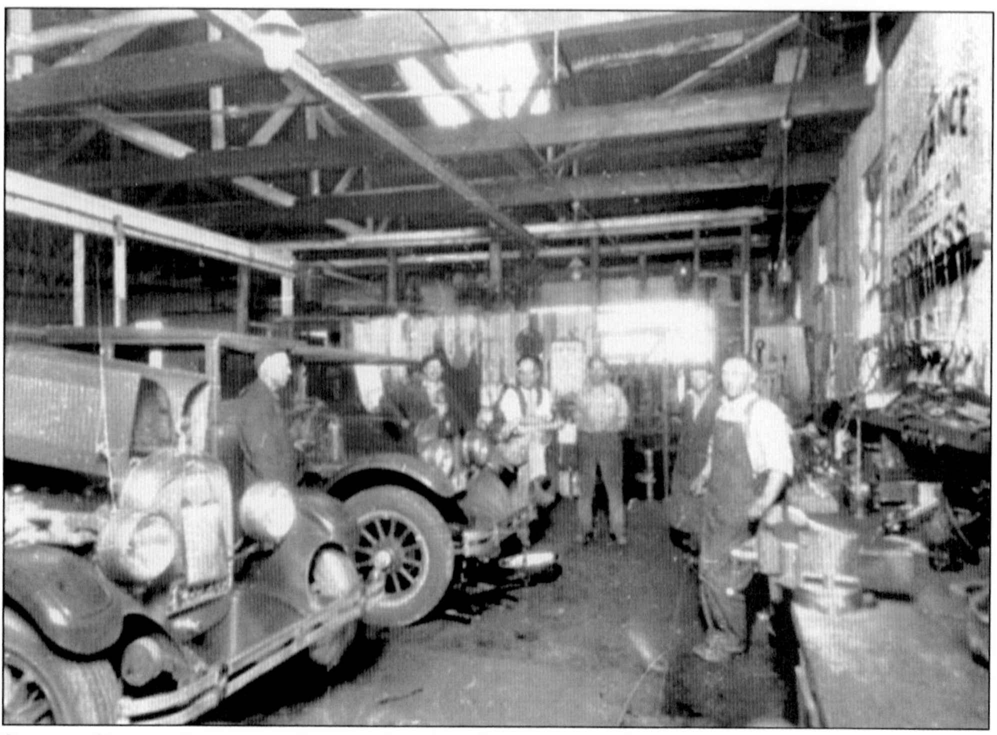

Solano Garage Interior. Cars are lined up for repair inside the Solano Garage in 1928.

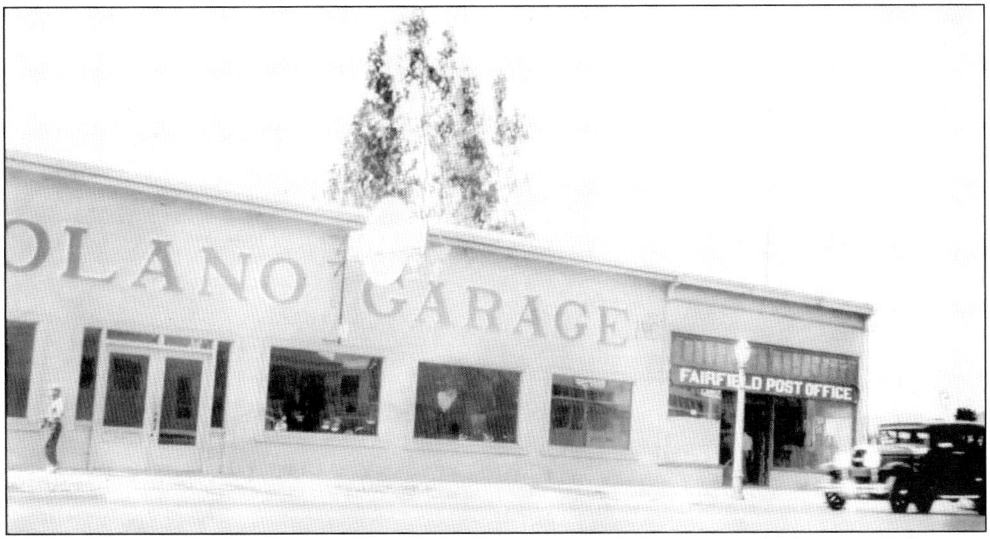

GARAGE AND FAIRFIELD POST OFFICE. The new courthouse replaced the post office on Courthouse Square in 1911. The post office found a new home in this building next to the Solano Garage.

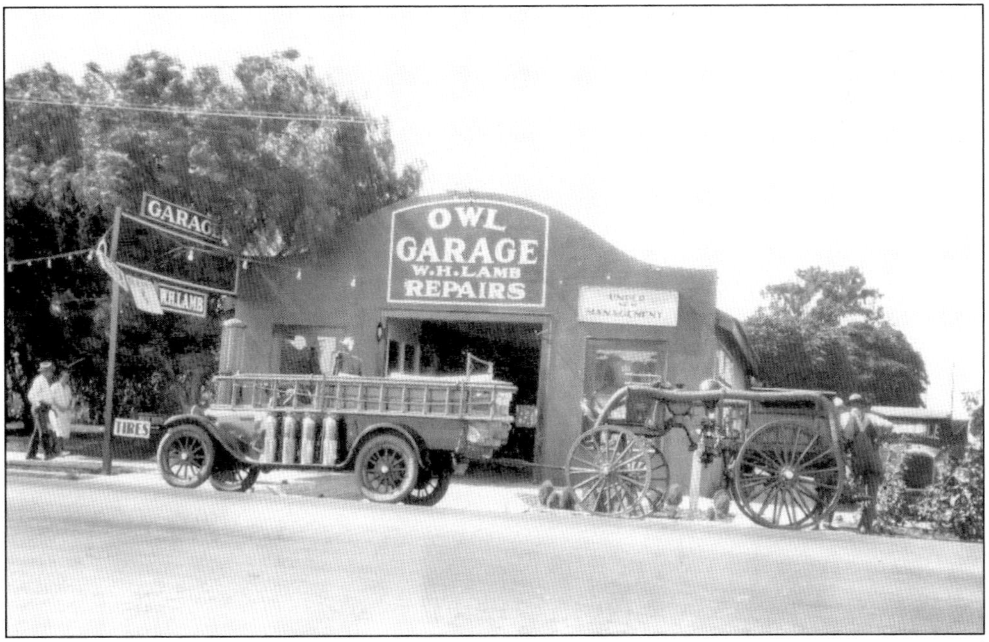

OWL GARAGE. The Owl Garage, seen here with ladder and hose carts parked in front, operated in the 1930s.

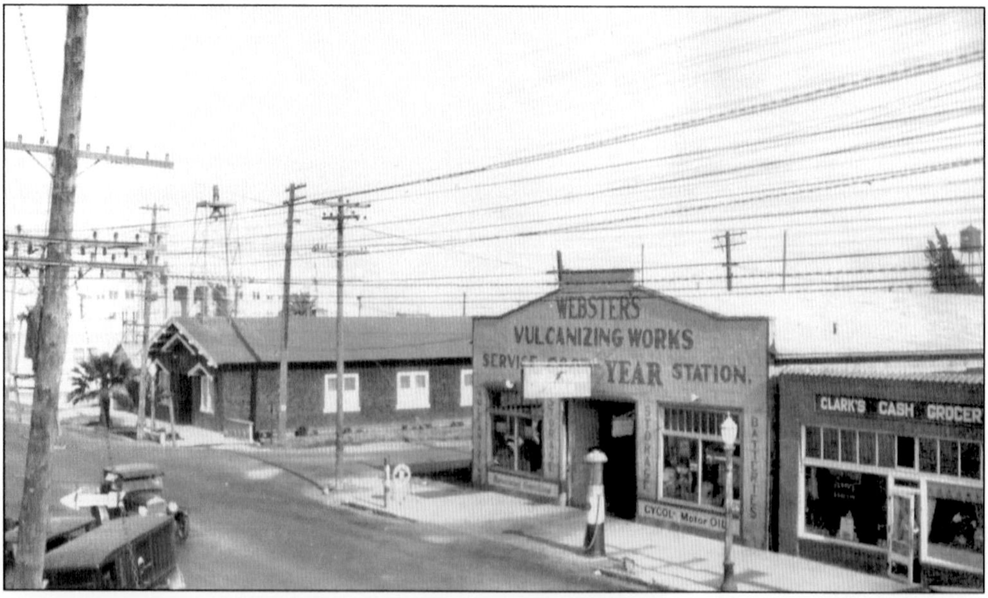

WEBSTER'S VULCANIZING WORKS. Synthetic rubber was made here, but customers could also fill up the gas tank when the works was open for business at the corner of Texas and Jefferson Streets.

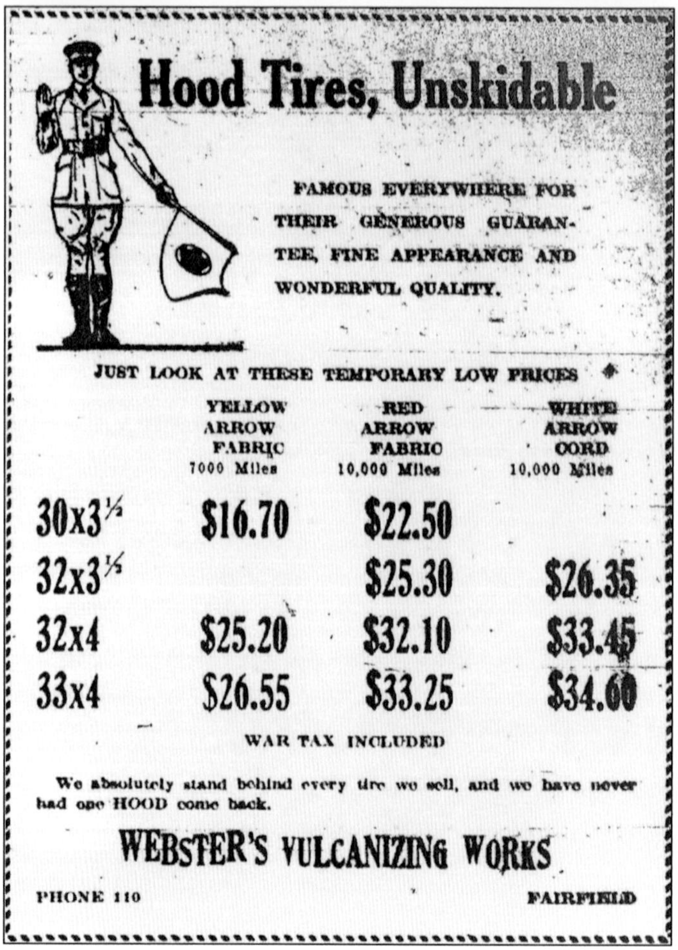

AD FOR WEBSTER'S SERVICES. In 1922, Webster's Vulcanizing Works advertised their products in the *Solano Republican*.

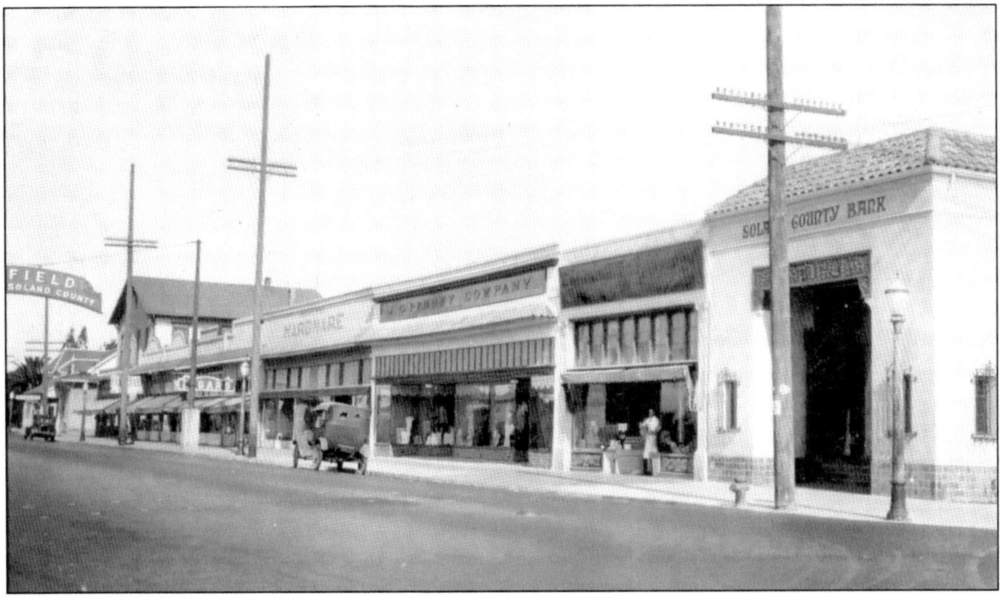

TEXAS STREET, 800 BLOCK. Construction of the new Solano County Bank at 800 Texas Street began on September 27, 1928. The building on the left housed Parr's Electric Shop during the 1920s and then became the Safeway Grocery store. The shop at 810 Texas Street changed from a store named Gordon's to Fairfield's first chain clothing store when Joseph Soares installed the J.C. Penney Company here in the late 1920s. Merchandise was lifted in baskets to the balcony where it was wrapped and paid for. The store at 816 Texas Street belonged to Evans and Pyles, "the world's best hardware store," according to local residents. They moved their business from Suisun to downtown Fairfield in 1923. The store had an old Franklin stove inside—painted pink!

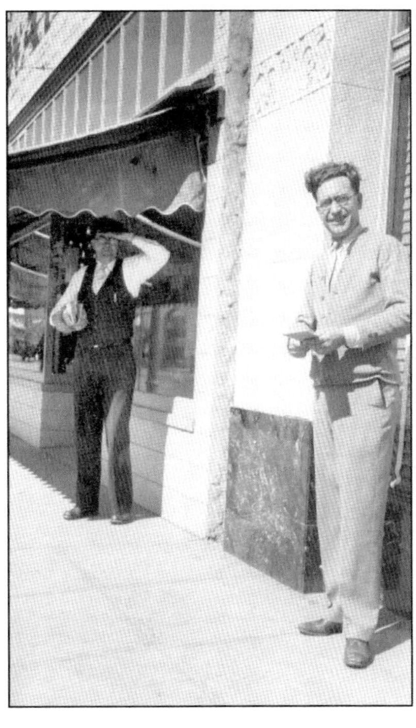

IN FRONT OF SOLANO BANK, 1932. These two gentlemen posed for the photographer in front of the Solano County Bank and Parr's Electric Shop in 1932.

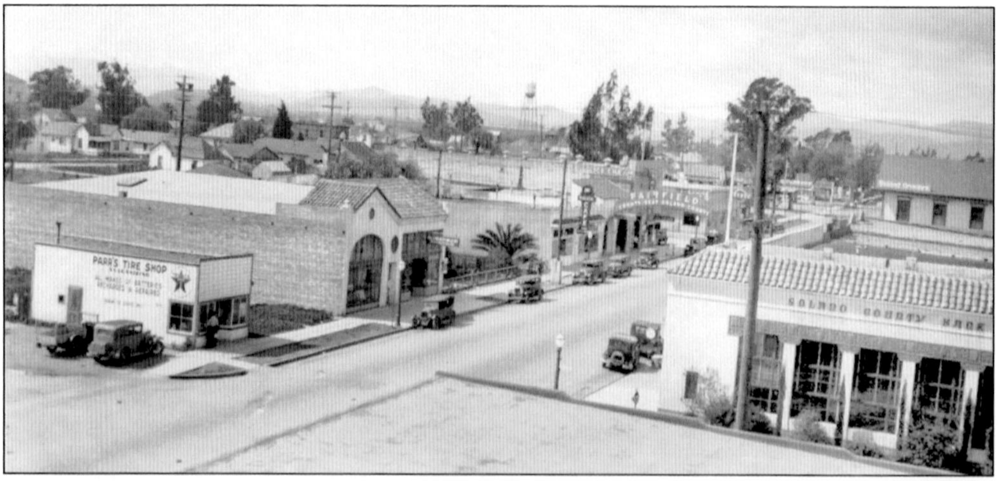

SOLANO REPUBLICAN OFFICE, TEXAS STREET. By 1930, Parr's Tire Shop had established itself on the corner of Texas and Webster Streets. The building next to it housed *Solano Republican* Printing. Further down are a café and a Sprouse Reitz Store, which had opened in the McInnis Building in July 1930. Beyond the Fairfield sign, Allan Witt's Barber Shop is visible, established in the 1920s. Witt also served as a mayor and city councilman, and his shop was a center for local news and views for many years.

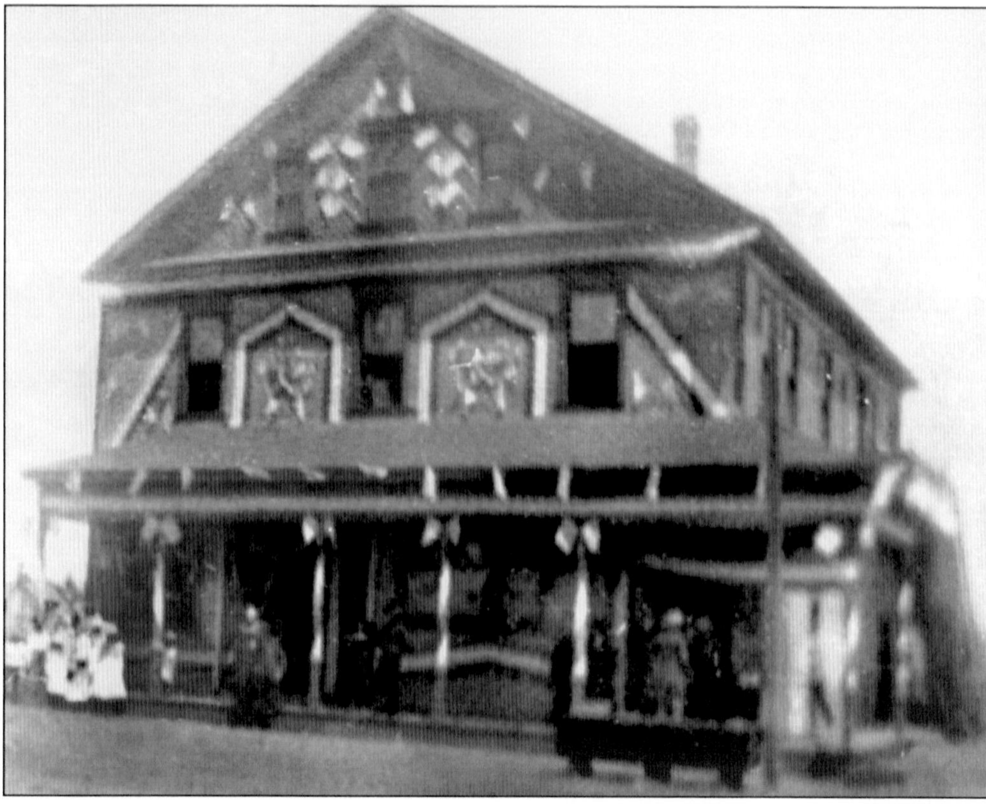

ANDERSON BAKERY. Several bakeries established themselves downtown over the years. One of the earliest and the most colorful shops was the Anderson Bakery on Union Avenue during the 1880s.

STENT MARKET, 1890s. The Stent Market sold groceries to residents during the 1890s. Note the large saw, likely used to butcher animals.

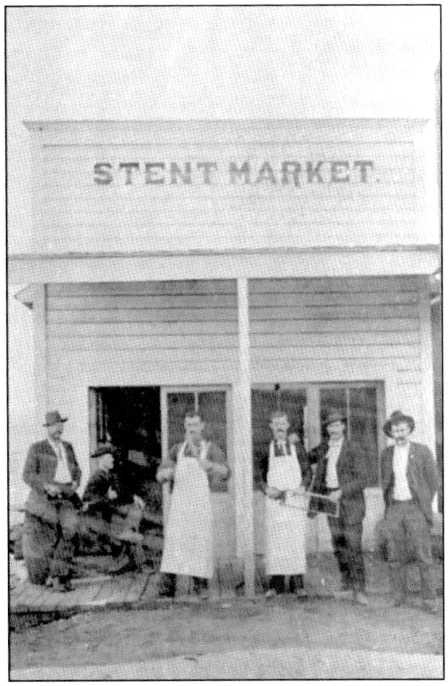

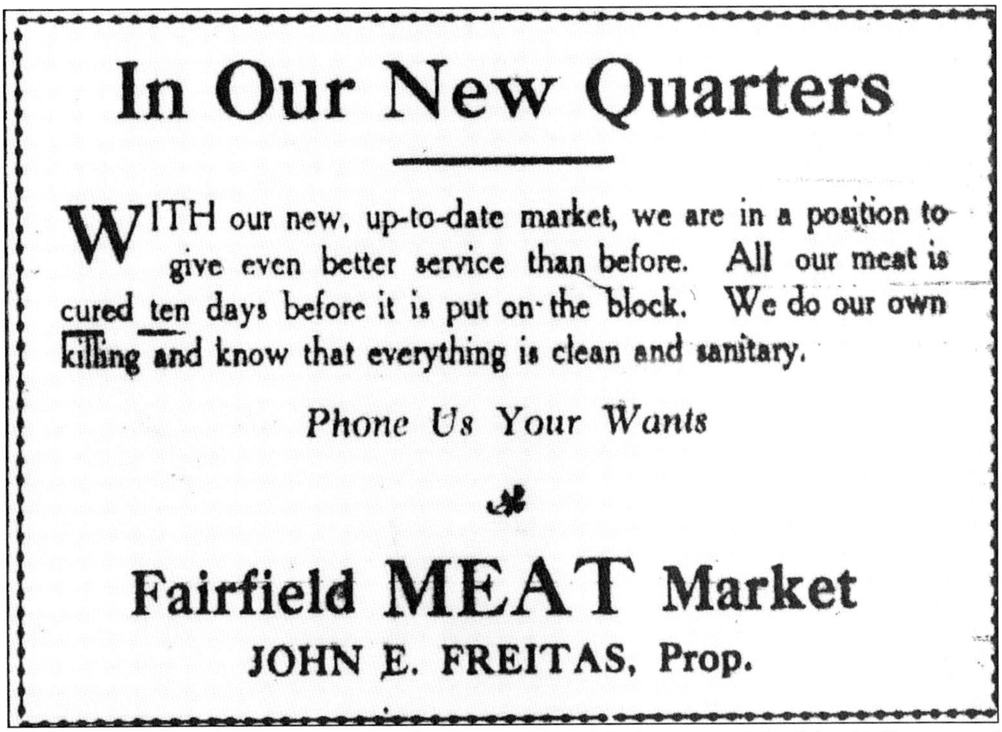

In Our New Quarters

WITH our new, up-to-date market, we are in a position to give even better service than before. All our meat is cured ten days before it is put on the block. We do our own killing and know that everything is clean and sanitary.

Phone Us Your Wants

Fairfield MEAT Market

JOHN E. FREITAS, Prop.

FREITAS MEAT MARKET AD, 1921. The Freitas Meat Market, owned by John E. Freitas and later his son Bud, operated from the early 1920s until the 1940s. Mr. Freitas believed in constant advertising. Another advertisement in 1922 informed customers, "Tell it to us! Just call 51-W any time before 10 a.m. and we will deliver your meat in time for lunch—the best meat obtainable."

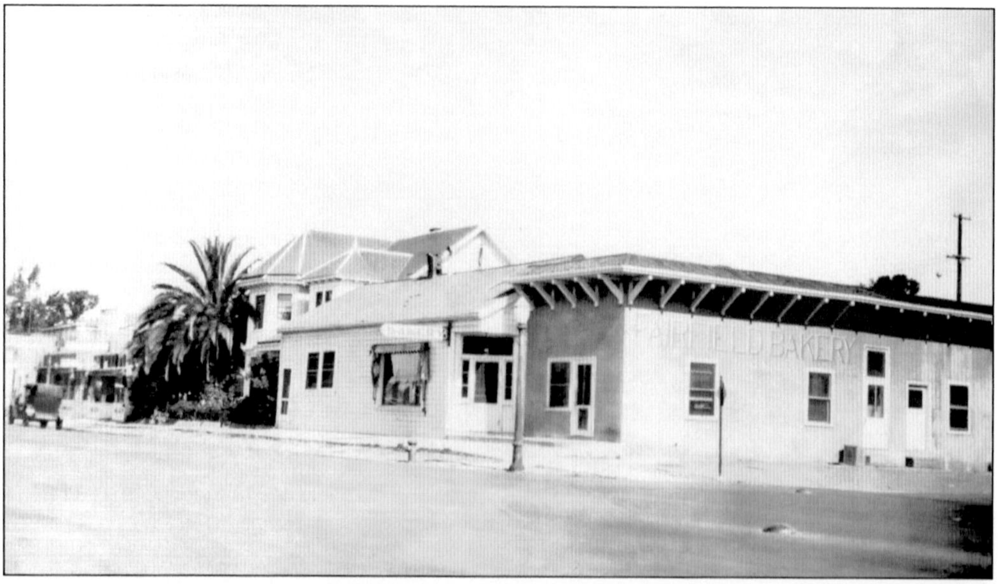

FAIRFIELD BAKERY. The Fairfield Bakery and Meat Market, operated by John F. Meyer, served residents with tasty baked goods and quality meats in the 1930s.

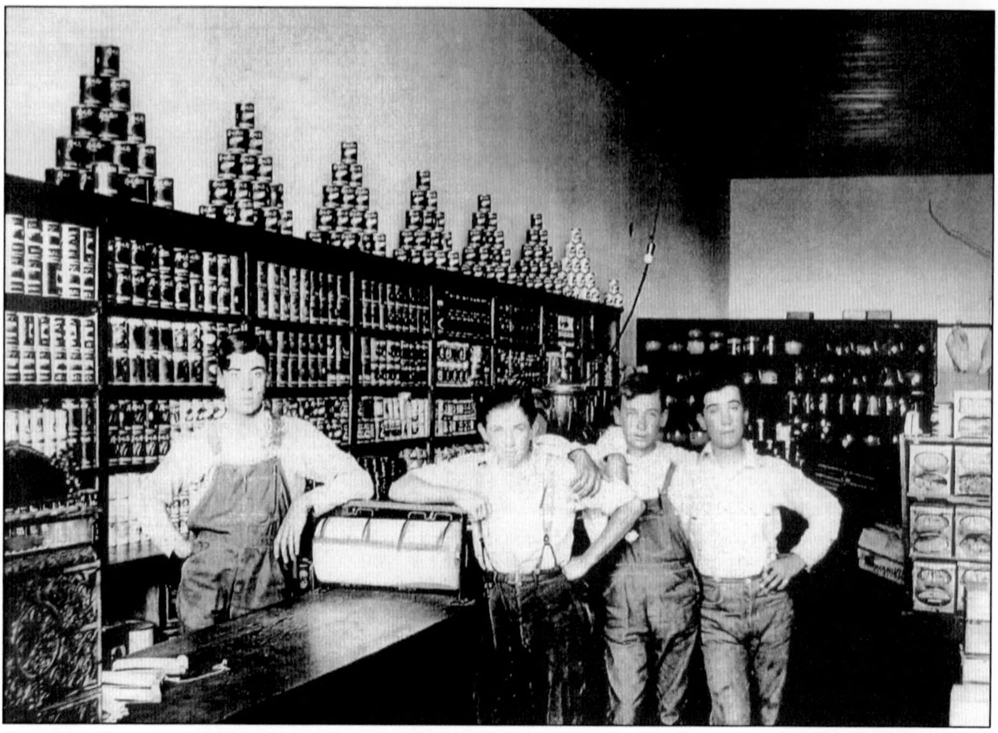

GEREVAS BROTHERS GROCERY STORE, 1920. The Gerevas brothers operated their grocery store on the 800 block of Texas Street during the 1920s. Lillian Whitby remembered, "One of the grocery stores got in a case of thread. We were all so happy because before, if we needed thread, we had to go to Suisun." Pictured, from left to right, are Laurie Gerevas, Bud Huck, Lee Yatsie, and Joe Serpas.

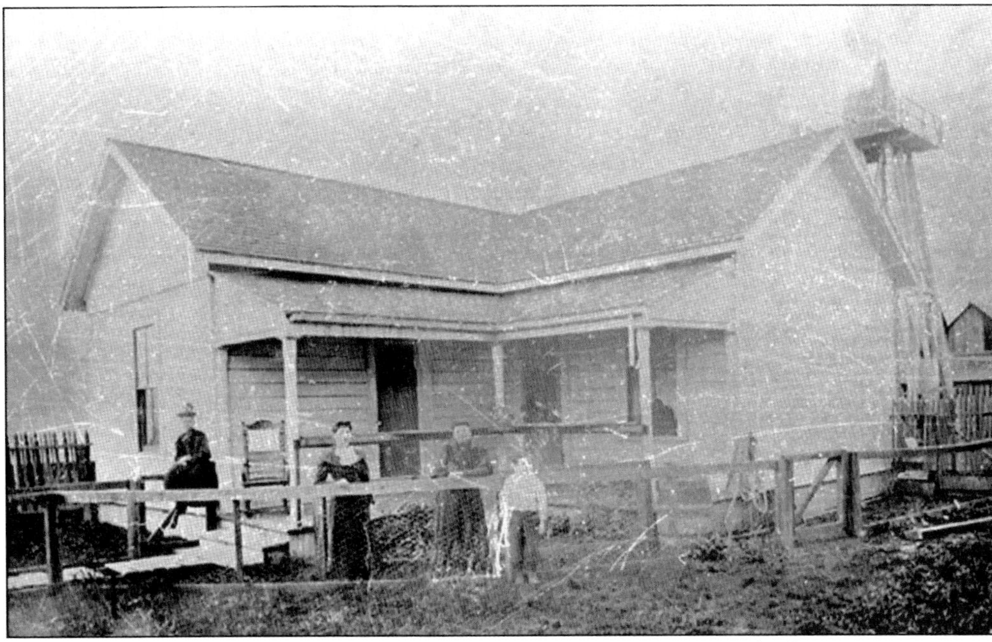

MACY HOME. In the 19th century, residences were mixed in among the businesses on Texas Street. This photo, taken during the 1890s, shows the Macy home on the north side of the 700 block. From left to right are Mabel Ethel Macy, Alice Macy Springer, and young Mervin Macy.

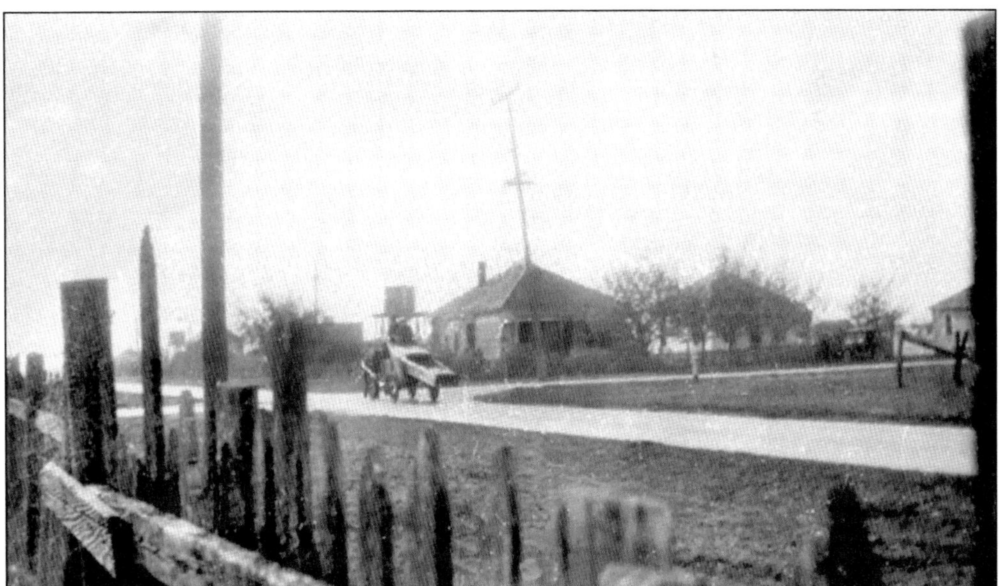

GREAT JONES. This view of the corner of Great Jones Street and Broadway was taken in the early 1900s. Captain Waterman allegedly named Great Jones after his former girlfriend. A narrow strip of asphalt had been put down in the middle of the street. Note the city water tank in the background. A communal water and sewer system was established in 1913.

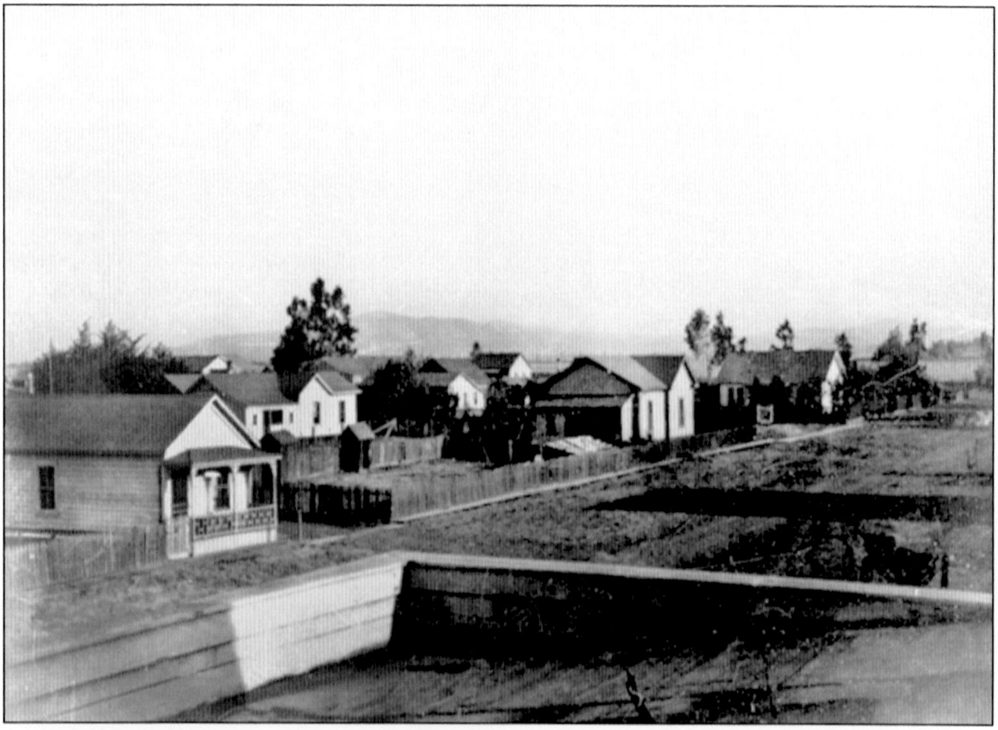

Street Scene. This is another unidentified street scene in Fairfield, possibly Union Avenue looking south, with Mount Diablo in the distance.

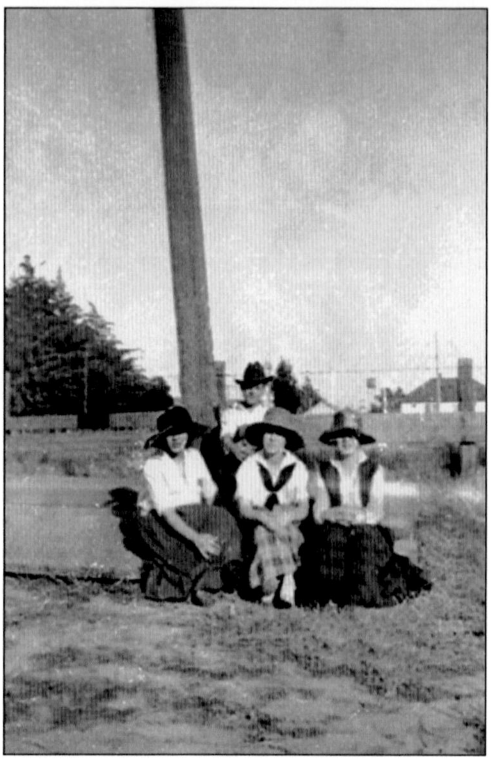

Taylor Street. A group of friends gather around a pole on Taylor Street, before the street was paved. From left to right are Clara Waugh, Ruby Brady Grigsby, and Leah Babe Shively Carpenter. The gentleman behind the group is Verne Morrill.

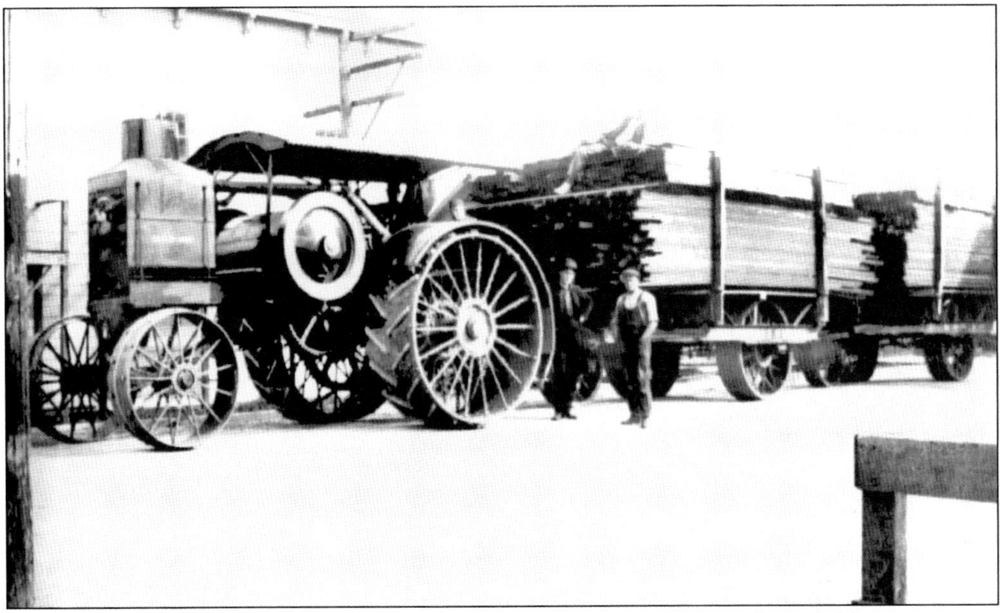

Steam Engine. At the turn of the century, many residents still viewed Fairfield as a not very desirable place to live. When Lillian Whitby informed her mother-in-law, Martha Whitby, that the young couple planned to build a house on Jackson Street in 1901, Martha sniffed, "Why are you building in Fairfield? Everyone knows that Suisun is the big city!" By the 1920s, that attitude had changed. Fairfield slowly began to grow, with more residents moving from the surrounding valleys into town. Here, a steam truck pulls a large load of lumber, needed to build all those new homes and stores.

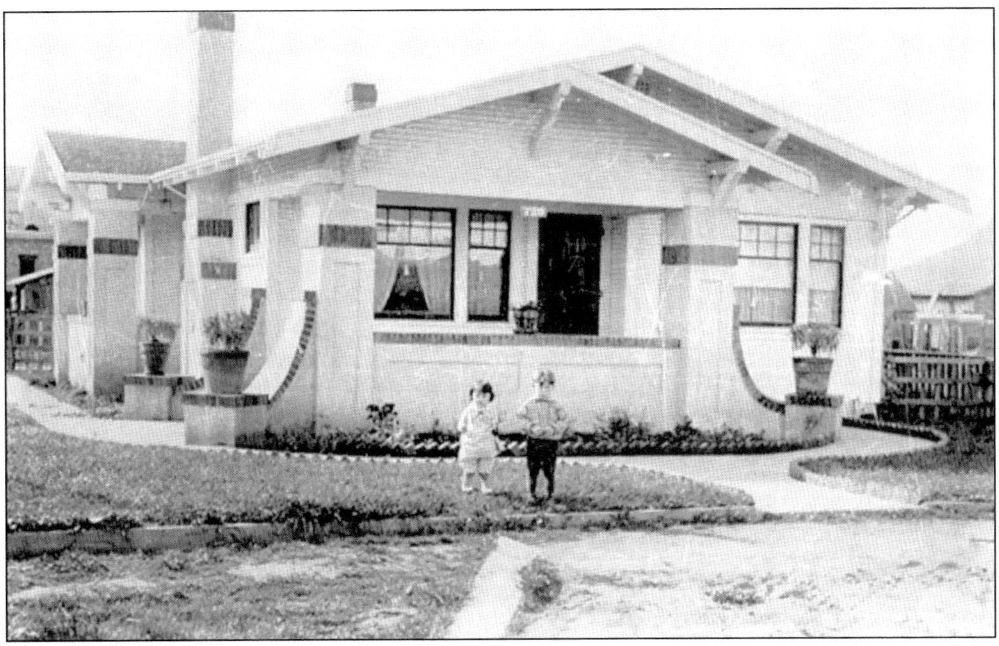

Empire Street, Gerevas Home. While Texas Street was the main commercial artery of the town, Empire Street became the premier residential address. The Gerevas family built this house at 725 Empire Street.

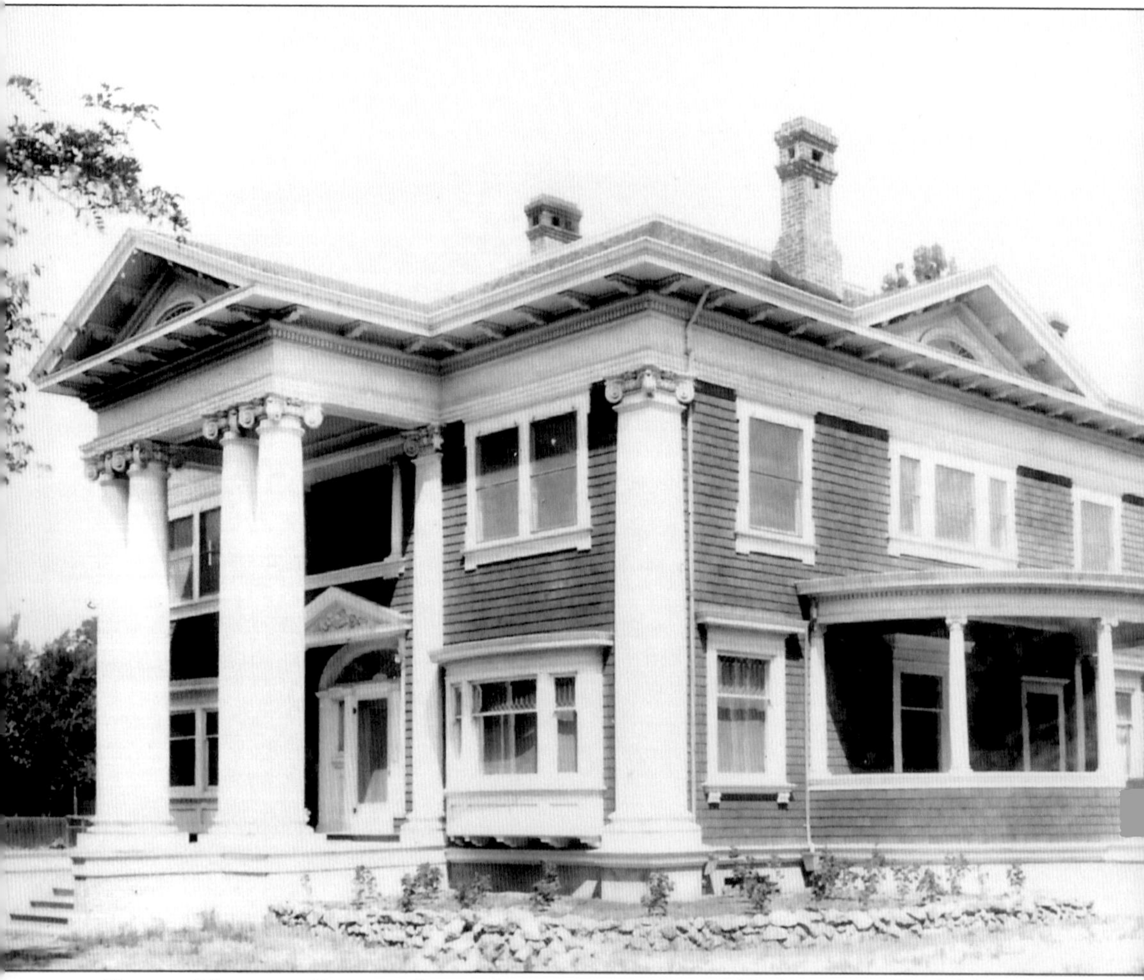

Goosen Mansion. Prior to the city's incorporation in 1903, houses in Fairfield had been simple, often just simple frame dwellings with minimal decoration. Typically, more imposing mansions were built on the ranches of more affluent orchardists in surrounding valleys. An exception is the imposing Goosen mansion at 1010 Empire Street. Henry Goosen owned both Goosen Hardware Store on Texas Street and the Fairfield Water Works, which he purchased in 1902. As a highly successful businessman, he contracted McCullum, McDougal, and Cameron to build the house in 1910. The architect, if one was used, is unknown. The Goosen Mansion is a two-story, 12-room, Colonial Revival–style house, covered with painted wood shingles. Onyx for the three impressive fireplaces was quarried at Tolenas Springs. A front portico with massive Ionic columns greets visitors. The house is nicknamed, "The Mayor's House," because Fairfield's second and fourth mayors, Mr. Smith and Manuel Campos respectively, owned it.

Map of Fairfield, 1946. Fairfield continued to grow slowly, numbering 1,312 residents by 1940. Its name—Town of Fairfield—changed to City of Fairfield in 1938. But the real change came in 1942 when construction of the Fairfield-Suisun Army Airfield began. By 1945, the airfield was reconfigured as a major airfield for the Strategic Air Command. It was renamed Travis Air Force Base after the fatal crash of General Travis in 1952. The Base brought large numbers of new residents looking for homes. On January 15, 1946, the City of Fairfield annexed land north of Kentucky Street, the first annexation since Captain Waterman filed the original plat in 1858.

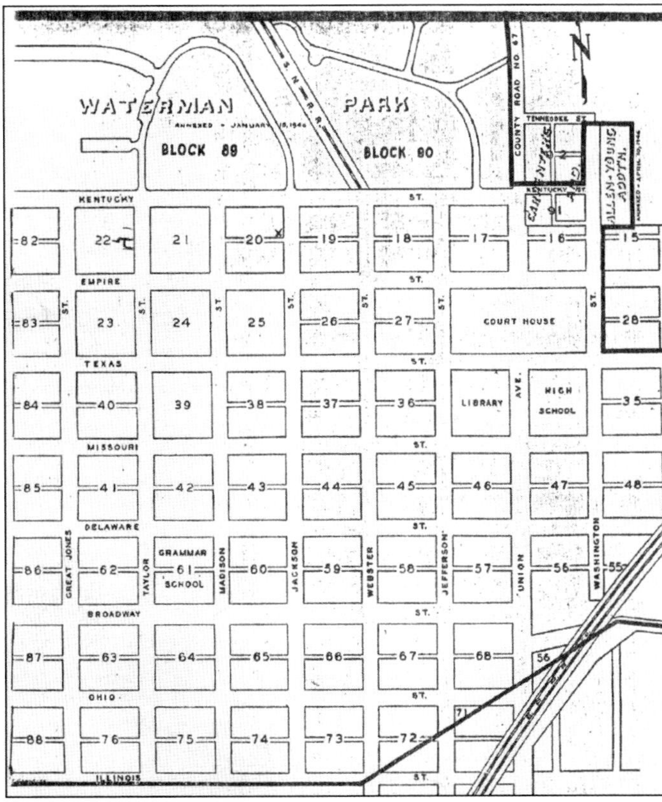

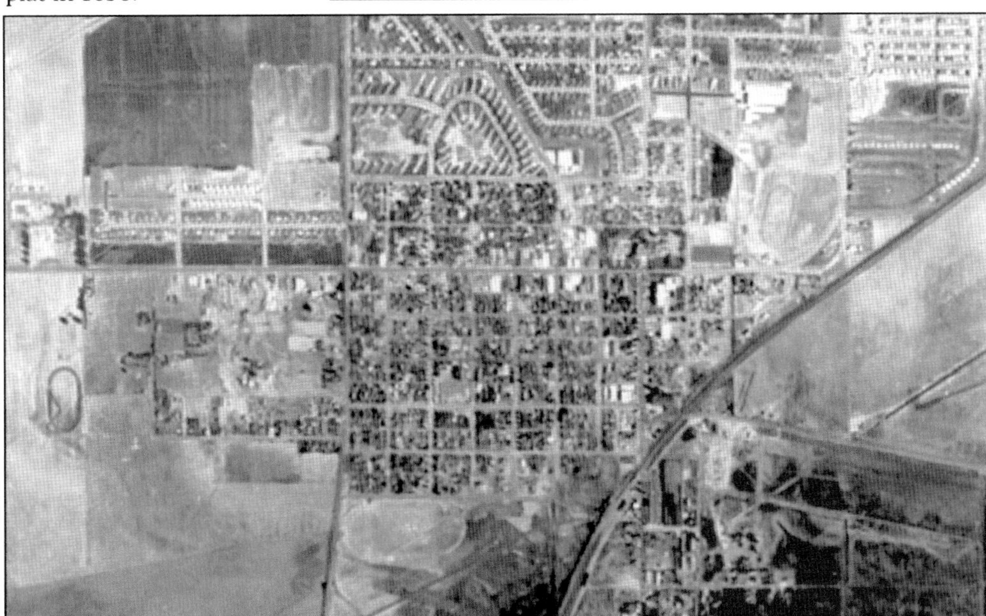

Aerial View of Fairfield, 1952. Between 1940 and 1950, the number of residents nearly tripled to 3,118.This aerial photograph of Fairfield was taken in the summer of 1952. It clearly shows the addition of the Waterman Park Housing area, as well as growth along Texas Street beyond downtown.

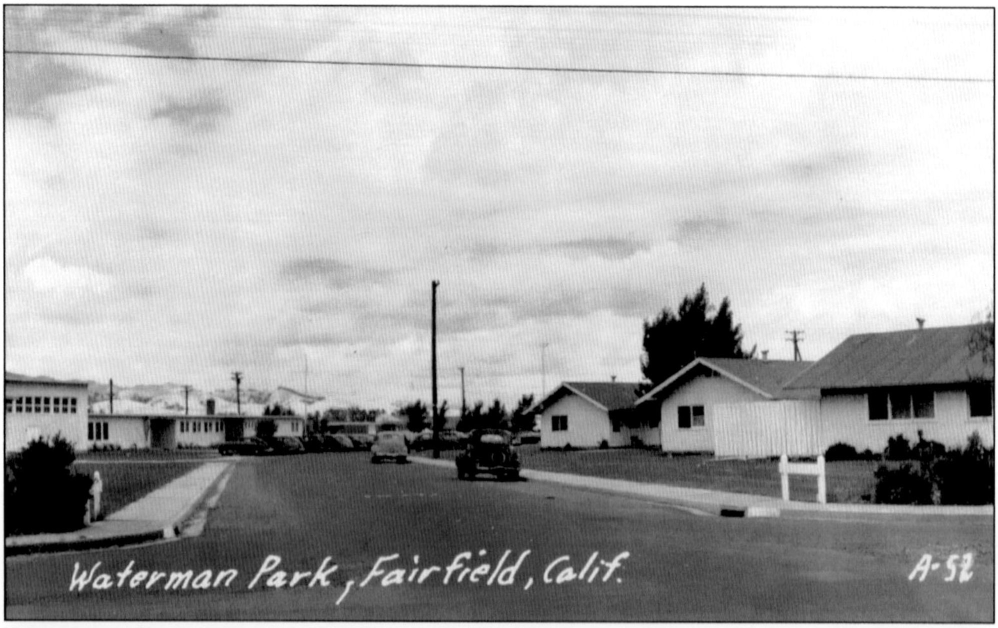

Waterman Park Housing. The houses built in Waterman Park were government housing, strictly for military personnel stationed at Travis Air Base. Rent was around $60 per month. The complex included its own theatre, beauty shop, and café. It even had its own newspaper.

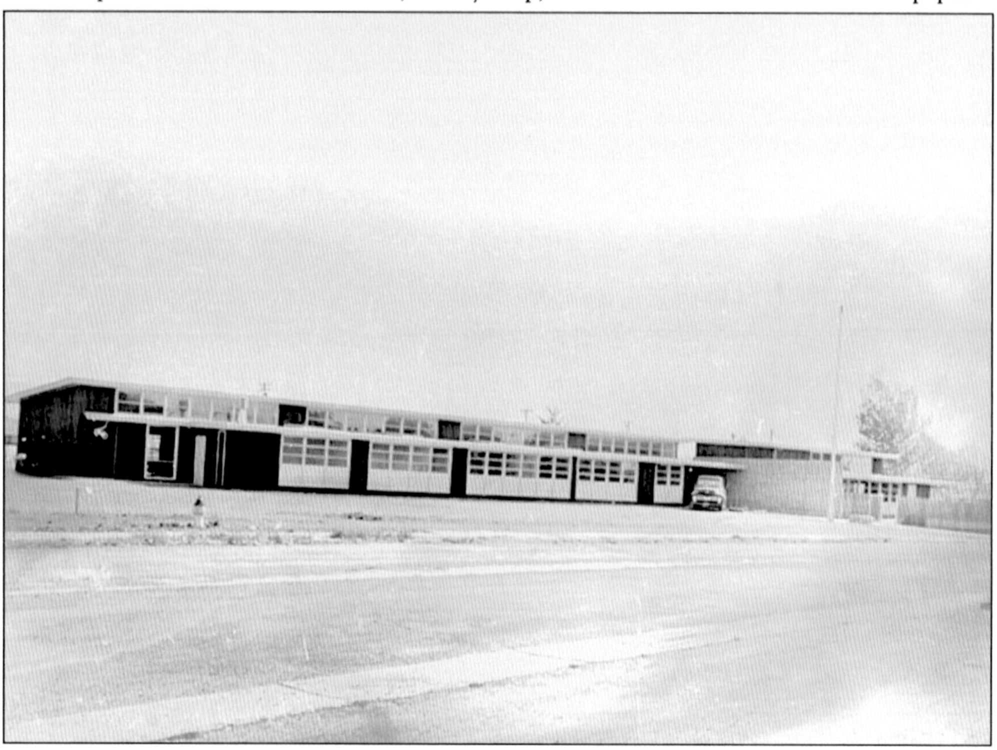

Waterman Elementary School. Another feature of the development was Waterman Elementary School. Older students attended Armijo High School. Located on Civic Center Drive, the old elementary school building today houses Fairfield Adult School.

Six

SERVING THE COMMUNITY

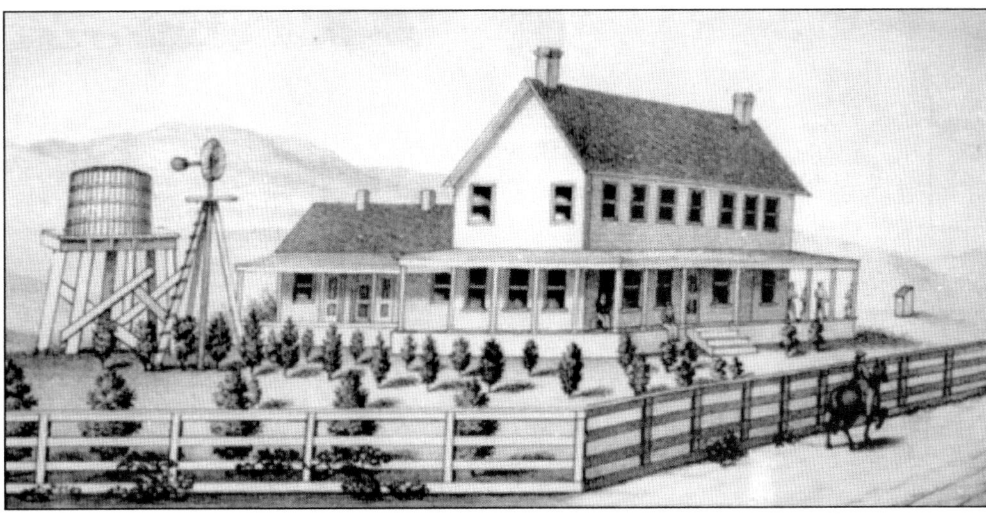

COUNTY HOSPITAL, *THOMPSON & WEST HISTORICAL ATLAS* MAP OF SOLANO COUNTY, 1878. The first Solano County Hospital, a combination of poorhouse and hospital, was built in 1876 on 60 acres in the Tolenas area. It consisted of a two-story, plain, white, frame building, shown here in an 1878 drawing. Besides the hospital, it had several barns, a water tower with a capacity of 10,000 gallons, a laundry building, carpenter's shop, prison, wood shed, and a cottage housing the hospital's superintendent. In accordance with beliefs at the time that fresh air and sunshine improved health, the covered veranda of the hospital allowed patients to stay outside. Inside the building, the first floor offered a reading room, dining room, dispensary, storerooms, three sleeping rooms for ambulant patients, and a "last chance" ward for dying patients.

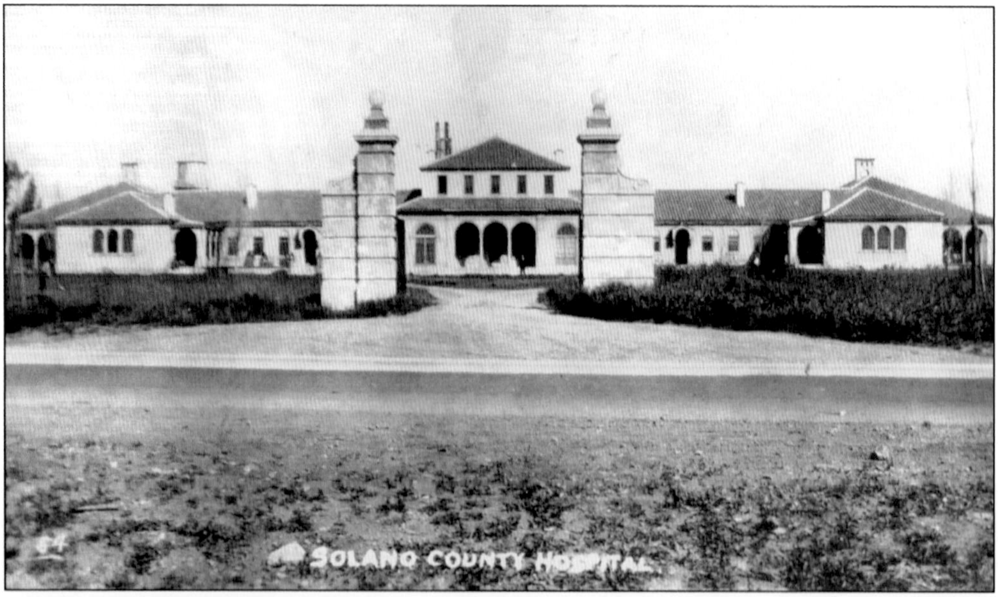

NEW COUNTY HOSPITAL. By 1917, the county hospital on Tabor Avenue needed to be replaced. Plans for a county hospital existed, but were delayed by World War I. In 1920, a new county hospital was built on Rockville Road, one mile west of the courthouse, outside town limits. C.E. Perry of Vallejo designed it in the newly popular Spanish Colonial Revival style. A low, sprawling building, constructed at a cost of more than $100,000, opened its doors to the public on November 7, 1920. It was expected that all the ill of the county could be treated here.

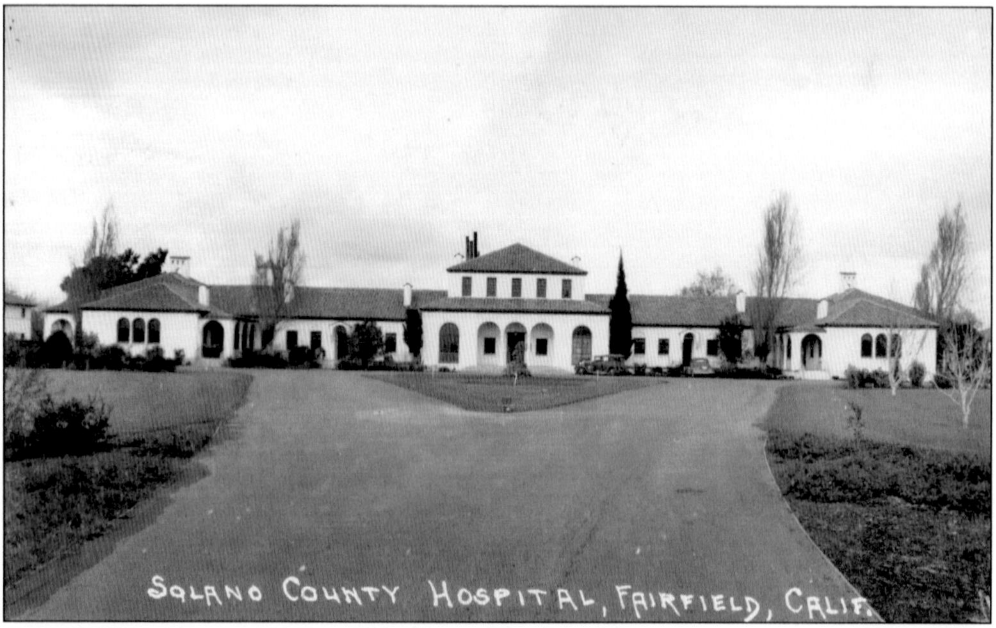

COUNTY HOSPITAL, 1940. By 1940, the entrance had been changed and widened. With the population rising, additional buildings had been added to the complex. After the end of its service as a hospital in the 1970s, the buildings were used for county offices. The board of supervisors finally decided to raze the buildings in 1998. In 2004, an apartment complex replaced it.

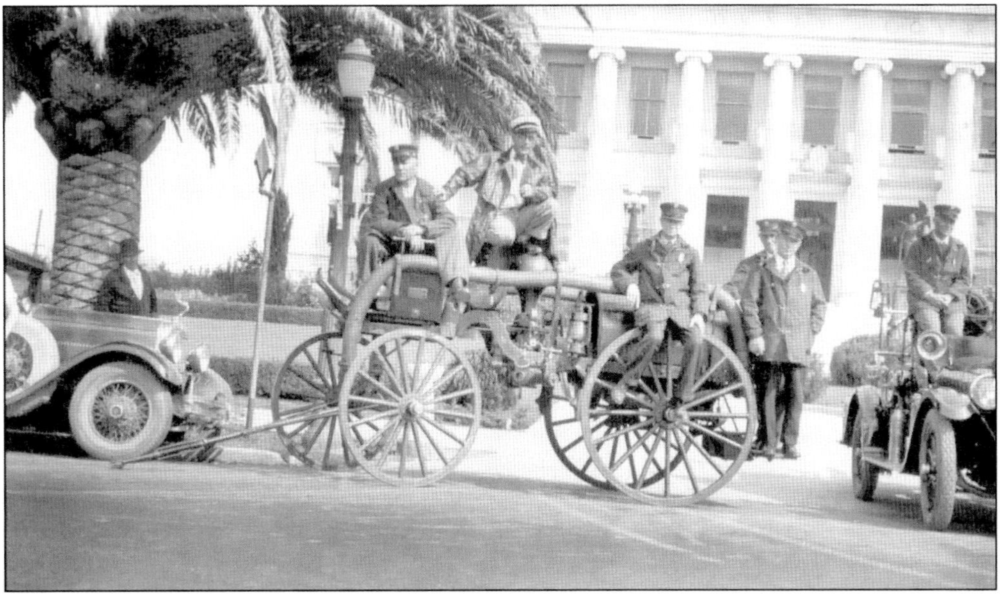

FIREMEN AT COURTHOUSE, 1932. The devastating fire of 1929 that destroyed Armijo High School and the first Solano County Library made evident the need for more modern firefighting equipment. Still, it took a couple of years for the Fairfield Fire Department, at the time housed on Webster Street, to acquire a new engine. Here, one of the older fire engines is shown.

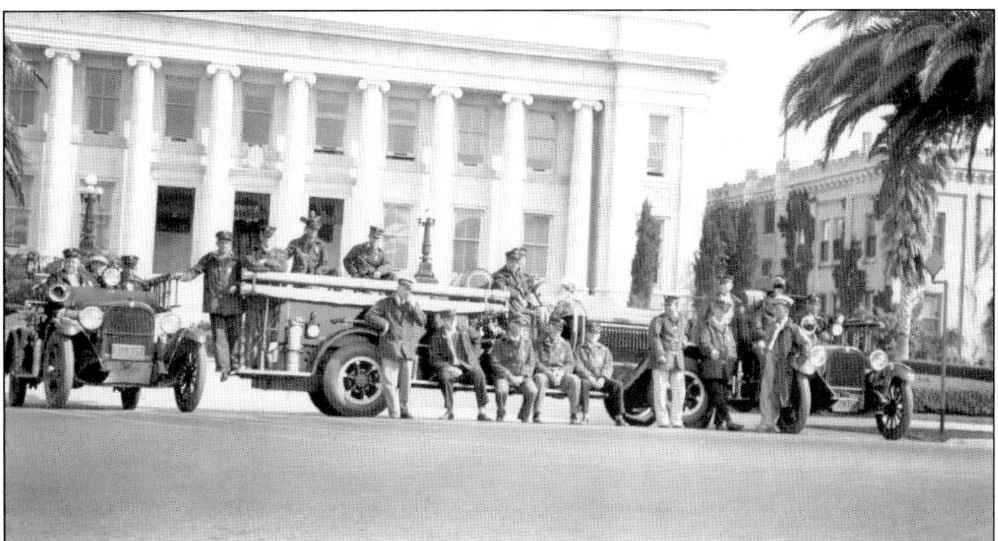

NEW ENGINE, 1932. A group of firemen sit on the steps of their new engine in front of the courthouse. Featuring a longer ladder than the earlier version, this engine could battle a blaze in multistory buildings. To the right, the county jail is visible.

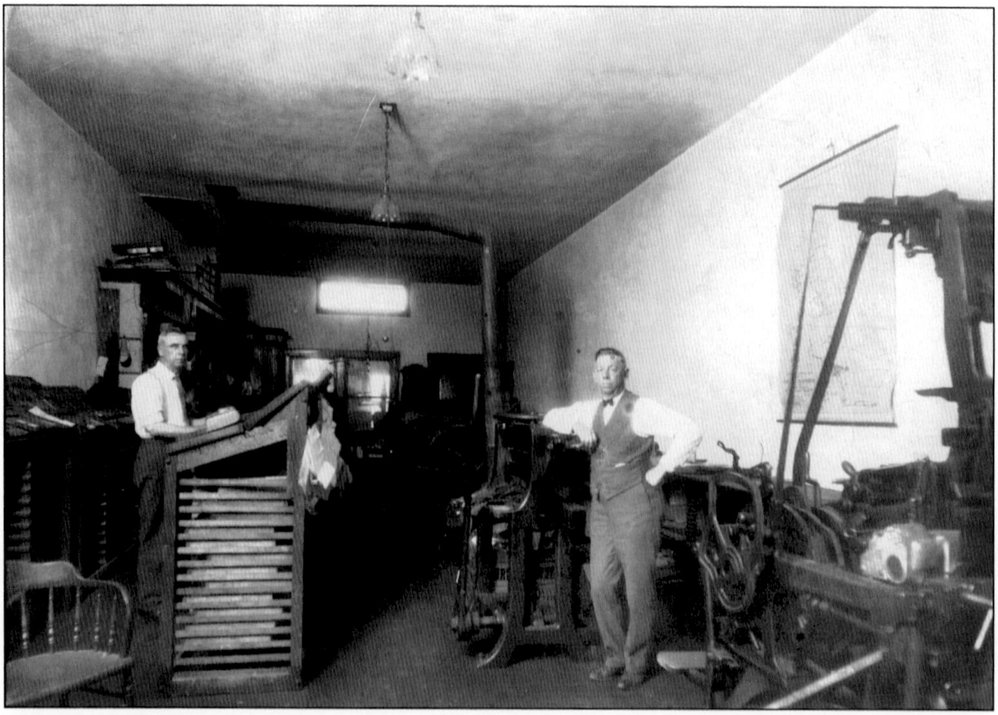

NEWSPAPER PRINTING ROOM, C. 1910. A look into a narrow basement shows the man on the left at a composing table, and the man on the right leaning on a cutting machine. A linotype machine is in the foreground at right. Press, cabinets, and typecases with individual letters are in the background.

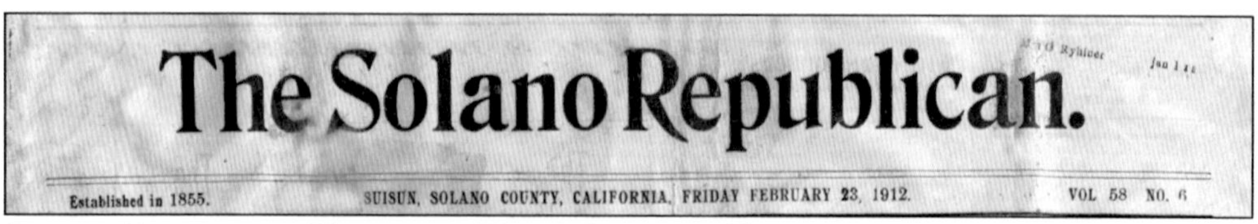

The Solano Republican.

Established in 1855. SUISUN, SOLANO COUNTY, CALIFORNIA, FRIDAY FEBRUARY 23, 1912. VOL 58 NO. 6

SOLANO REPUBLICAN HEADLINE. The *Solano Republican* was founded in 1855 as the *Solano County Herald*. It operated out of Benicia until the relocation of the county seat to Fairfield. On September 11, 1858, the editor announced that the newspaper would move to Fairfield onOctober 1, and stated that, "we avail ourselves of this location to come into more intimate communication with the people of this county, we shall expect an increase in patronage."

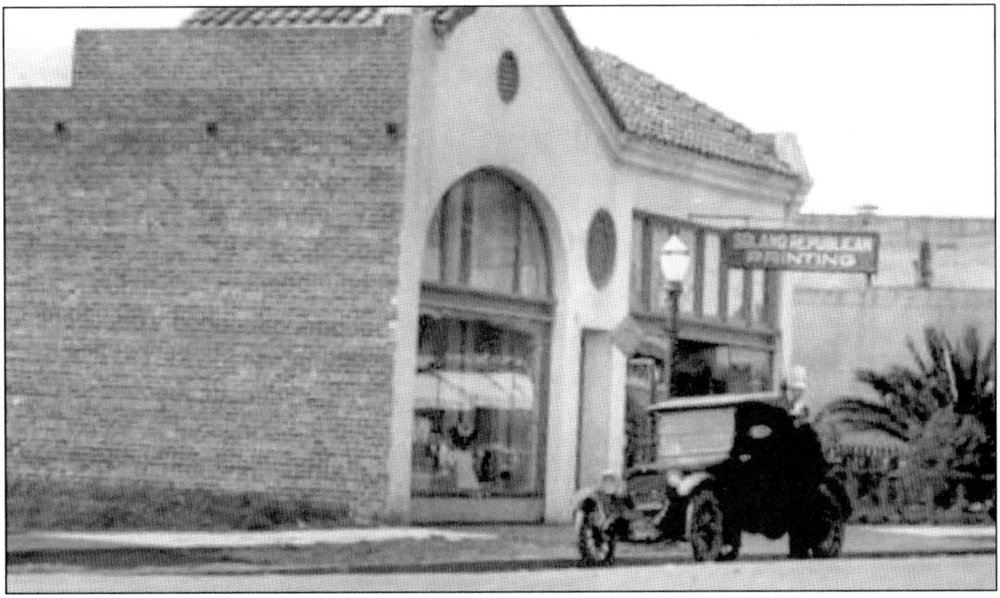

SOLANO REPUBLICAN PRINTING. Competing newspapers, the *Solano Press* and the *Solano County Herald*, eventually merged in the fall of 1869 to become the *Solano County Republican*. In October 1875, the paper was purchased by new owners, Montgomery and Bowen, who finally moved the paper to Fairfield. By the late 1920s, the *Solano Republican* was operating near the corner of Texas and Webster Streets. At that time, it was published weekly, changing later to a biweekly schedule. David Weir became its publisher in later years.

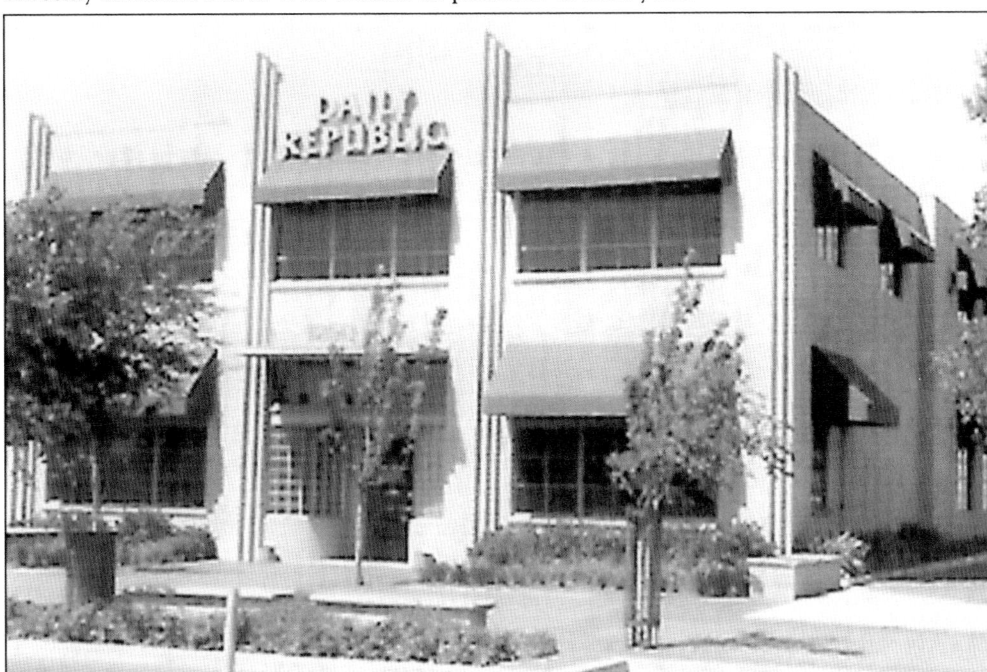

DAILY REPUBLIC BUILDING, 1935. Eventually, the *Solano Republican* acquired the building at 1250 Texas Street from Bernard Gillespie and moved its printing business here. The newspaper was renamed the *Daily Republic* and still serves area residents as a daily newspaper.

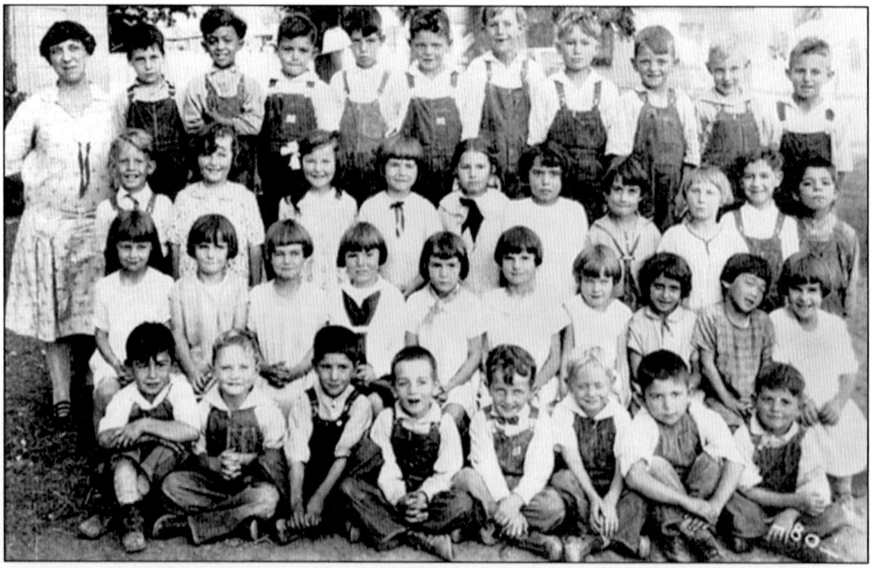

PRIMARY SCHOOL, FIRST GRADE, 1928. By the 1920s, if not earlier, Fairfield had a primary school at Delaware and Madison Streets. Pictured, from, left to right, are (front row) L. Gerevas, M. McInnis, unidentified, E. Swasey, G. Cusick, G. Smith, T. Billalon, and E. Tavalaro; (second row) F. Lawrence, unidentified, J. Juan, H. Venning, unidentified, F. Silveria, B. Wright, unidentified, A. Kajima, and E. Lewis; (third row) W. Turner, K. Stauffer, three unidentified, A. Vallado, D. Freitas, and three unidentified; (back row) teacher Miss Moss, two unidentified, J. Lawrence, A. Gonsalves, R. Erickson, A. Athey, B. Hance, R. Tavalaro, K. Jones, and J. Hopkins.

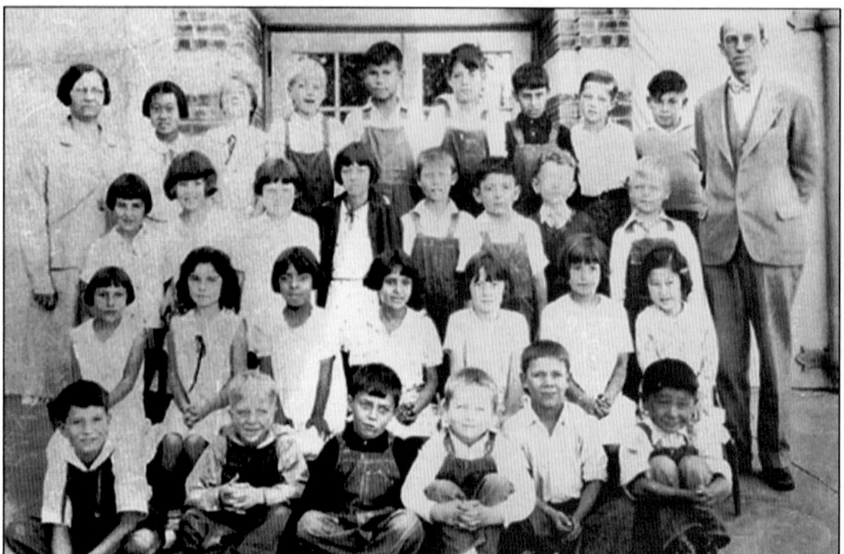

PRIMARY SCHOOL, SECOND GRADE, 1930. From left to right are (front row) two unidentified, T. Perez, B. Chadbourne, E. Alonzo, and W. Ichimoto; (second row) one unidentified, J. Soares, five unidentified; (third row) G. Campos, two unidentified, A. Cabral, B. Lambrecht, T. Billalon, J. Mortensen, and M. Markey; (back row) Mrs. Kerr, K. Takanaka, H. Anderson, E. Jacobas, P. Huerta, A. Gonsalves, T. Perez, C. Woodard, L. Gerevas, and Mr. Mark Woods.

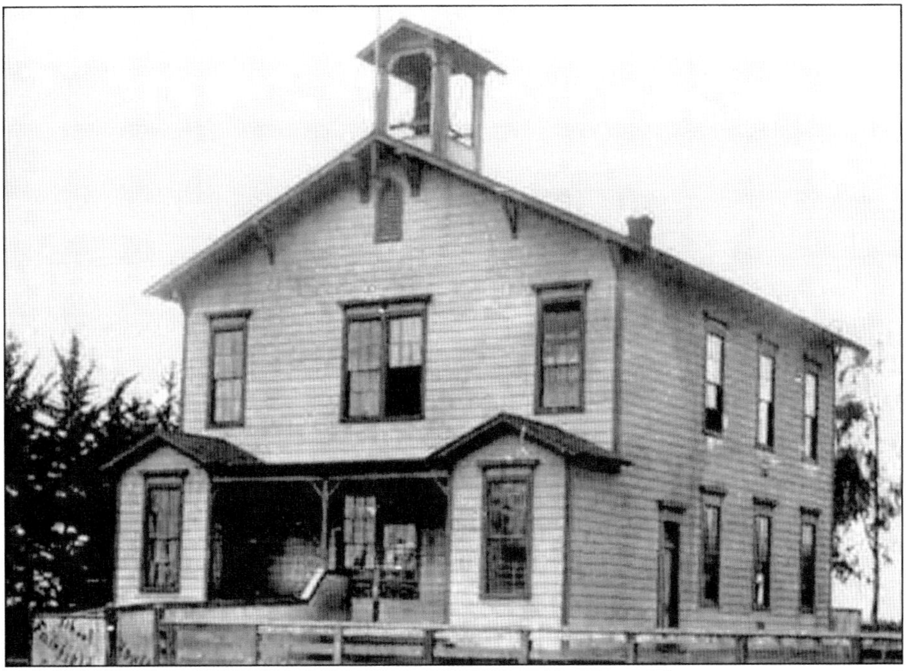

Fairfield Grammar School Before 1908. A growing town needs its own grammar school. This handsome structure with a bell tower on the corner of Delaware and Madison Streets fit the bill for growing Fairfield until 1908, when increasing enrollment required a larger building.

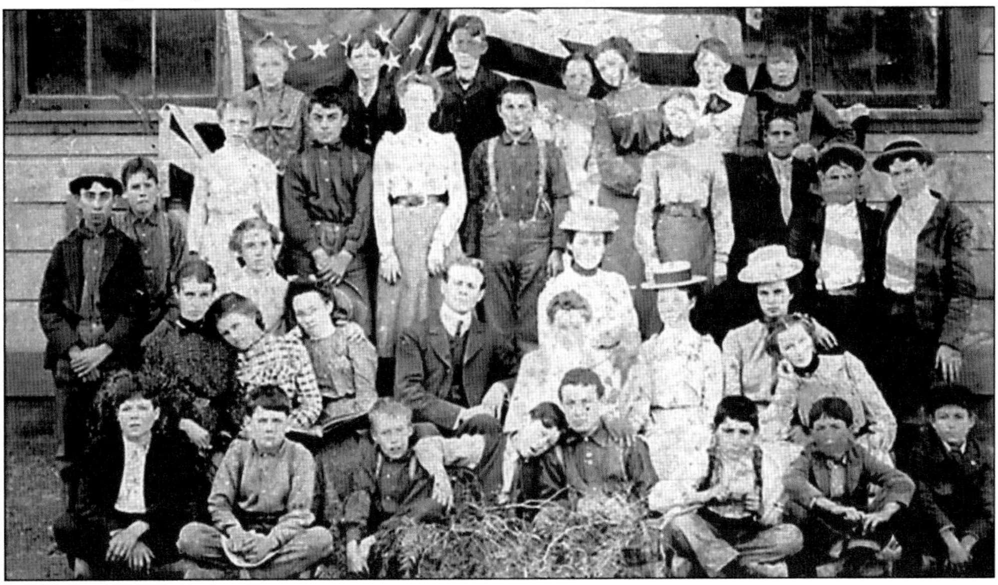

Grammar School Class, Seventh and Eighth Grade, 1903. This photo shows the seventh and eighth grade grammar school class with their teacher. Shown, from left to right, are (front row) A. Battersby, L. Morrill, E. Staples, W. Donssout, W. Matthes, T. Braghetta, J. Carroutt, and F. Kellog; (middle row) P. Lambert Wright, S. Clark, R. Woods, G. Lawlor, G. Lockie Wring, J. Gerreras, G. Durren Howard, J. Serpas, J. Quigley, E. Meyers, G. Fix, W. Taylor, F. Serpas, R. Murphy, S. Merrill, I. Fix, L. Scarlett, G. Cox, teacher Will C. Wood, E. Battersby, S. Pearson, E. Barth, and R. Fix; (back row) E. Cox, B. Kelly, and E. Lockie.

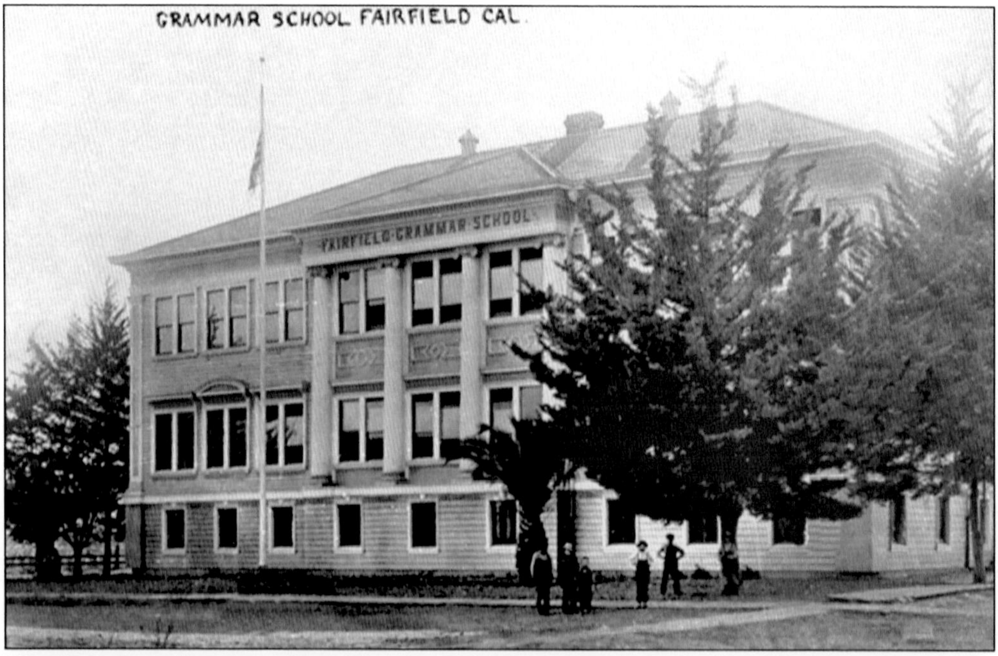

New Grammar School, 1908. The new Fairfield Grammar School was built in 1908, on the old school lot on Delaware and Madison Streets. At the time, the father of longtime resident Vera Oliver had a contract painting houses in the town of Cement. He was asked to come back to Fairfield to paint the new school building. It turned out to be a bigger job than anticipated. His wife finally decided to move the whole family from the Central Valley to Fairfield.

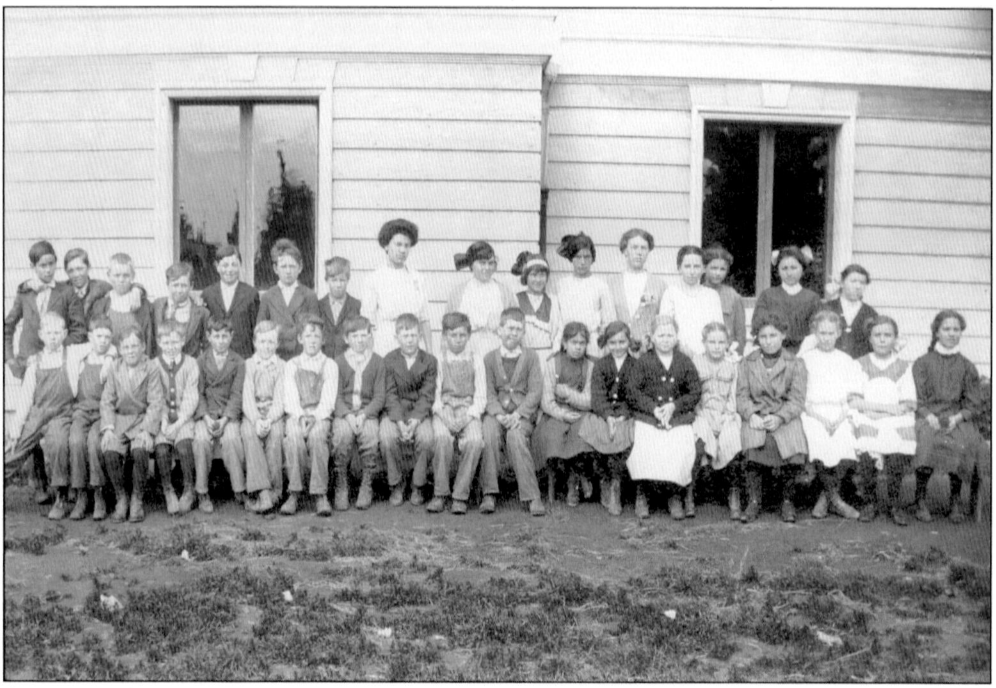

Grammar School Class, c. 1908. School children are gathered for their first official photograph in front of the new Grammar School.

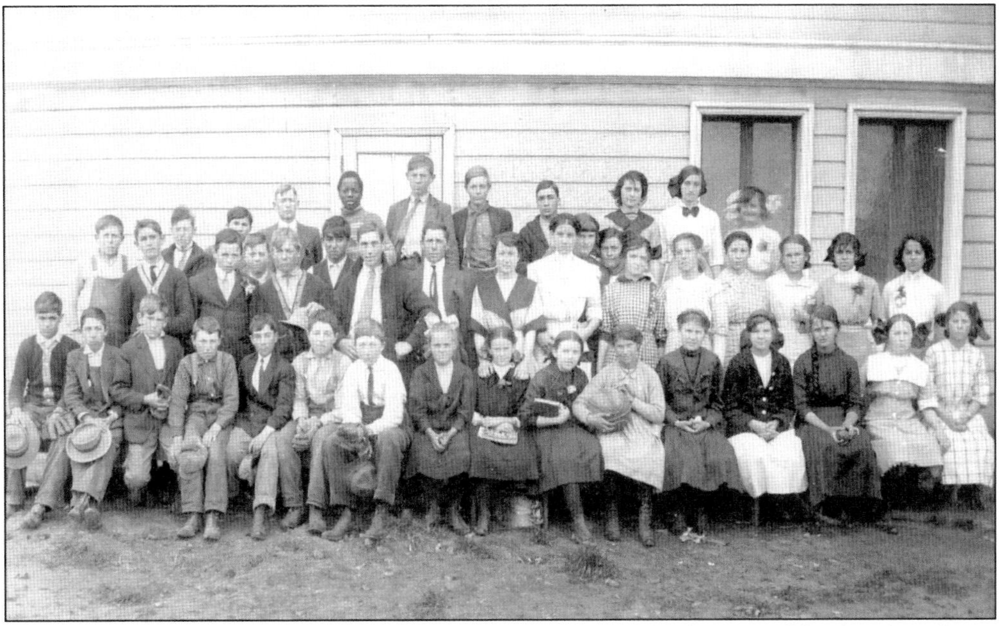

GRAMMAR SCHOOL CLASS, C. 1908. A slightly older group of children posed for this class photo. Of interest is the fifth child from the left in the back row. Few African Americans lived in Solano County before World War II, although the newspaper did mention "a half dozen colored children" in 1871. This child is most likely the son of Tillie Fann.

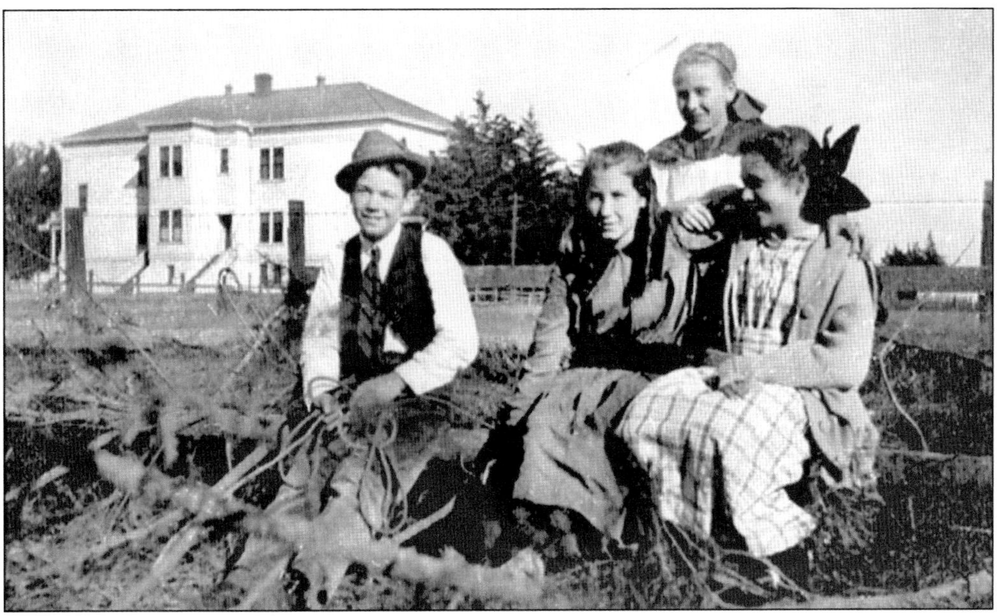

BONDS FORM. Friends Verne Morrill, Ruby Brady Grigsby, Grace Burdick Mason, and Hazel Burdick Sarasin are gathered on a sunny afternoon in front of their grammar school around 1908. Several of these children stayed lifelong friends, as witnessed by their appearance on page 78 of this book.

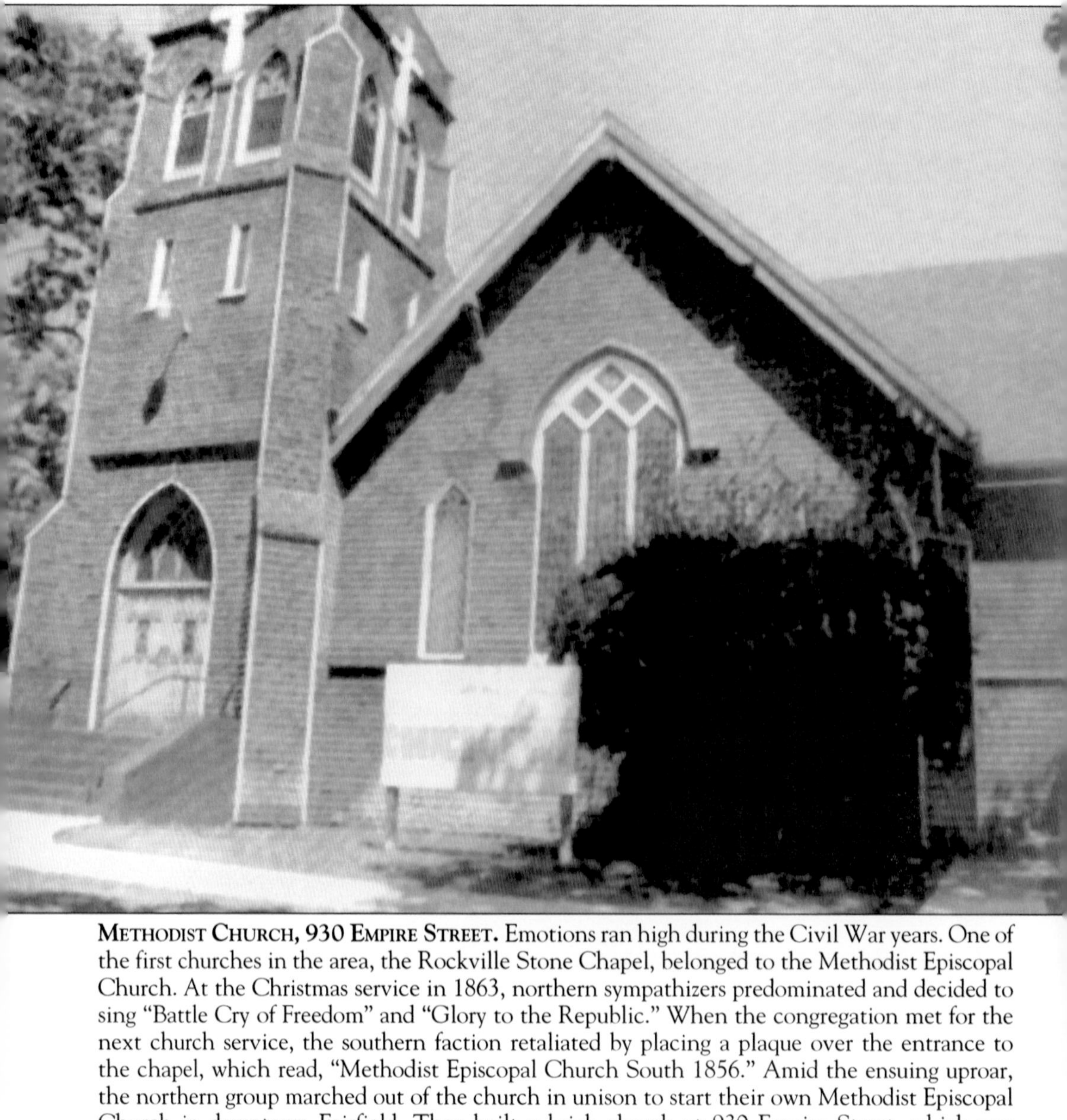

METHODIST CHURCH, 930 EMPIRE STREET. Emotions ran high during the Civil War years. One of the first churches in the area, the Rockville Stone Chapel, belonged to the Methodist Episcopal Church. At the Christmas service in 1863, northern sympathizers predominated and decided to sing "Battle Cry of Freedom" and "Glory to the Republic." When the congregation met for the next church service, the southern faction retaliated by placing a plaque over the entrance to the chapel, which read, "Methodist Episcopal Church South 1856." Amid the ensuing uproar, the northern group marched out of the church in unison to start their own Methodist Episcopal Church in downtown Fairfield. They built a brick church at 930 Empire Street, which was destroyed in the earthquake of April 1892. Their new church, a Gothic Revival–style building covered with wood shingles, shown in this photo, was completed by 1863.

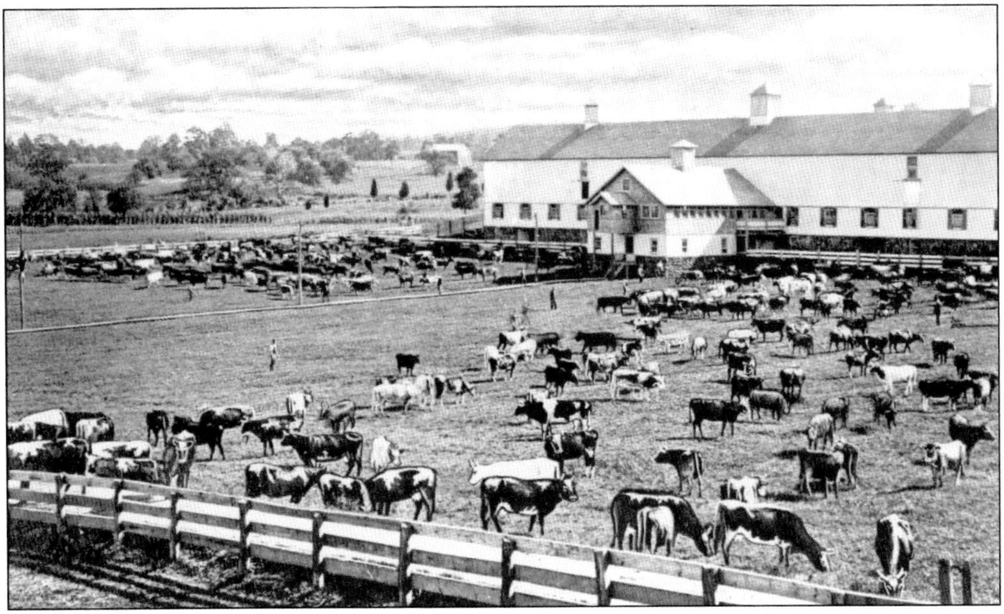

FAIRFIELD DAIRY. A postcard preserves the image of the Fairfield Dairy, "Producers of Fairfield Dairy Certified Milk." The image was taken around 1921. The dairy was located outside the town limits, north of the intersection of today's Travis Boulevard and North Texas Street.

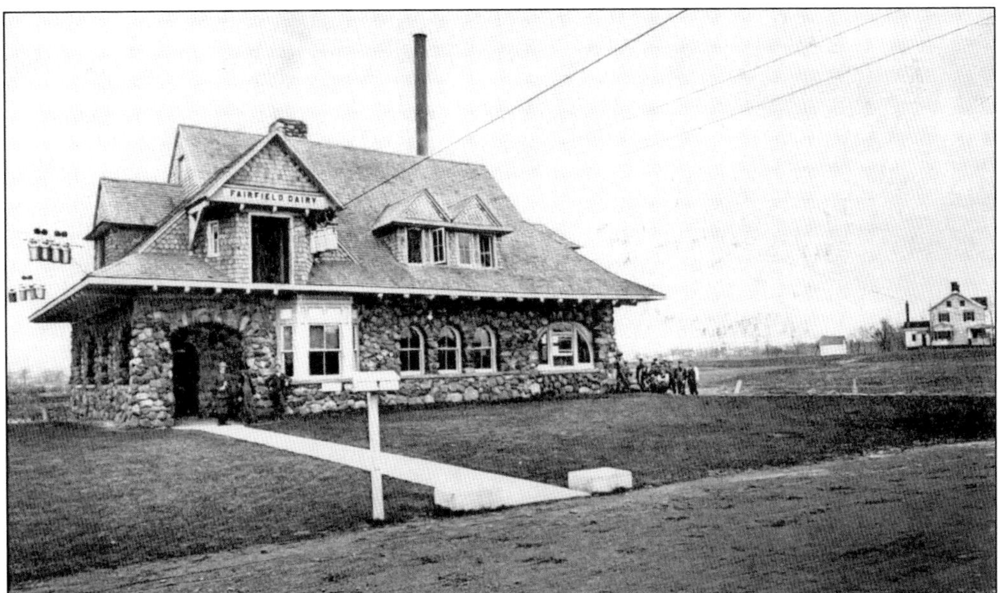

HOUSE OF DAIRY SUPERINTENDENT. The Solano County superintendent of dairies lived in this house. While its location is unknown, its Colonial Revival style appears to date from the late-19th or early 20th century.

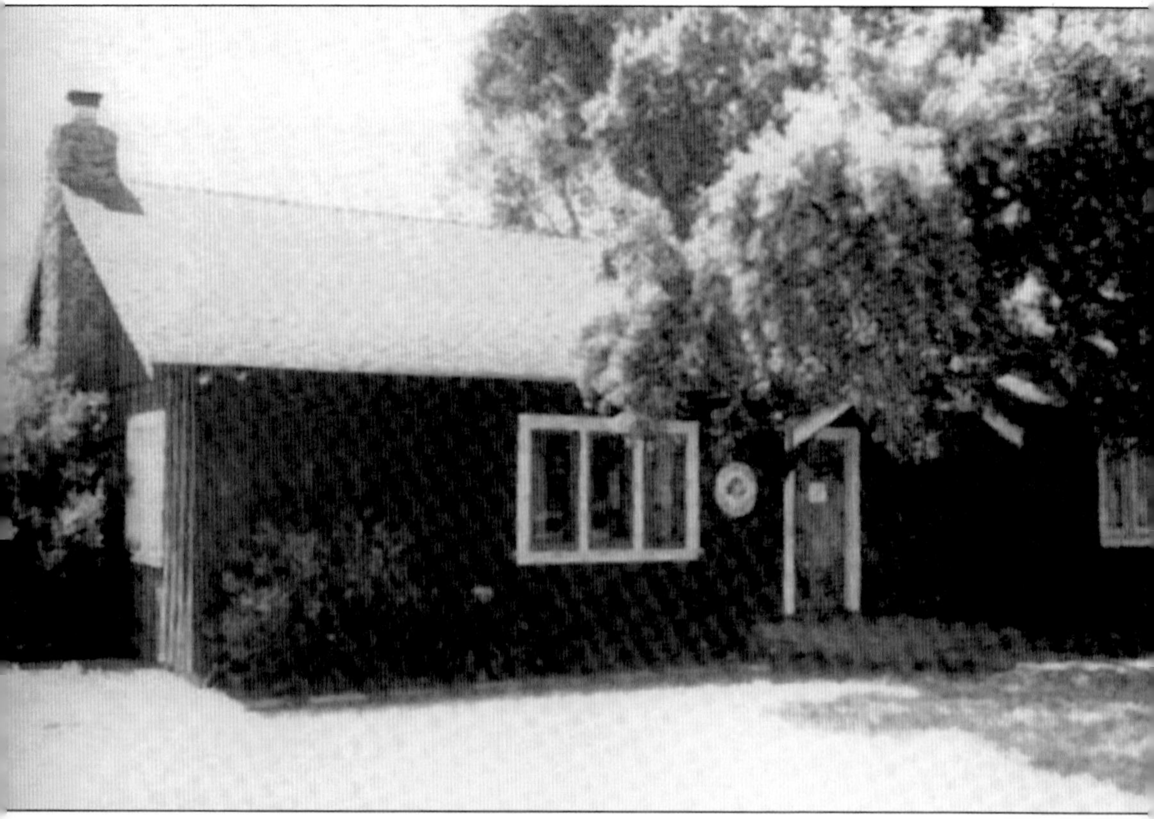

GIRL SCOUT HOUSE. In 1931, the Girl Scouts received their own house, a modest wooden structure, on Union Avenue. Mrs. Ruth Sheldon and Armijo High School home economics teacher, Miss Jane Beck, were responsible for rallying the community and pulling the project together. Local businessmen donated money and spent countless hours building it. In 2001, despite strong objections from the community, the building had to make way for the parking garage of the new government center. The Girl Scouts will receive a new home in the Rolling Hills area.

Seven

ENJOYING THE GOOD LIFE

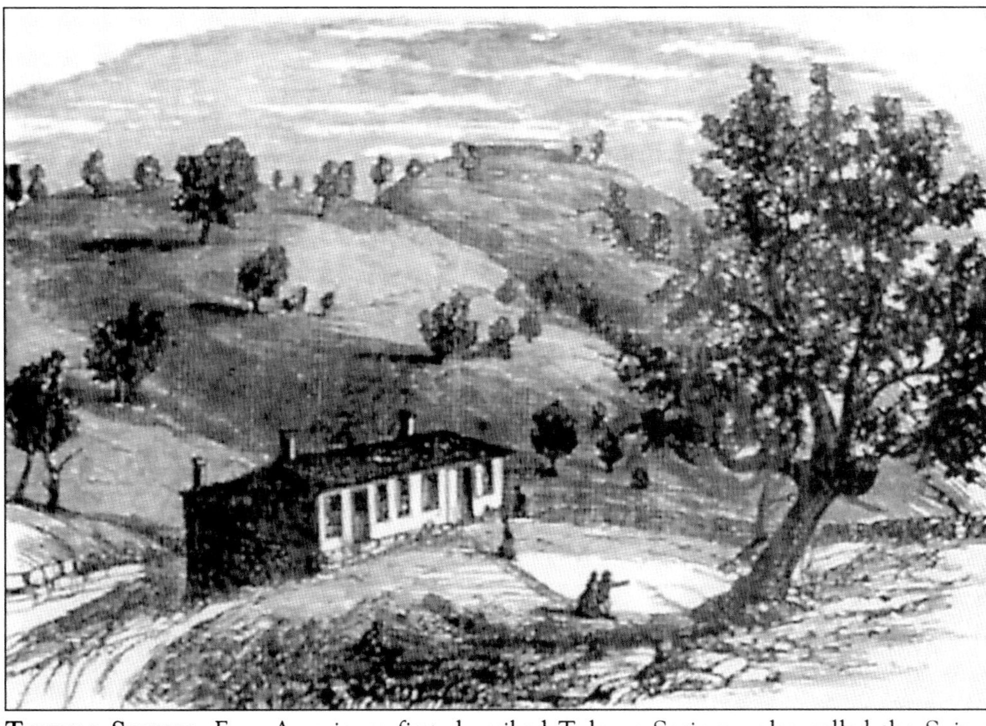

TOLENAS SPRINGS. Euro-Americans first described Tolenas Springs—also called the Suisun Soda Springs or Solano Mineral Springs—in 1855. The discovery of a quarry of high-quality marble nearby drew much attention, leading to the formation of the Suisun Marble and Quarry Company. At the same time, local resident Thomas Swan acquired the springs, had the mineral water analyzed for its health benefits and spent much of his energy in the development of a health resort. Besides the construction of a bathhouse, shown here in a drawing, he also had the mineral waters bottled and sold as Tolenas Springs Soda. While so engaged, he was elected district attorney of Solano County, and two years later in 1853, county judge. He also served in the lower house of the California legislature in 1855. While the springs never became the elegant spa he envisioned, it remained a popular excursion destination. It was a favorite gathering spot for the annual May Day festivities, when hundreds of residents spent the day picnicking, playing games, and dancing.

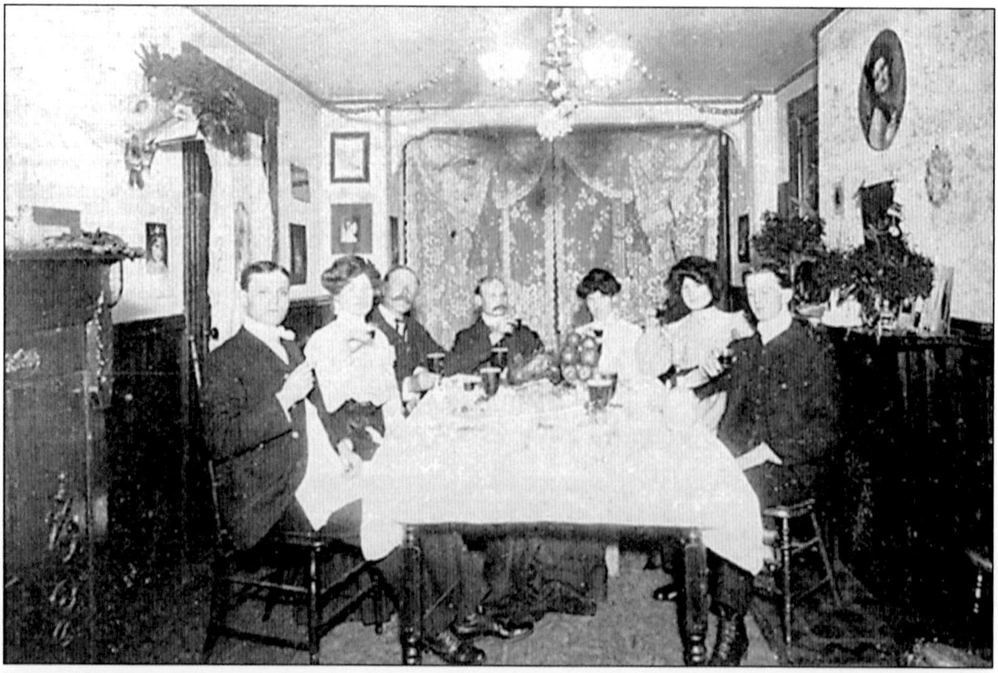

Fields Family at Dinner. Much of the entertainment in the 19th century took place in private homes. Families like the Fields gathered around the dinner table to talk and enjoy each other's company during long, leisurely meals.

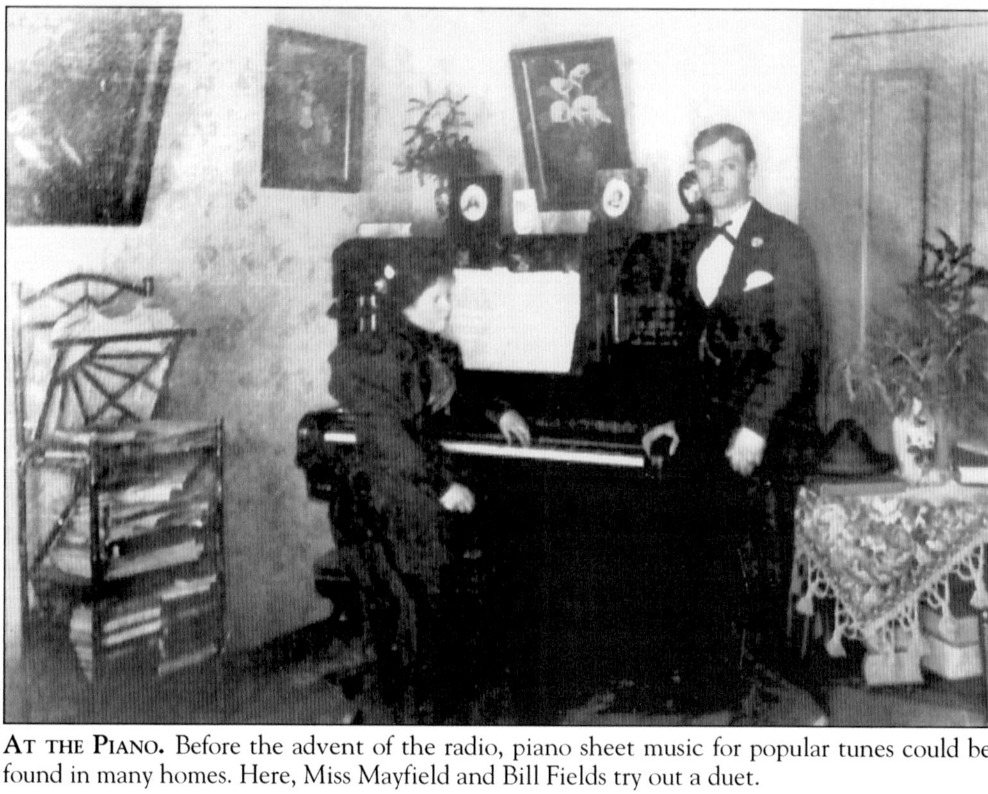

At the Piano. Before the advent of the radio, piano sheet music for popular tunes could be found in many homes. Here, Miss Mayfield and Bill Fields try out a duet.

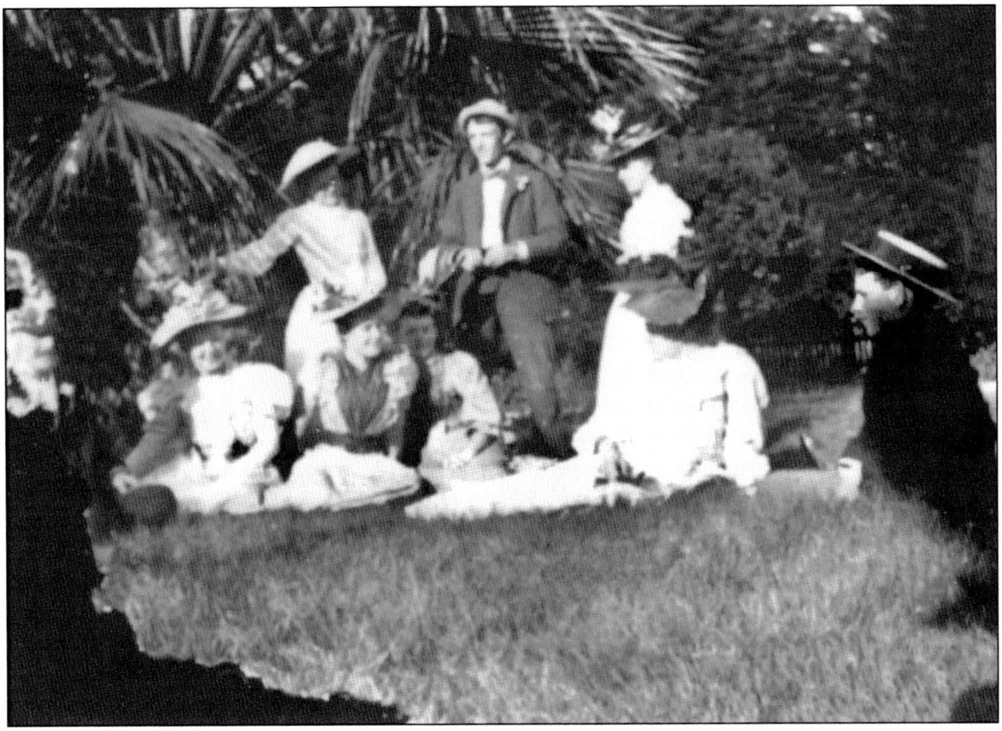

VISIT ON THE PIERCE RANCH. During the summer months, families on ranches throughout the valleys entertained friends and relatives who wanted to escape the heat of the city and enjoy the fresh country air. Though some visits were purely social, like the one shown here on the Lewis Pierce Ranch at the turn of the century, most guests came to help with the fruit harvest.

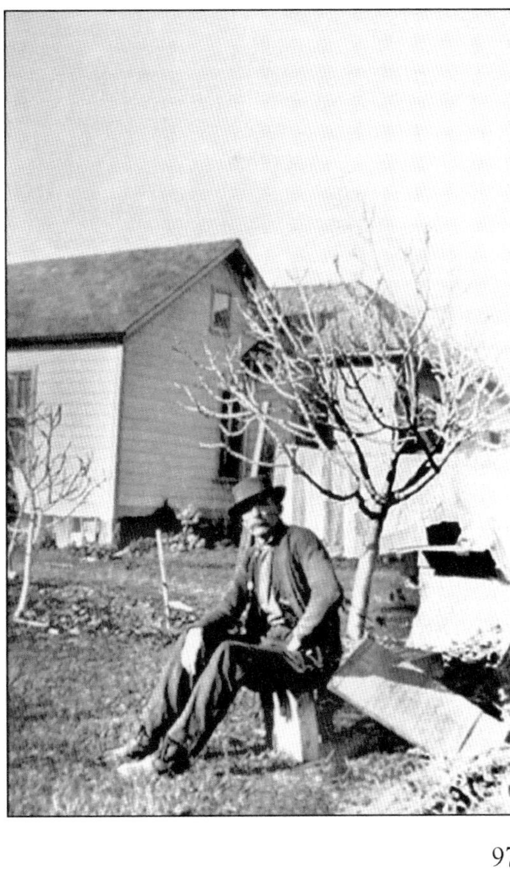

FIELDS OF TOIL. Much of the work in field and orchard was arduous and dirty. Here, "Papa" Cox is seen resting between garden chores in early spring.

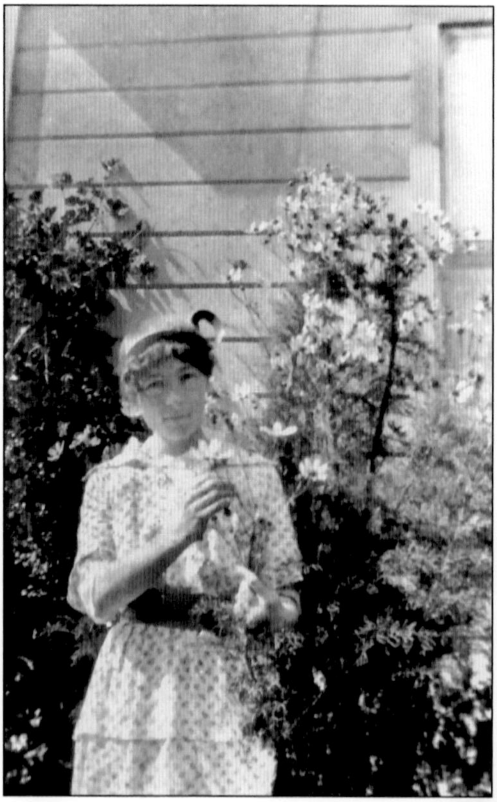

Elsie Cox, Late Spring c. 1910. "Papa" Cox's daughter Elsie enjoys a sunny aftrernoon, dressed in her Sunday best.

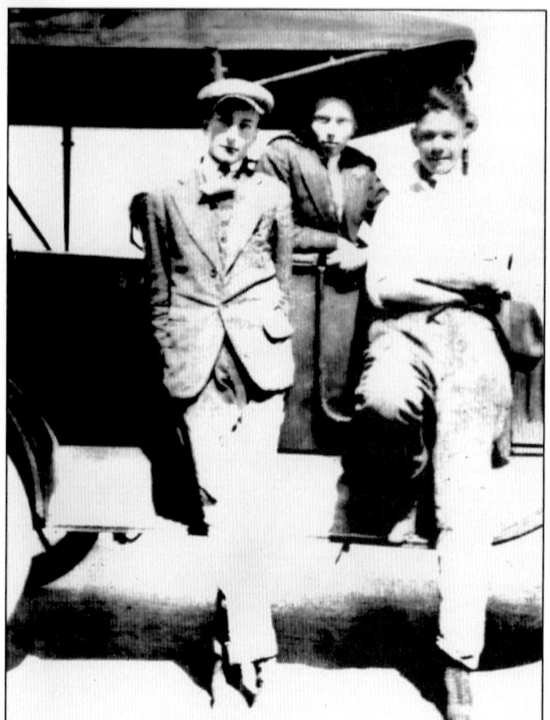

Watching the Girls Go By. Seen here ogling pretty girls like Elsie Cox are, from left to right, Earl Crandell, Ralph Prather, and Verne Morill.

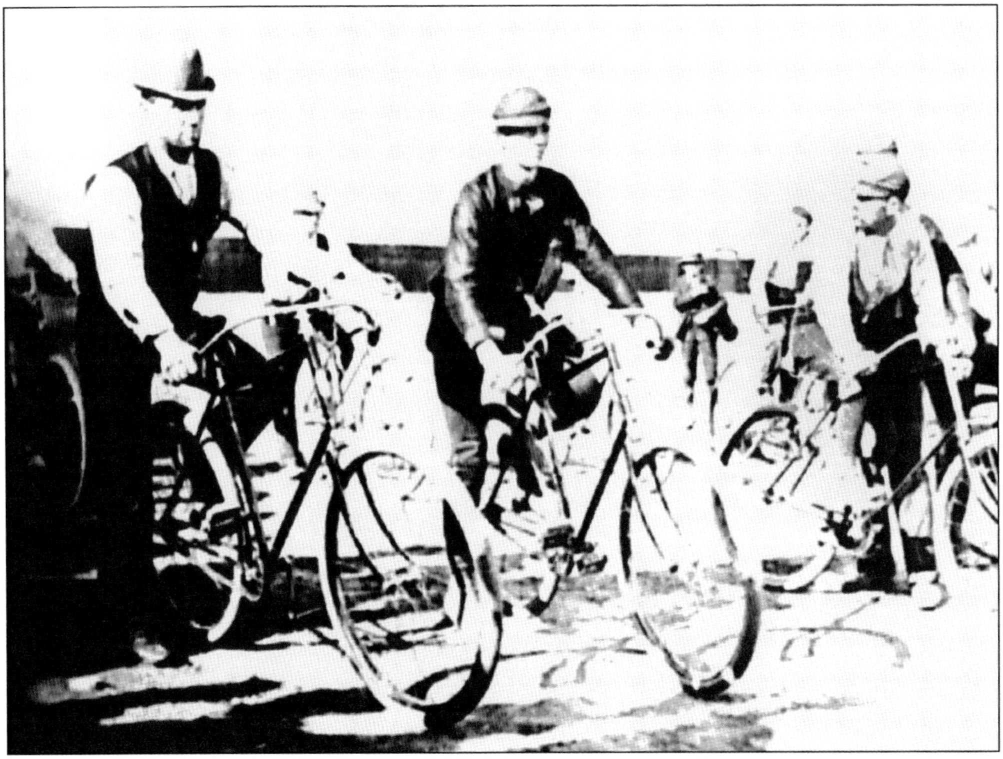

Turn-of-the-Century Biking Craze. A bike race was another way to pass a pleasant afternoon in the company of friends in Fairfield. Bicycle clubs, like the international Wheelmen organization, often held weekly races and long-distance expeditions and were extremely popular in the late-19th and early 20th centuries.

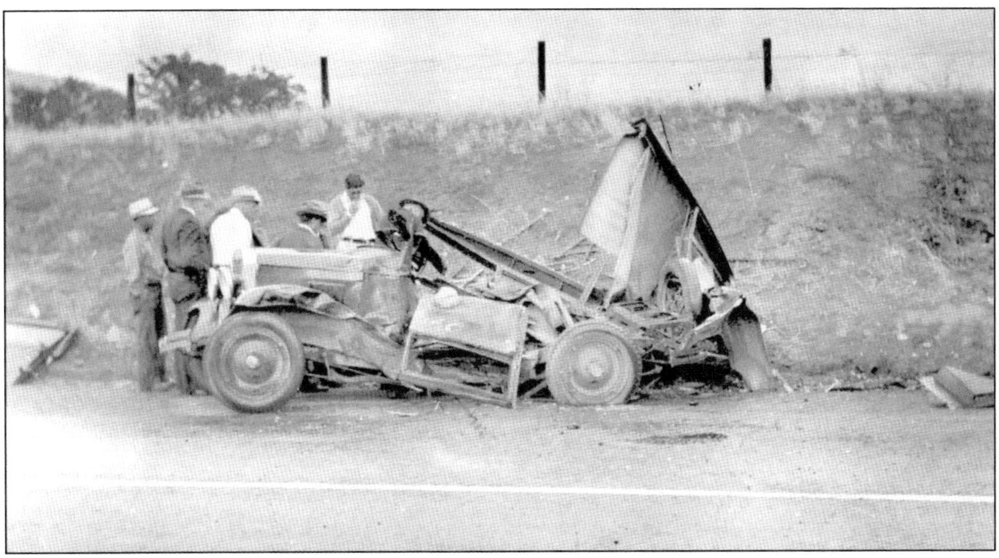

Highways Fill. With cars increasing, day trips became more possible and popular. Unfortunately not all ended well, as this car wreck somewhere on the road between Fairfield and Vacaville on November 11, 1937, demonstrates.

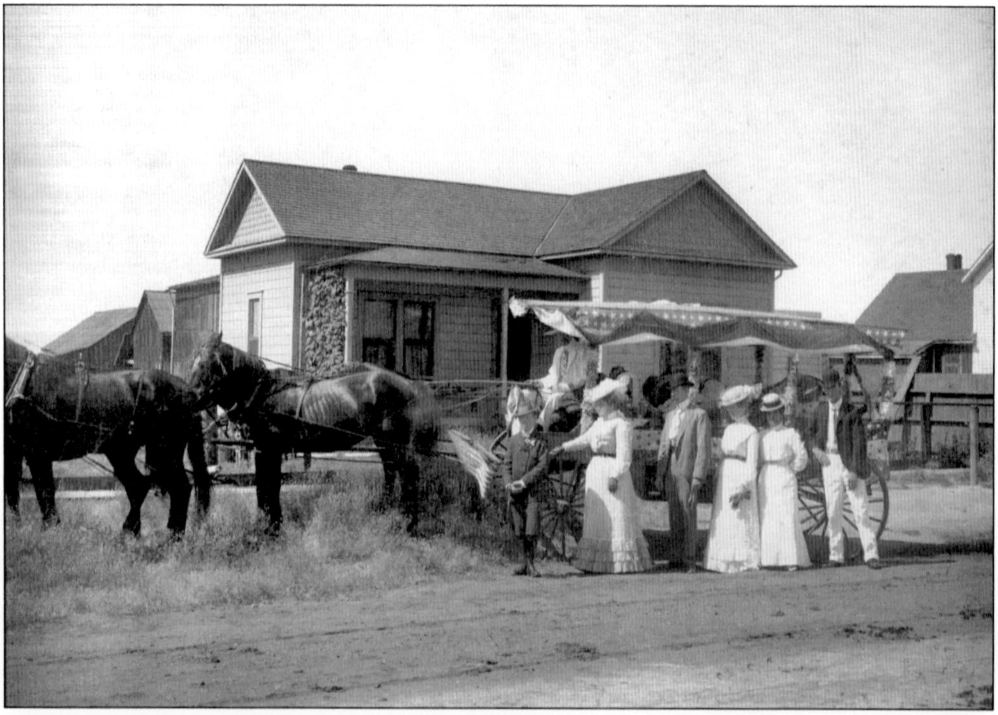

July Fourth Float. Parades were always popular, especially for July Fourth, and residents often went to great lengths to create a float. Sometime in the early 1900s, this group stands next to their float, drawn by four horses. They seem to be waiting for the parade to start.

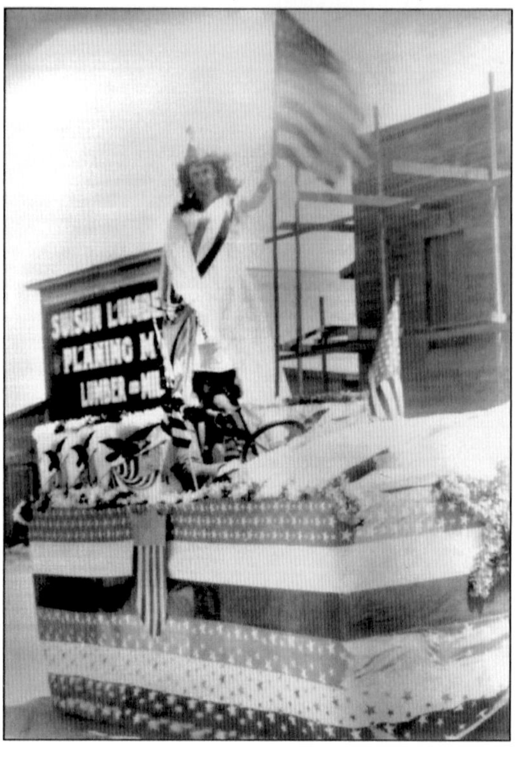

Ellie Buzzini, Miss Liberty. The Fairfield July Fourth parade would go along Union Avenue and onto Main Street in Suisun. In this 1910s photo, Elsie Buzzini waves from a float as "Miss Liberty."

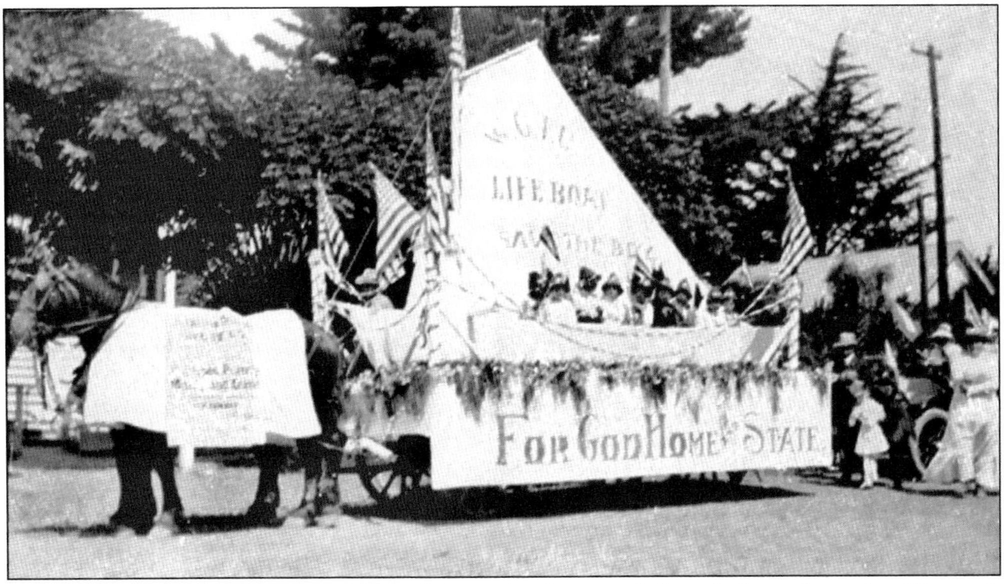

No Liquor on the Fourth. This elaborately decorated float belonged to the Women's Christian Temperance Union, known—and feared—locally as the WCTU. Their float is appropriately titled, "Life Boat–Save the Boys."

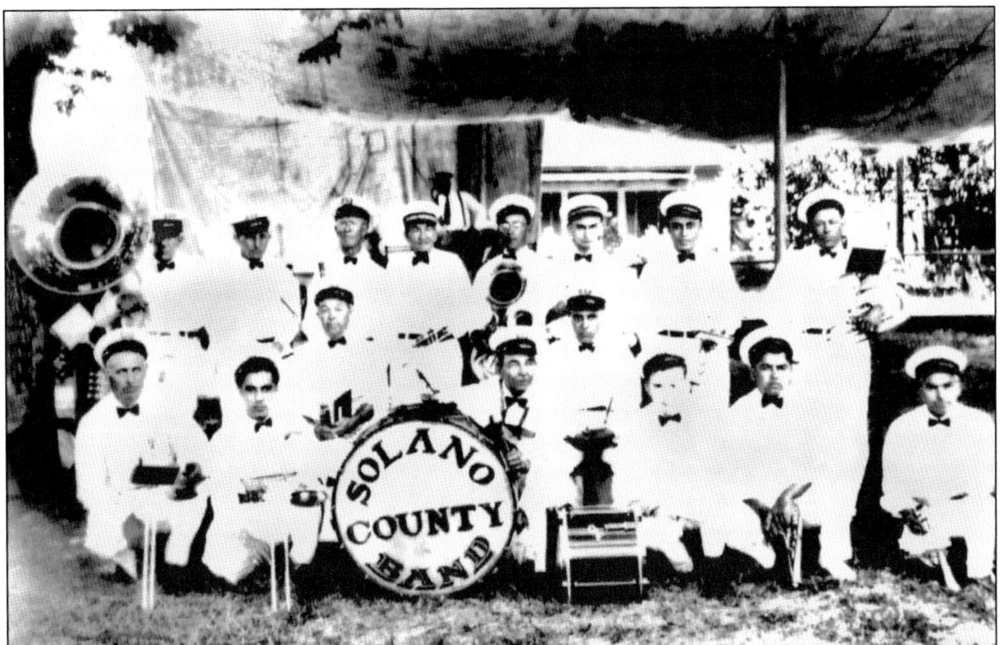

Solano Band. The Solano Band was one of several popular musical groups that played at local festivities, parades, dances, and public concerts. In 1928, Adam Grigsby (first from the left in the back row) played the sousaphone, with Joe Gerevas (fifth from left) on the euphonium, while Laurie Gerevas (seventh from left) wields the tenor saxophone.

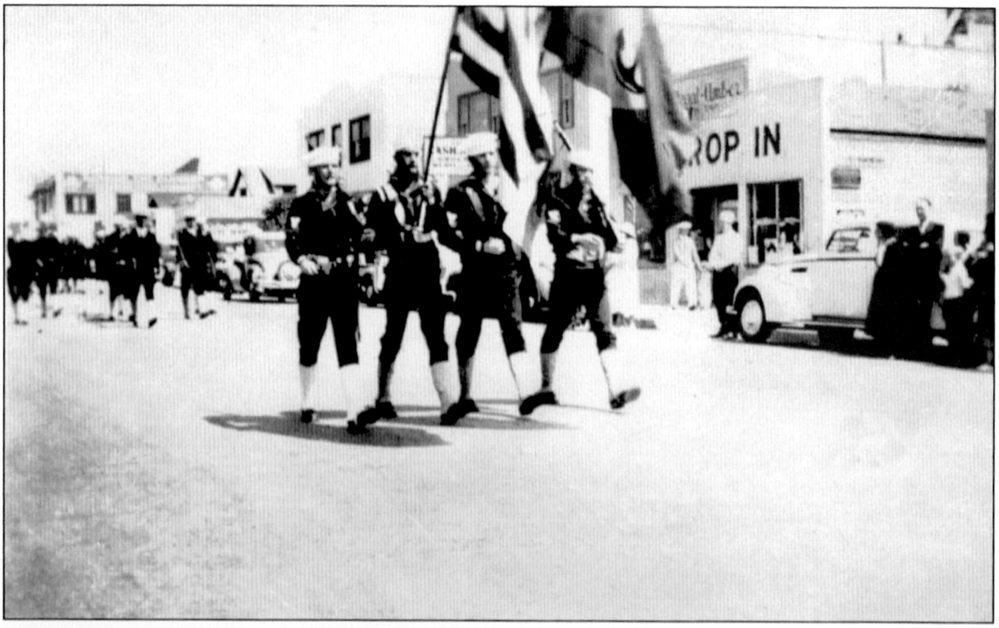

The Approaching War. As World War II drew near, military formation formed part of a July Fourth parade.

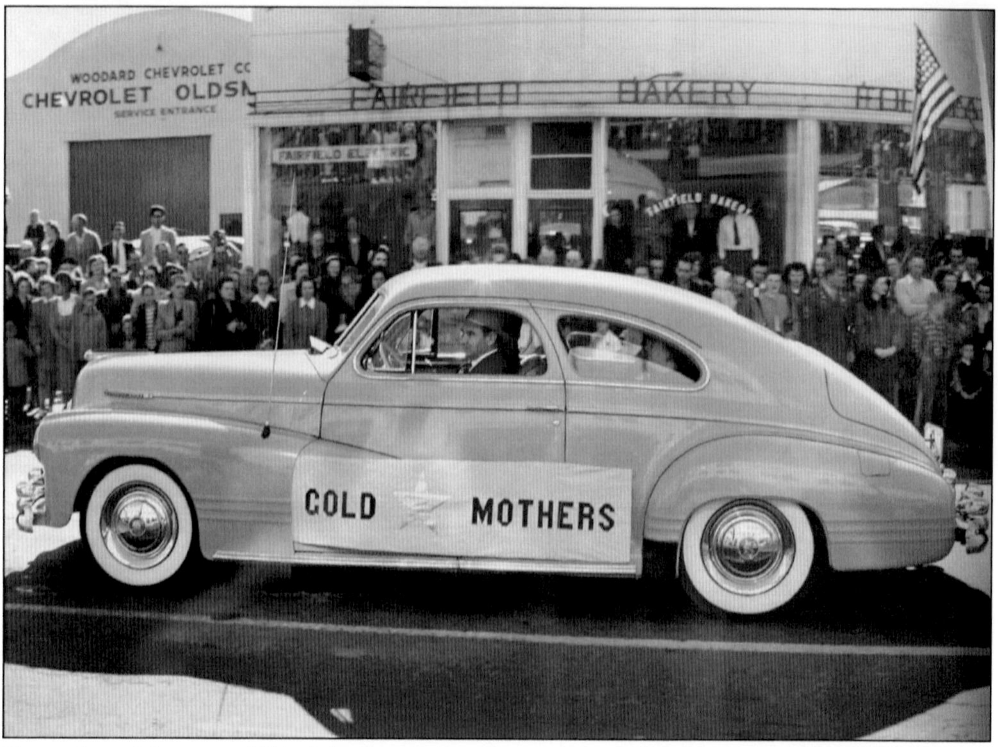

Gold Star Mothers. This July Fourth Parade seems to take place around 1943. Here, the Chevrolet carries Gold Star Mothers of World War II—women who had lost sons in combat—along Texas Street. Note Woodard Chevrolet to the left and the Fairfield Bakery in the center of the buildings shown.

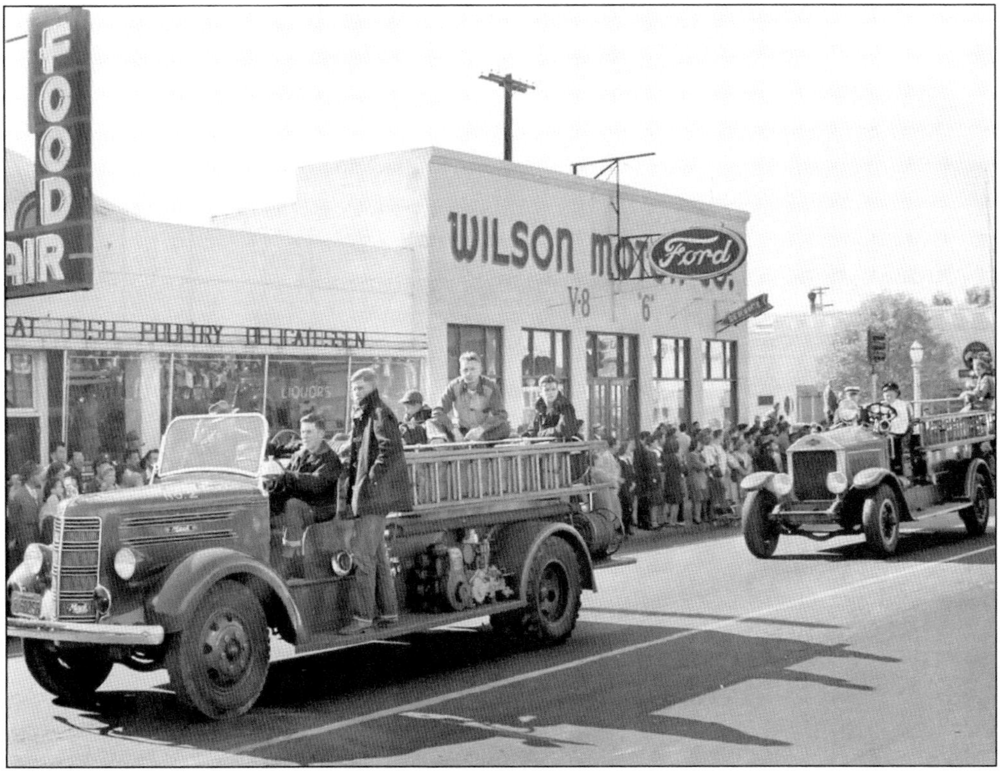

Fire Trucks on Parade. This shot of the fire trucks that followed the Gold Star Mothers allows us a view of Texas Street further to the west.

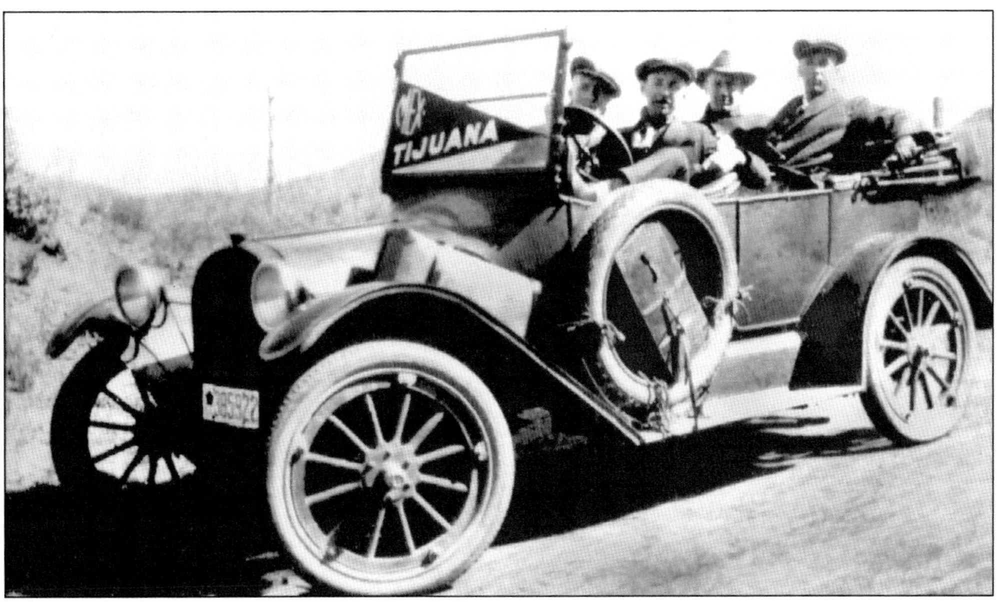

Feeling Mobile. With the automobile came greater mobility. Long trips to explore new areas of the state or even the continent became more common in the 1920s. Here, Bill Braker at the wheel, a friend, Fire Chief Matt Knolty, and Howard Yatsie set out on a trip to Tijuana.

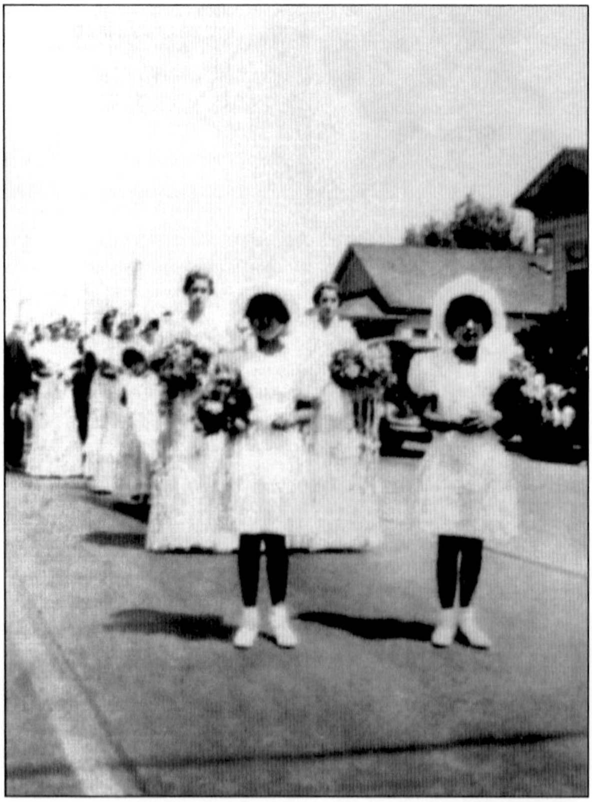

Holy Ghost Festival. Portuguese immigrants brought the Holy Ghost festival—*Festa do Espirito Santo*—with them. The festa goes back to the year 1296, when Portugal suffered through a long drought and famine. Queen Isabel tried to alleviate the suffering by secretly taking bread from the palace and giving it to the poor. Her husband, King Diniz, confronted her one day, wanting to see what she had hidden in her apron. When she opened her apron, instead of bread, red roses fell to the floor. In the festival to commemorate her, Queen Isabel leads a parade, wearing a crown, white dress, and elaborate velvet cape. Several "little queens" and other helpers accompany her. After the parade, *sopas e carne*—a soup of beef bread and gravy—is passed out in huge quantities. Here, young Miss Oliveras is seen accompanying the Queen.

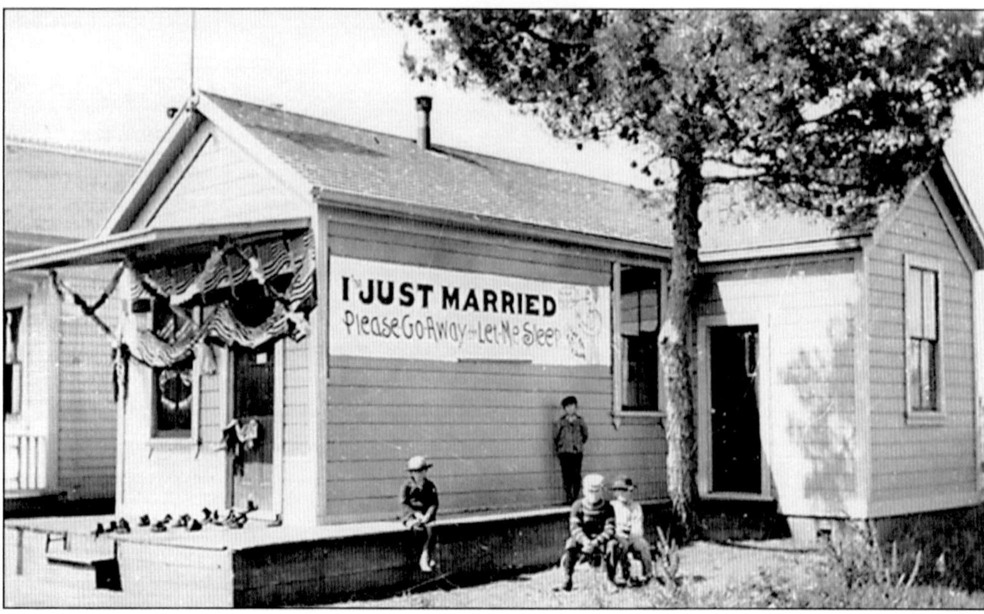

Fun in Fairfield. Here, the office of attorney Wilbur U. Goodman is shown on Union Avenue. Mr. Goodman got married in March 1904, and pranksters nailed this large sign and shoes to his porch.

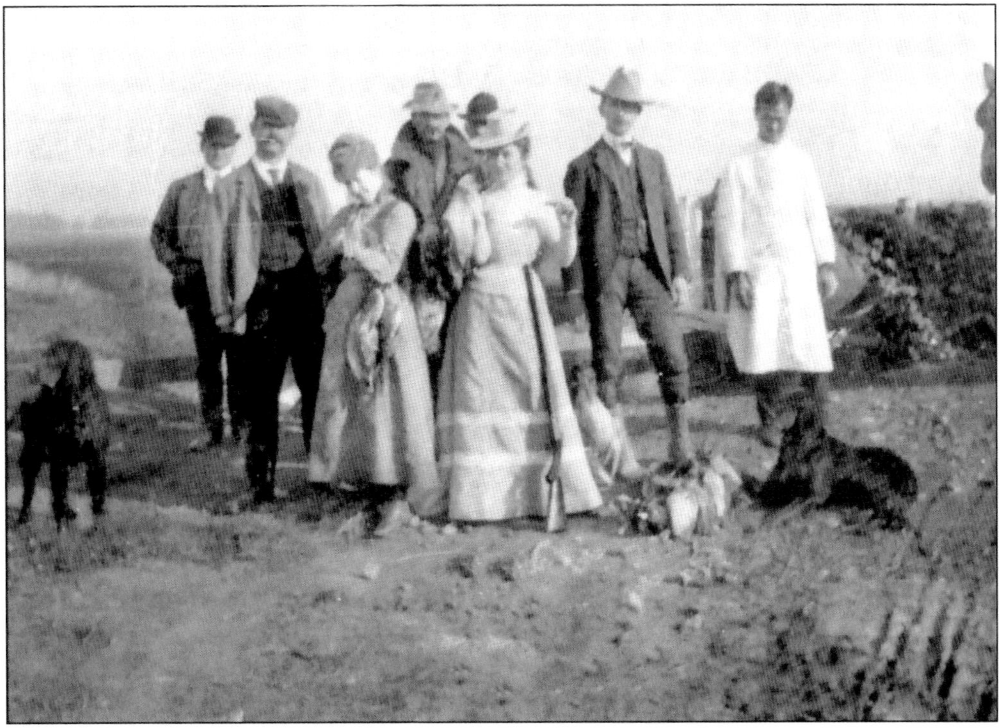

Day in the Marshes. With the Suisun Marsh so close, duck hunting has always been a popular sport in Fairfield. Here, a party gathers for a day of hunting around 1890. Note the shortened skirt of the lady's hunting dress on the left. The man in the white coat on the right may be the Chinese cook.

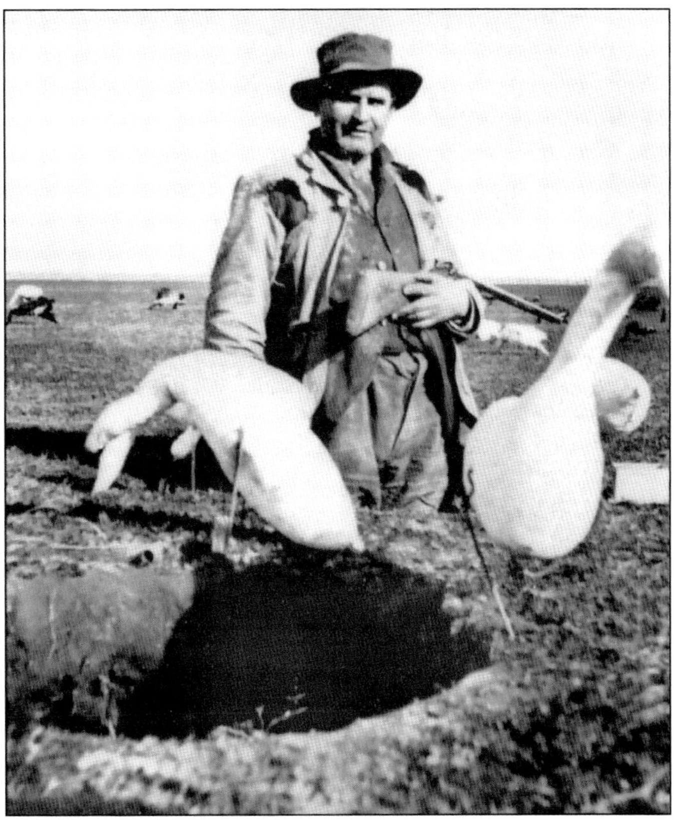

The Sporting Life. This duck hunter is shown setting out duck decoys. By the 1920s, a large number of hunting clubs had established themselves throughout the marsh. While members enjoy the annual hunting season, they also maintain the levees and marshlands in their club's area, thus protecting the marsh and the migrating waterfowl.

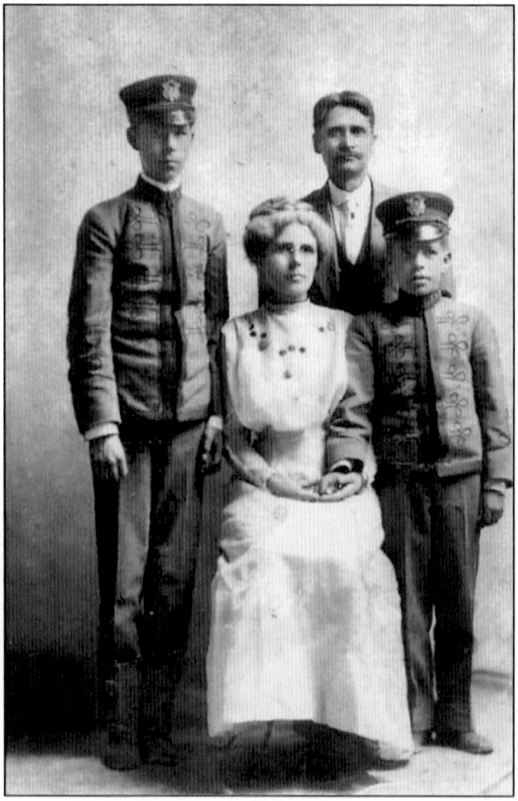

Harold and Harvey Richardson. This photo shows young Harold Glenn Richardson and his younger brother Harvey Ingle Richardson in 1917, shortly before H. Glenn attended a military academy in San Diego. Their parents are Charles Nelson Richardson and Ruth Cassels Richardson.

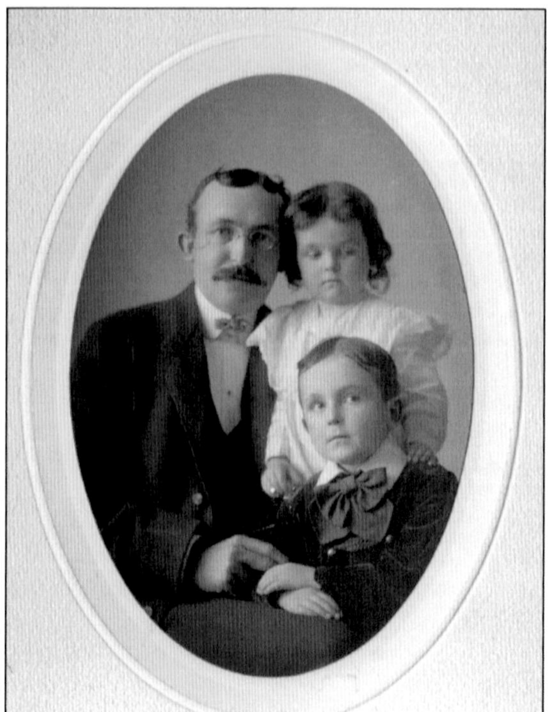

County Recorder. Mr. Corcoran, shown here with his two young children, served as Solano County Recorder at the turn of the century.

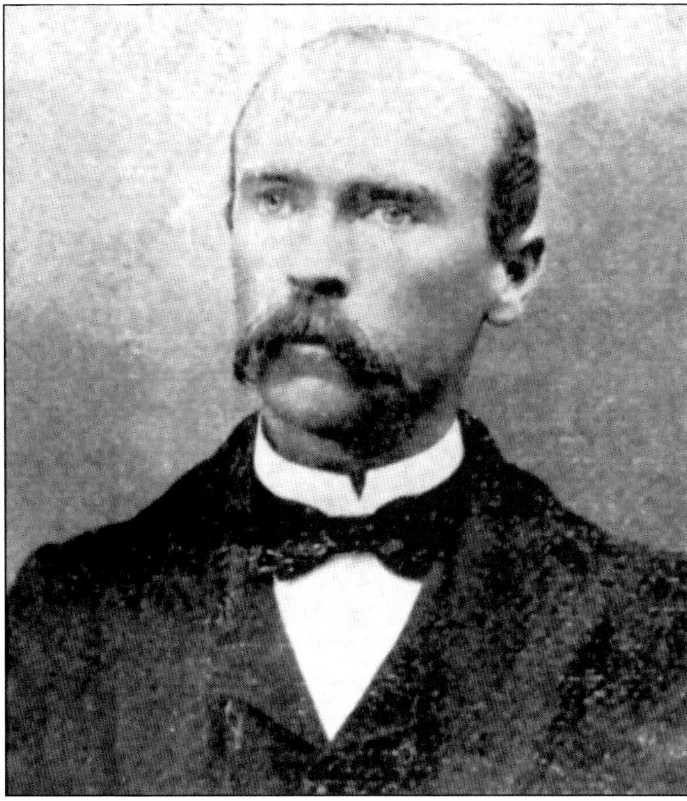

SCHOOL SUPERINTENDENT WHITE. Dan H. White served as the Solano County superintendent of schools from 1899 to 1938. Throughout his career, he kept his campaign promise of total devotion to his duties as the educational leader. He is recognized as the "Father of the Modern Educational System" in the county. Prior to his appointment as superintendent, he managed the *Cordelia X-Ray*, one of the local newspapers.

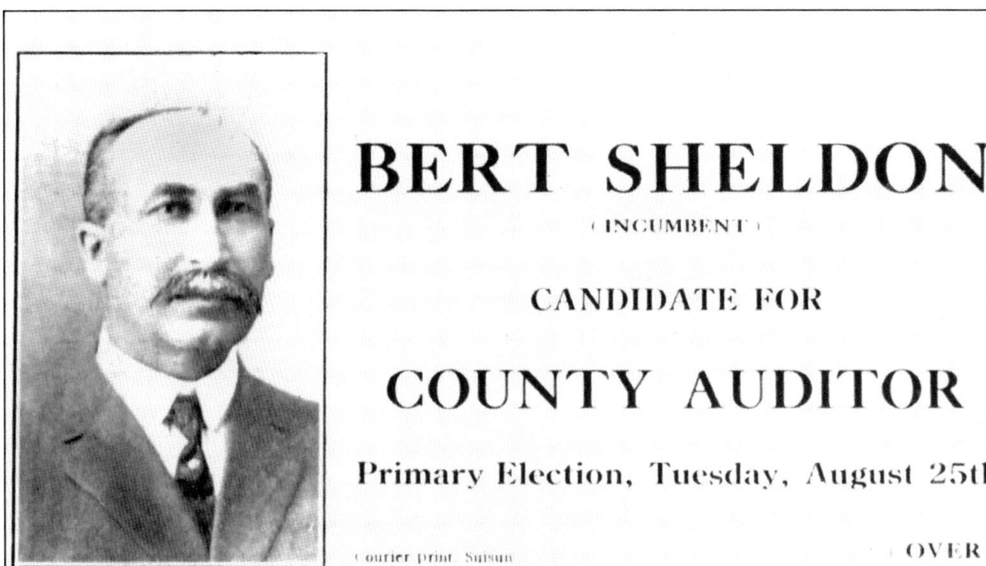

BEN SHELDON. Ben Sheldon campaigned for, and won, the seat of county auditor.

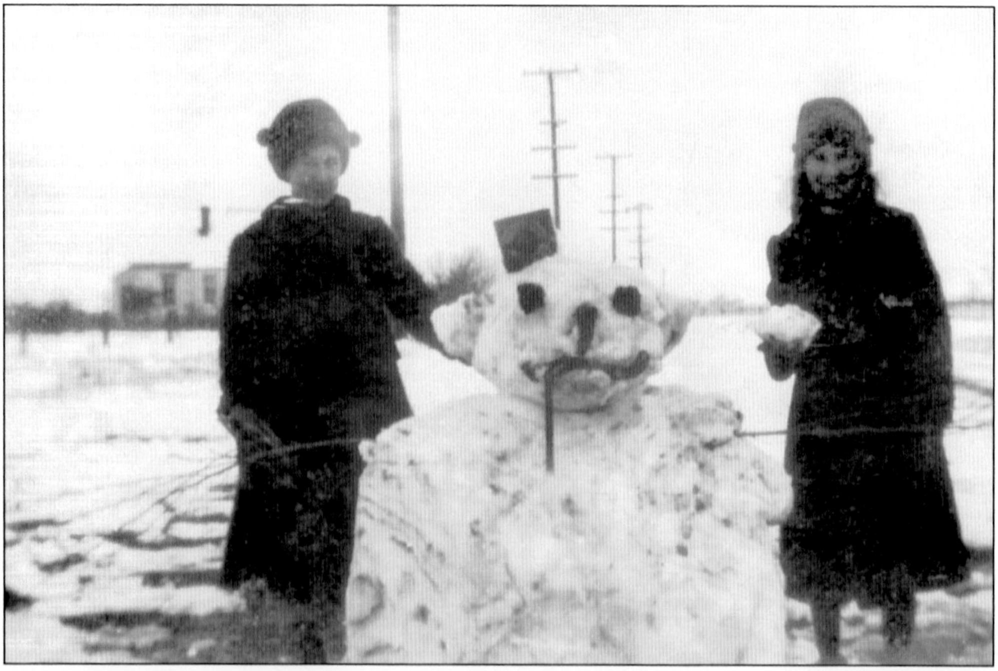

SNOW, 1913. The winter of 1913 surprised Fairfield residents with temperatures low enough to keep a light snowfall on the ground. Sisters Amy Brady Blanc and Ruby Brady Grigsby were able to build a snowman at their home on the corner of Taylor Street and Broadway.

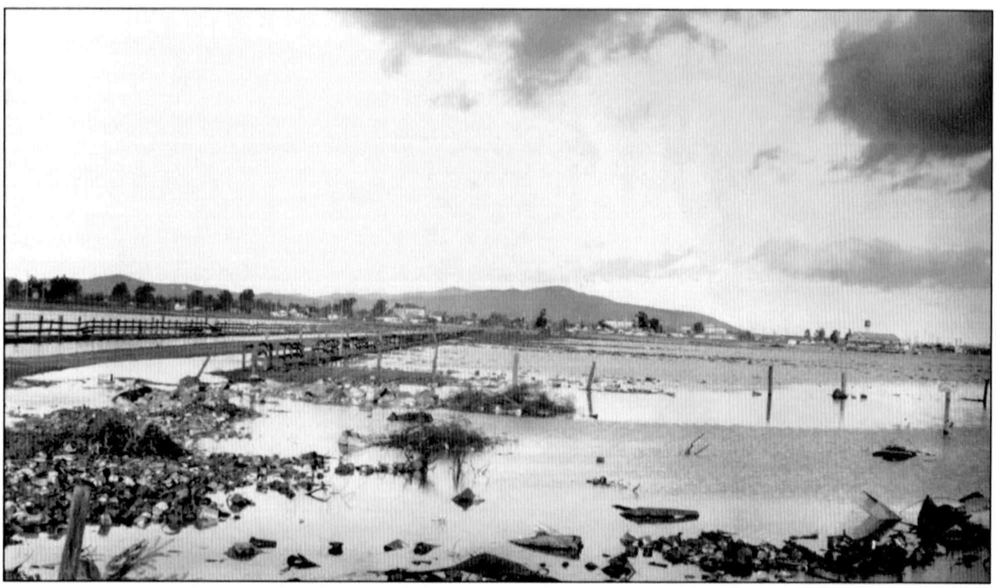

FLOOD, 1932. Heavy winter rains led to flooding in the Suisun Marsh area between Fairfield and Suisun. Here, the courthouse and Armijo High School are visible in the background.

Eight

Field and Orchard

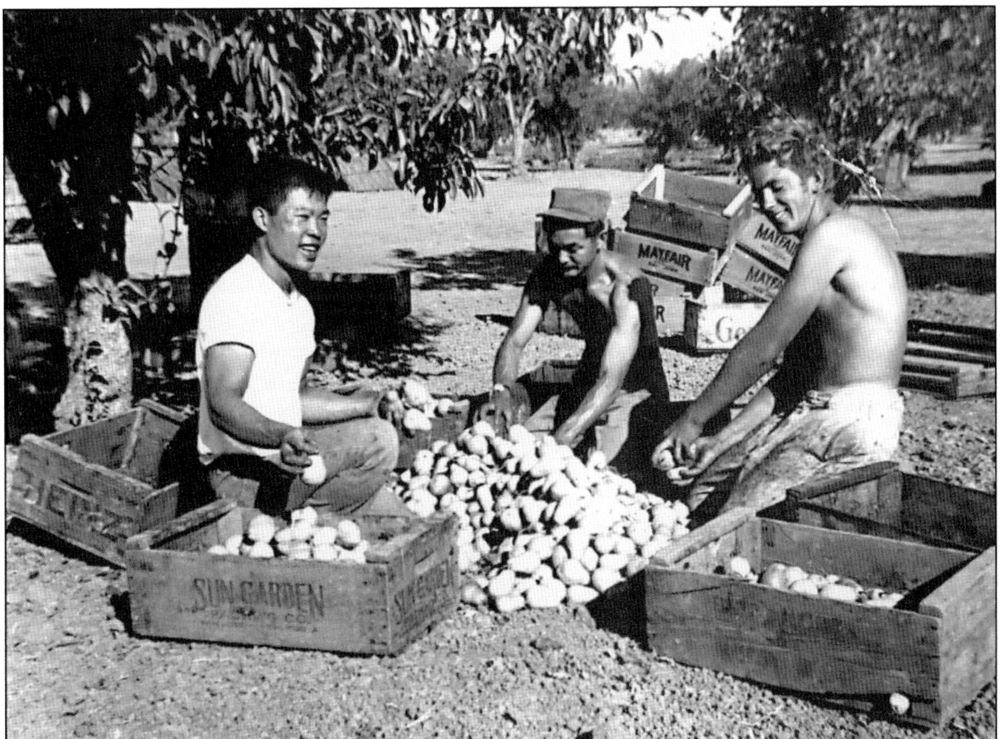

Fong Family and Friend, Sorting Pears. Vaca, Suisun, and Green Valleys were famous throughout the United States for the quality of their orchards. Due to microclimates, certain types of fruit ripened earlier than anywhere else in the state, giving farmers a competitive edge in shipping to the East Coast. The valleys surrounding Fairfield and Suisun specialized in pears, prunes, and cherries. Peach, apricot, and nectarine cultivation was limited due to the high water table in most of the area. Each year the season began with cherries in May and ended with prunes and walnuts in September. During those months, population in the area increased dramatically. Men, women, and children; friends and relatives from out of town; and migrant workers spent long days in the orchards, cutting sheds, dry yards, and packing houses to process the harvest. Young members of the Fong family sort pears, by ripeness, into the cutting shed.

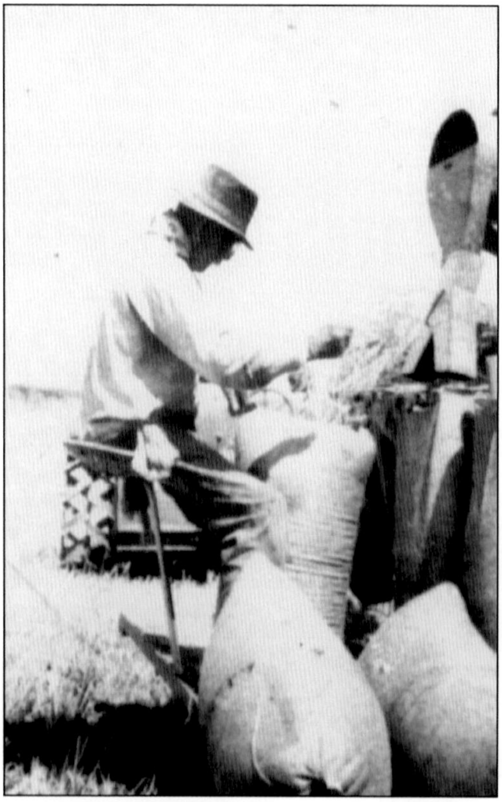

Filling Wheat Bags. Early agriculture in Solano County concentrated on market hay, wheat crops, and cattle. By the late 1860s, the national wheat market had collapsed, forcing local ranchers to search for new crops. A promising grape culture failed with the advent of phylloxera, a disease that withers the vines, in the 1870s. At the same time, the arrival of the railroad allowed rapid transport of perishable fresh fruit to larger markets. Home orchards suddenly became very profitable. Within the next decade, large commercial orchards covered the valleys. Areas closer to the marsh and towards the Potrero Hills, where the soil is marginal and water scarce, continued to grow wheat and graze cattle.

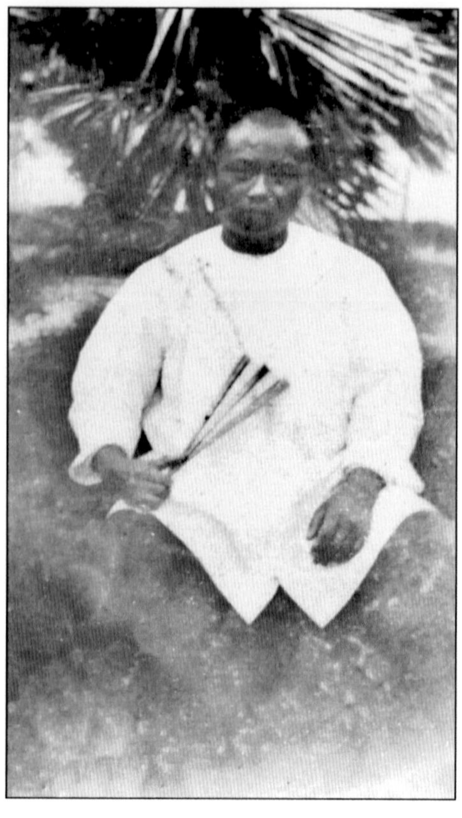

Chinese Houseboy. Many hands were needed to establish and maintain orchards. By the 1870s, Chinese workers arrived in large numbers, working both as house servants, such as this young man, and as hired workers in agriculture. Many came from rural areas in China. Their knowledge of fruit and vegetable farming was valued during the decades in which the California orchard industry was established. This period ended with the Chinese Exclusion Act of 1887, when most Chinese in rural areas were driven out, leaving only a few urban enclaves of Orientals.

Ranch Hand. Japanese immigrants replaced the Chinese workers after 1887. While many were employed as ranch hands, such as the gentleman shown here, large numbers of Japanese managed to lease land of their own. All local Japanese families were deported to the camps in 1942, and most never returned to Solano County. Around 1911, Spanish and Portuguese immigrants arrived. Most had migrated with their families from their homelands to the sugar cane fields in Hawaii. Disappointed by difficult working conditions and broken promises, they found their way to California. Both climate and landscape reminded them of their homes in Europe. Most of these immigrants leased or purchased their ranches.

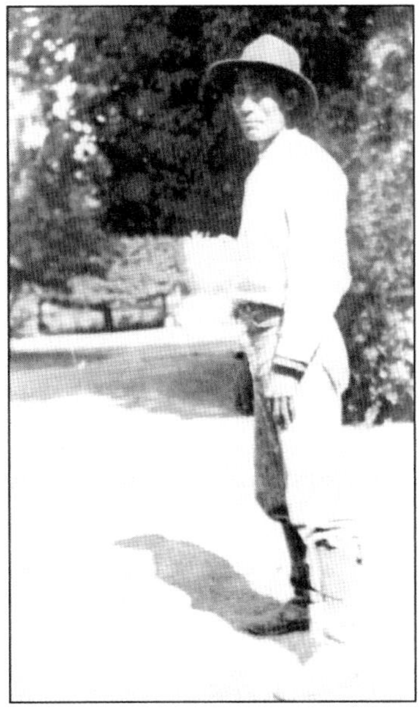

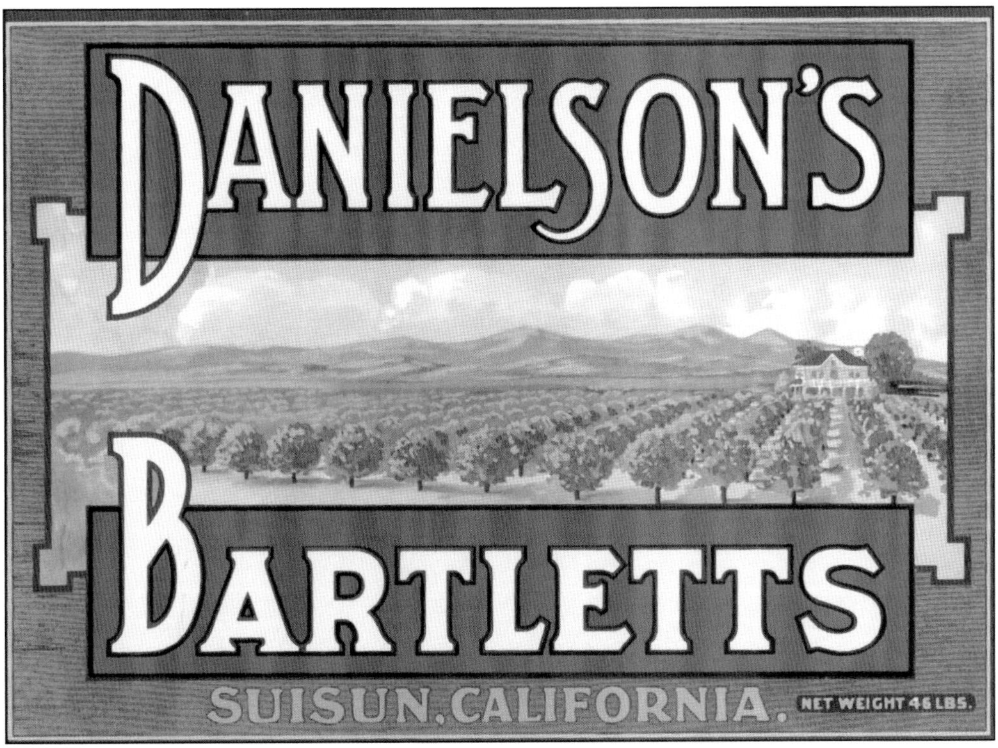

Danielson's Bartlett Label. Labels were developed in the 1880s, becoming a distinctive art form reflective of current trends. Many farmers had their own signature label. This allowed customers on the East Coast to recognize a favorite brand. Different colors or variations in a label design would spell out the quality grading for each box. Some farmers used a stock label, such as Mr. Danielson, adding just their name and product, while others used custom designs. This label was chosen well, showing a landscape very similar to the Suisun Valley surrounding his ranch.

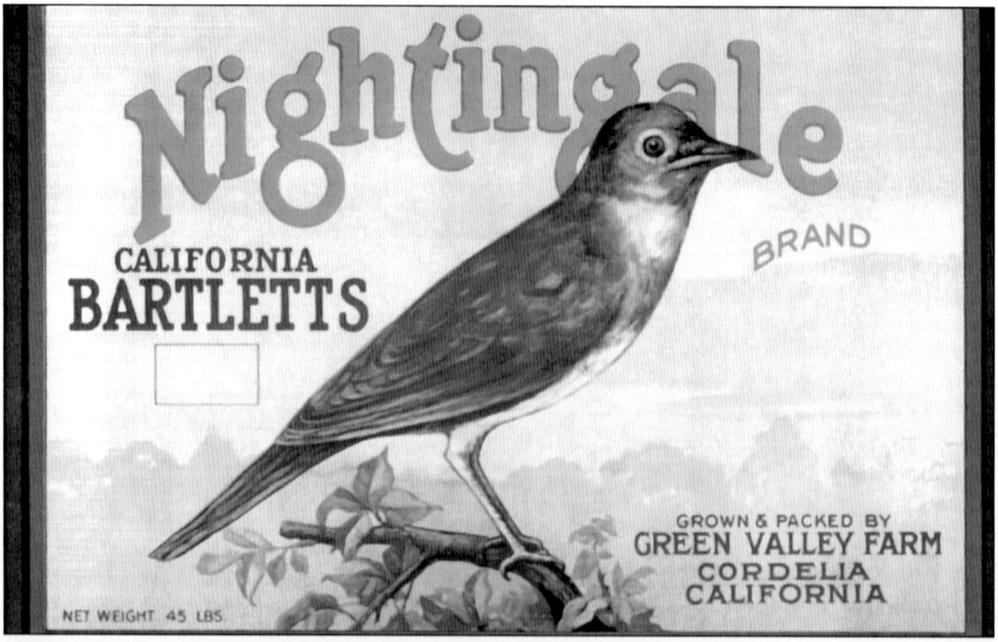

NIGHTINGALE LABEL. Fruit labels in the 1880s, such as this Green Valley one, used naturalistic images of animals, flora, and fauna. Each type of fruit or vegetable was packed in its own standardized box, necessitating label of various sizes. Most boxes were built by craftsmen on the ranch, using prefabricated wood pieces called "shook", which were hammered together at rapid speed. A good worker could build up to several hundred boxes a day.

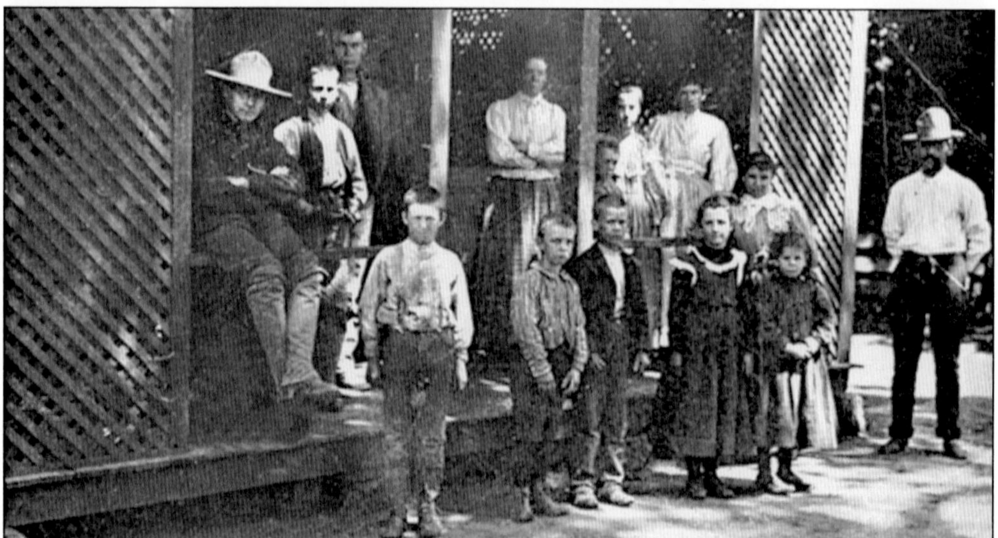

FRUIT PICKING RITE OF PASSAGE. Cutting and packing sheds varied from small lean-tos to large operations. They offered seasonal work for large numbers of women and children. Fruit was cut with specialized knives, varying with each type of fruit, followed by a flick of the wrist to get rid of the stone. Fruit was then laid out on drying trays, cut side up to let the juices pool. In the 1920s, cutting a 60-pound box of apricots earned the cutter 5¢. The trays were sulphured if necessary and laid out to dry in the sun. Until World War II, cutting and packing fruit was a rite of passage for many residents in the area.

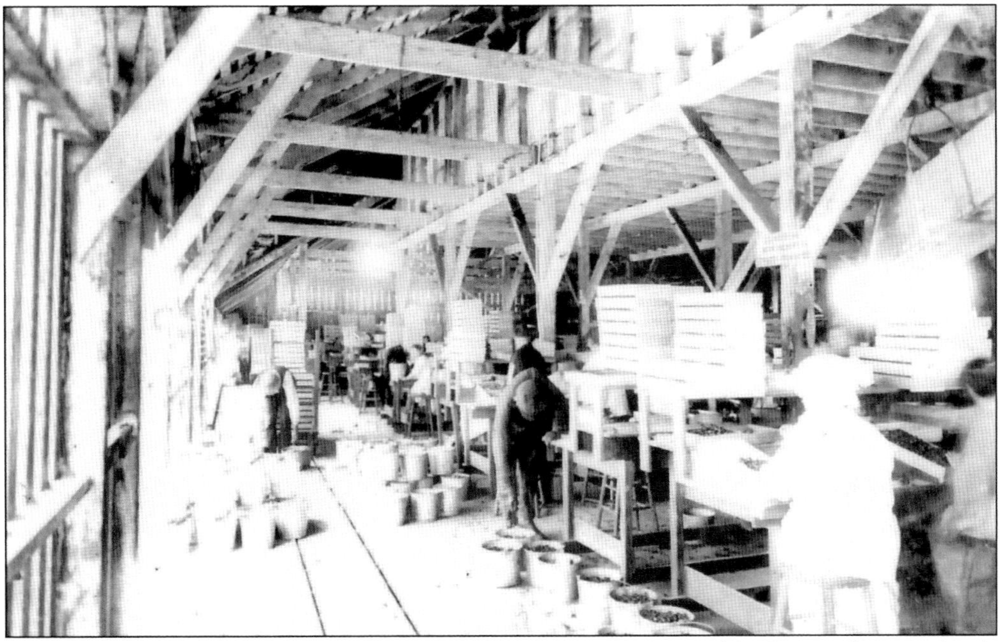

Cherry Packing Shed. In years past, the Jones Ranch operated one of the largest cherry orchards in the country. This shot of a large packing shed shows women at their tables, packing cherries for shipment to the East Coast. Cherries were often "fancy-packed," a special presentation with the top layer arranged in rows with one cherry next to the other.

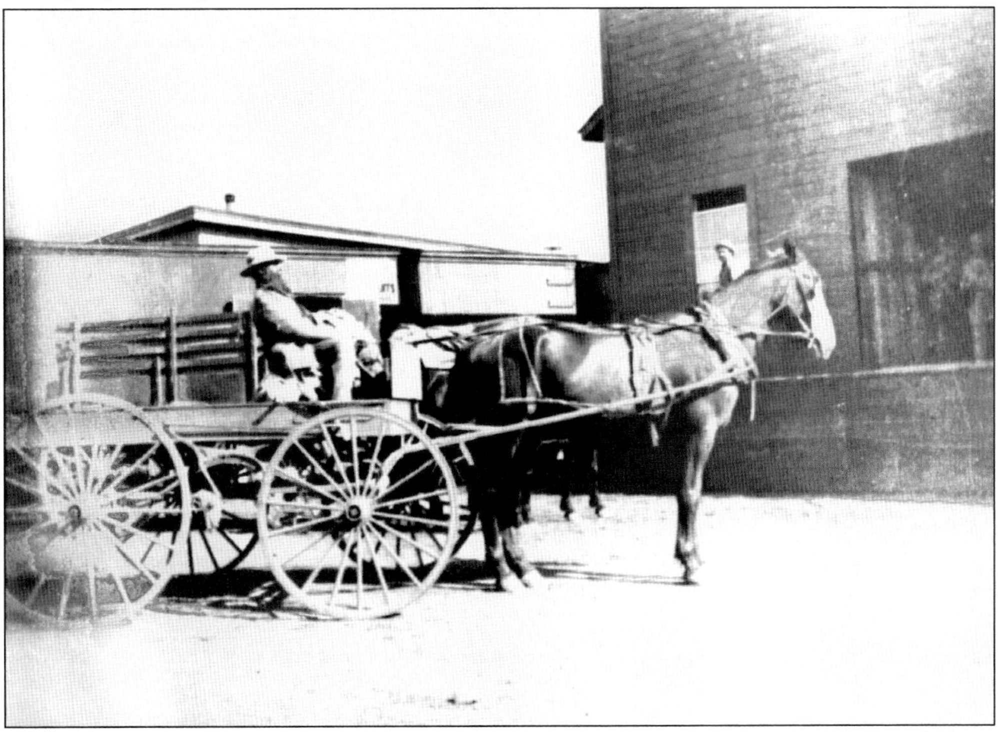

Fruit Wagon. Boxes filled with fruit were loaded onto a horse-drawn wagon, which took them to one of the fruit grower cooperatives or directly to the train station.

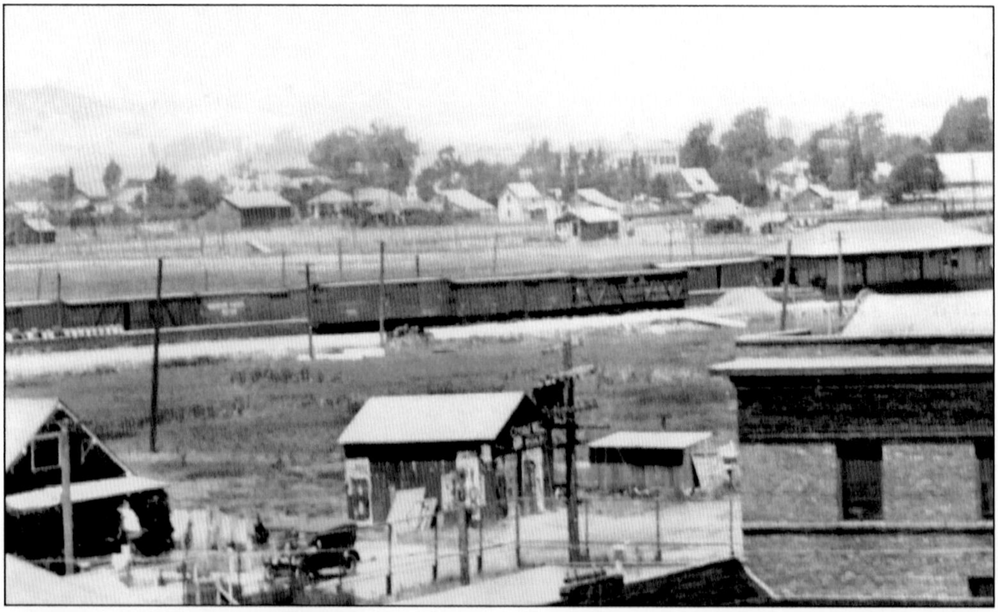

Fairfield-Suisun Train Station. The arrival of the transcontinental railway in 1869 opened up larger markets for local farmers. Refrigerated boxcars were developed by the 1880s, allowing shipment of fresh fruit to the East Coast without fear of spoiling. Locally, the Southern Pacific tracks were installed between Fairfield and Suisun. The train station was located between Webster and Jackson Streets, on today's Ohio Street. By 1878, it consisted of a platform, ticket office, and the Waterman House, a hotel and restaurant. Fairfield's new access to railway transportation contributed greatly to the decline of Suisun's wharf. By the early 1900s, Suisun's status as the business center of upper Solano County began to vanish. This shot was taken across Suisun's Main Street, with the Fairfield courthouse in the background.

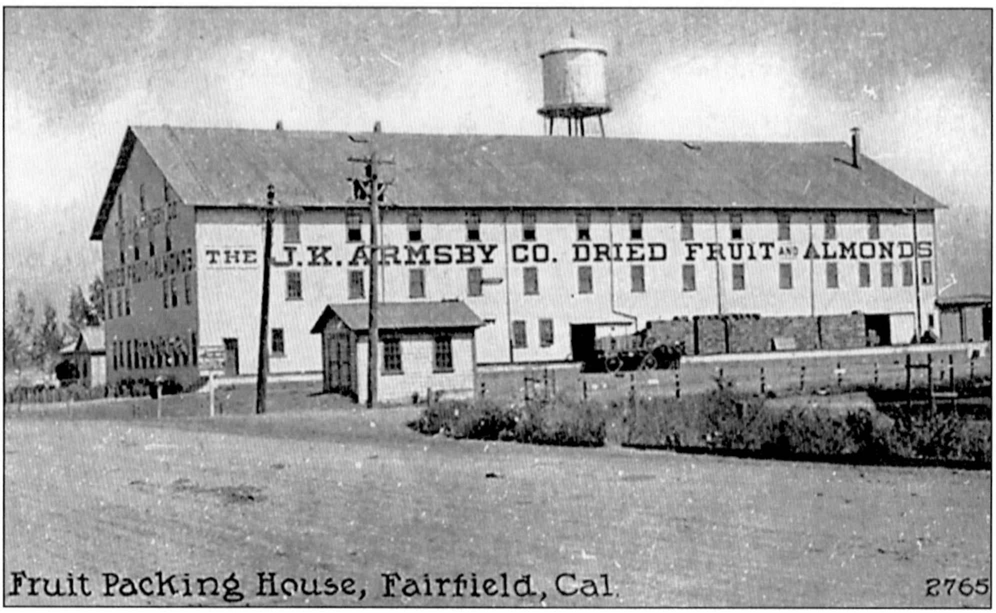

J.K. Armsby. The J.K. Armsby Packing House was one of the first packing and canning houses to establish a Fairfield branch along the railway. They began operation in 1890.

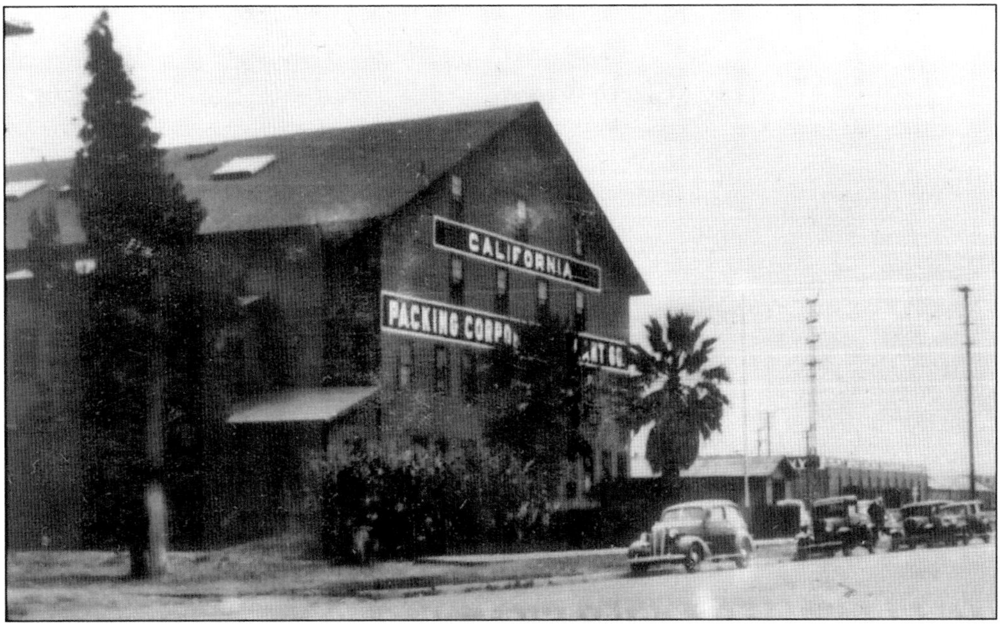

CALIFORNIA PACKING COMPANY. By the late 1920s, the California Packing Company operated a cannery in Fairfield. Del Monte later bought up the company. This photo was taken in the mid-1930s, when the orchard industry began to decline. Competition with irrigated orchards in Southern California challenged local growers during the 1920s. Higher labor costs led to an increase in prunes and nut orchards, less labor intensive than cherries and peaches. World War II once again increased the demand for prunes, shipped to troops overseas, but thereafter the industry declined.

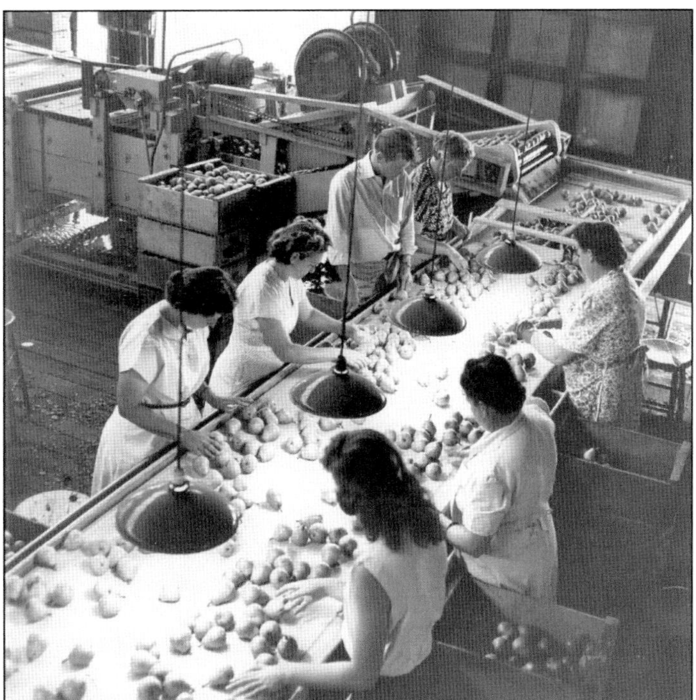

PACIFIC PACKING COMPANY. Despite the increased demand for dried fruit, the fresh fruit market continued to play a strong role in Fairfield. This photo shows a pear sorting line at the Pacific Packing Company sometime in the early 1940s. The ratio of six women to each man is typical for this type of work. Even before World War II, many families augmented their incomes with mom's seasonal wages at the packinghouse, and some companies even provided daycare for their employees.

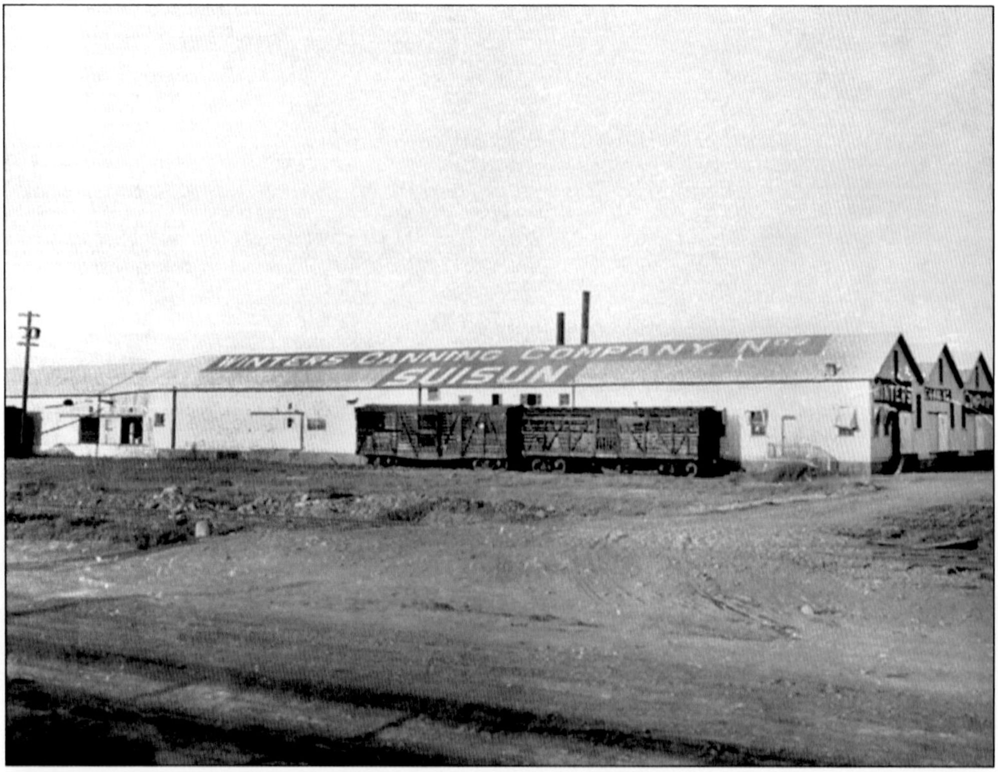

WINTERS CANNING COMPANY. With improved canning containers and sterilization methods, commercial canning was another method used to preserve seasonal bounty. The Winters Canning Company operated in Suisun, starting around 1910. During canning season, the company ran three daily shifts, employing hundreds of local women. The Hunt Brothers Company bought them up in the mid-1920s.

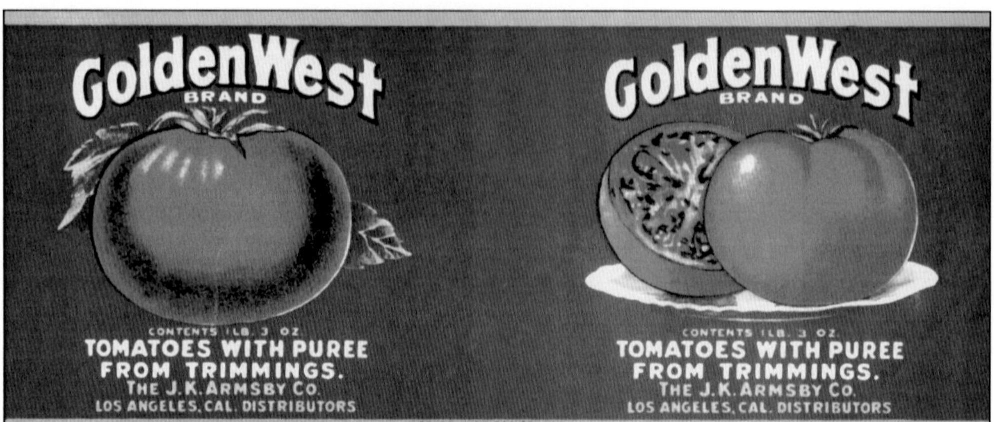

ARMSBY TOMATO LABEL. While fruit—fresh, dried, and canned—made up the majority of Fairfield's produce, in later years row crops like tomatoes were also processed by the J.K. Armsby Company. This tomato label has its headquarters in Los Angeles, yet the contents may well have come from Solano County.

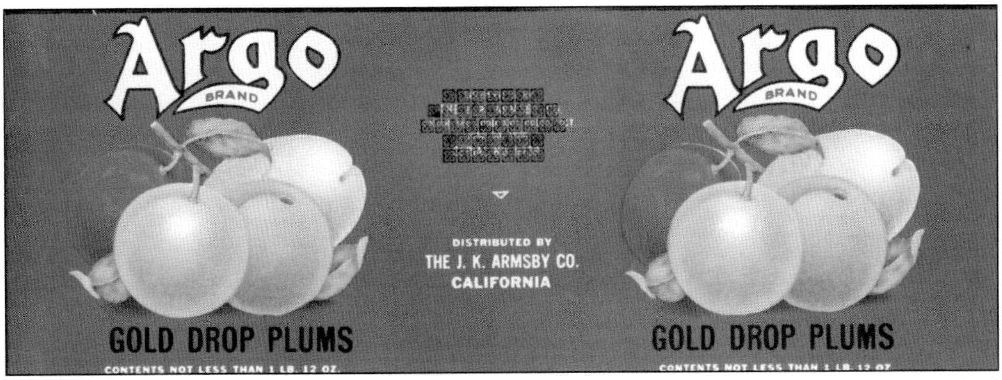

Argo Plums. Different brands and various fruit could be distributed by one cannery. Finished cans were warehoused until a buyer appeared, at which time that buyer's label was added to the can. Thus produce from the same orchard could end up being sold under a variety of labels.

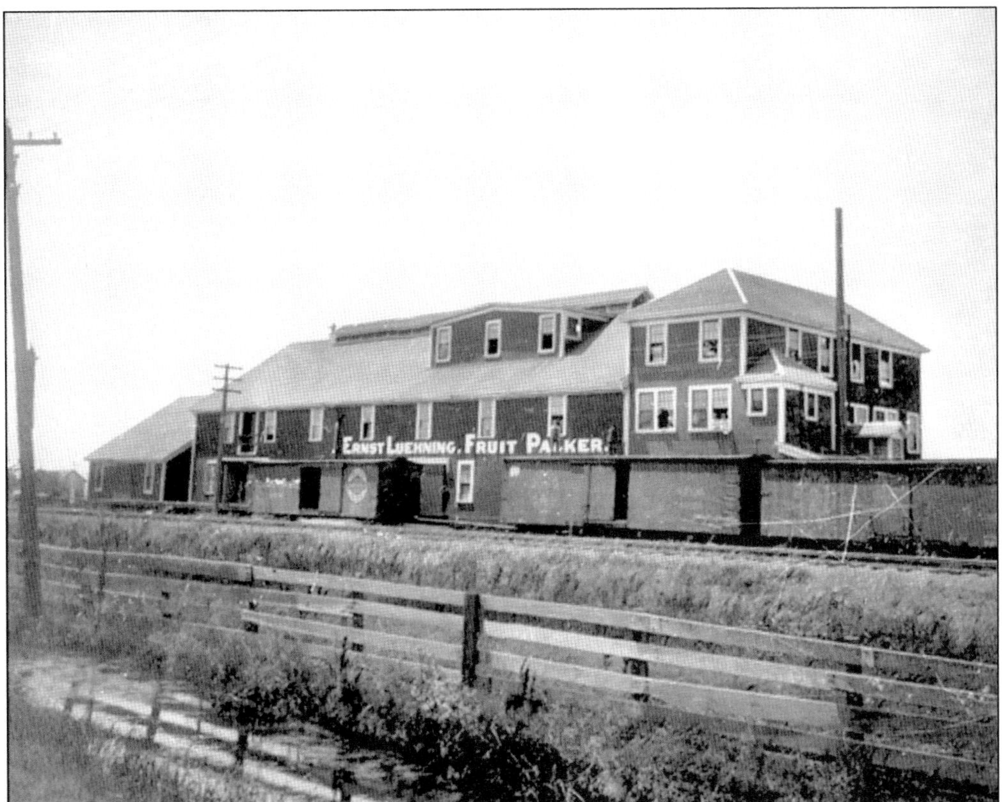

Luehning Company. The profitable fruit-drying business attracted interest all the way from Europe. Ernst Luehning of Hamburg, Germany, opened the packinghouse shown here that specialized in shipping dried fruit. By the 1910s, prunes were becoming the main crop, due to the reduced labor costs of growing them. They were packaged both fresh for the East Coast market, and dried for shipping all over the world.

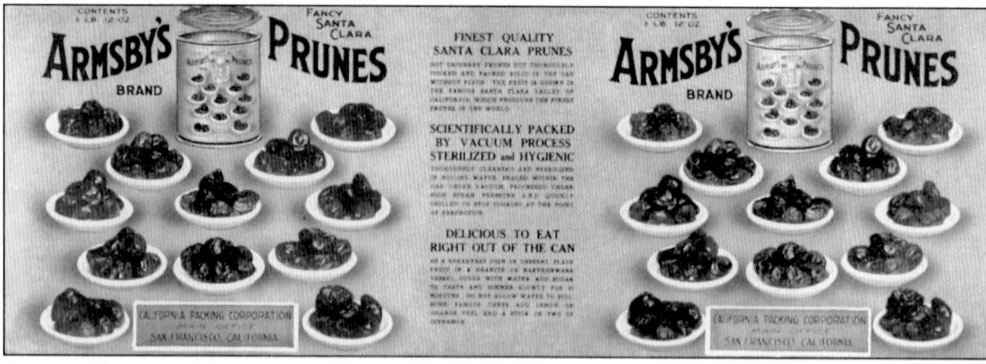

ARMSBY PRUNES ADVERTISING. In an age where fresh fruit remained a seasonal delicacy, dried fruit was a highly prized treat. A dish of stewed prunes was a staple on many restaurant menus.

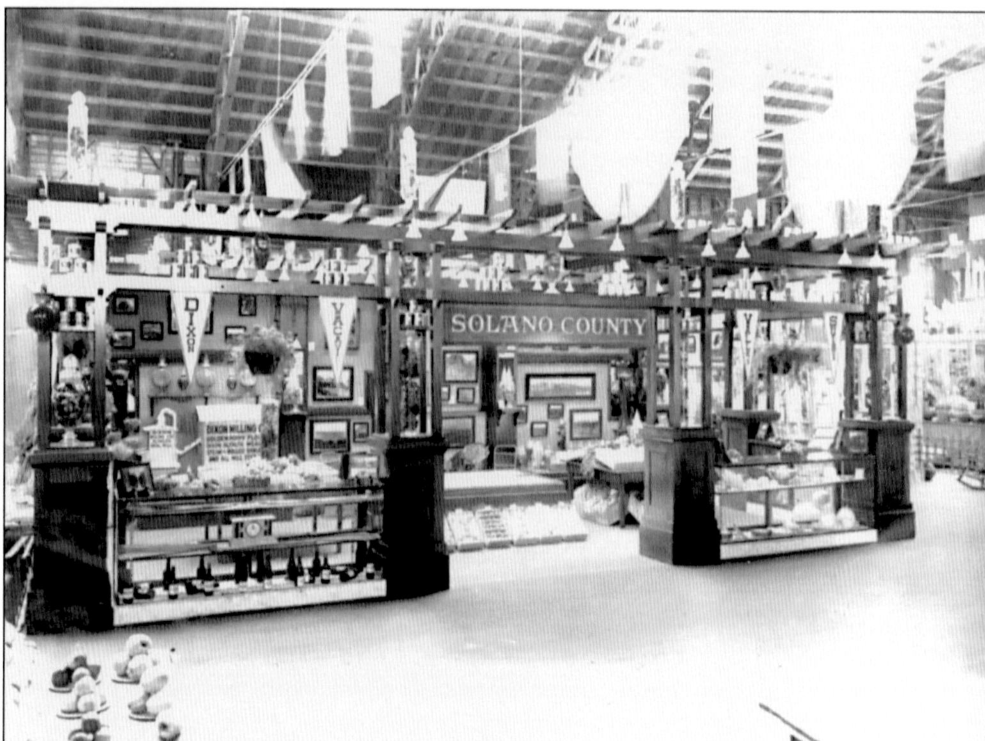

SOLANO COUNTY EXHIBIT AT STATE FAIR, 1915. As an agricultural county, Solano has always tried to promote its produce at county and state fairs. This elaborate display was created for the California State Fair of 1915.

Nine

The Town of Cement

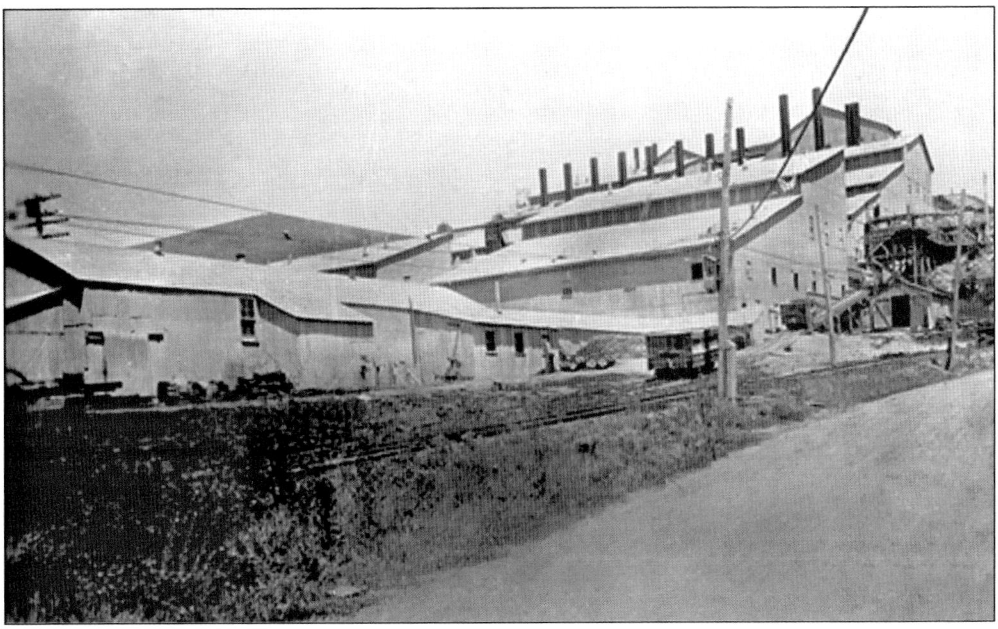

Cement Factory, the "Old Mill." New residents to Fairfield often inquire about the structure near Cement Hill, locally nicknamed "the Castle." In effect, this is the foundation of the rock-crushing machinery, one of the few reminders of a bustling town that centered solely on the production of cement. In 1902, the Portland Cement Company acquired 900 acres for $500,000 to mine a local quarry and process the material into Golden Gate brand cement. Much like several of their other cement cities across the country, the company town, Cement, employed about 500 workers, housed a population of nearly 1,000, and provided all the amenities and services necessary for their daily well being. For a quarter of a century, until its closure in 1927, the town of Cement provided work and cultural entertainment to people in upper Solano County.

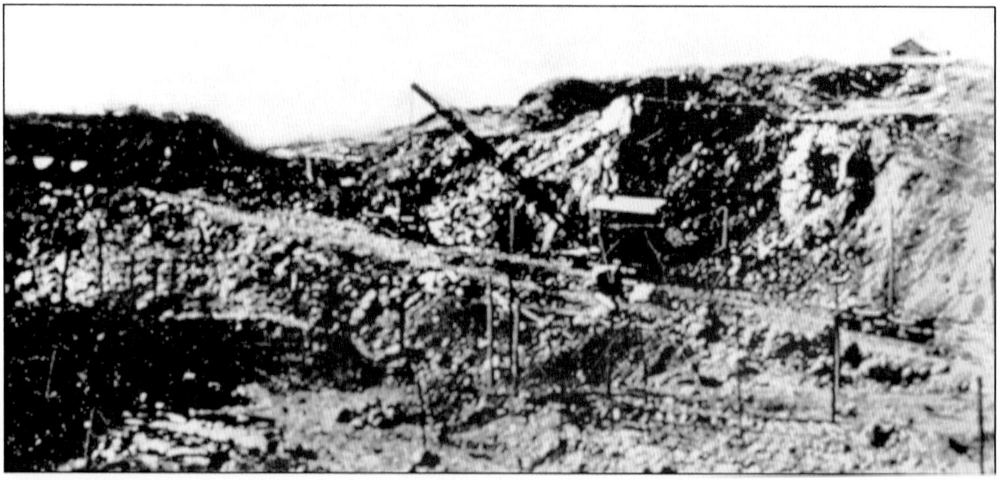

VIEW OF THE QUARRY. The rich deposit of lime on the former A.A. Dickie ranch was the main reason that the Portland Cement Company established its cement manufacturing operation in this area. Workers can be seen here quarrying the lime and loading it onto small railcars.

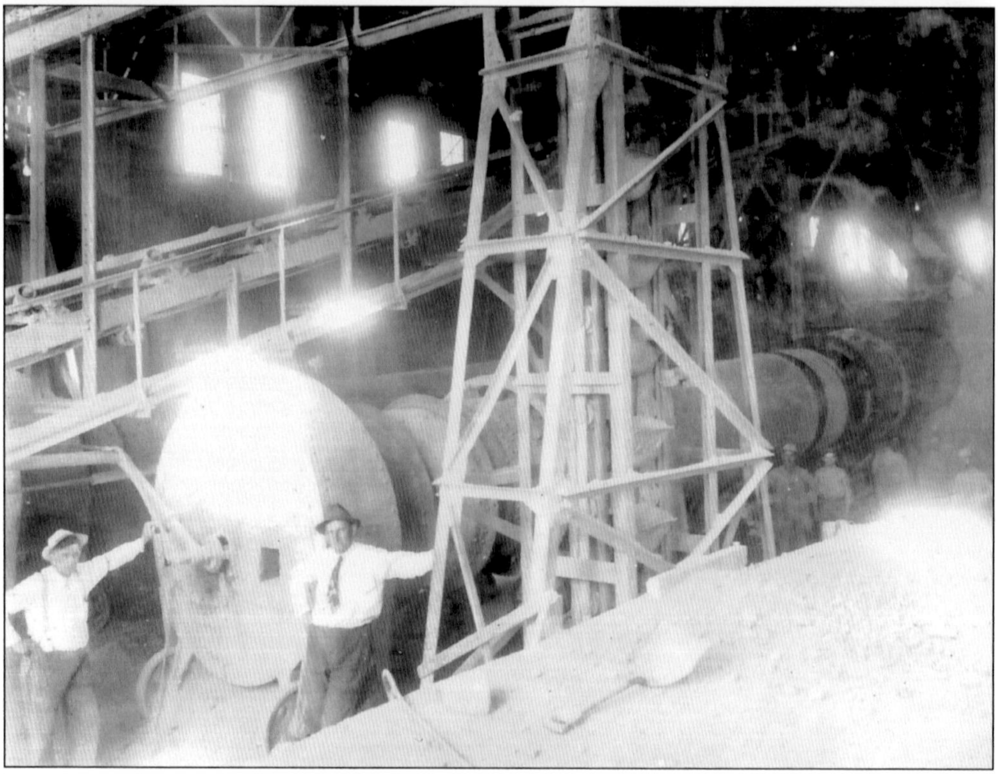

INSIDE THE CEMENT DRYER. Manufacturing cement was a complex procedure. Rock and clay were mixed in big silos and this mixture went into the rotating roaster to dry, such as the one shown here. From there it was transferred to the upper ball mills, mixed once again, and ground to a fine powder. Then it was on to the upper tube mills for a third mix, and from there the powder went into the kiln and was heated red hot, until it formed round cinders. These were then stacked in big piles and cured for a year. Finally, the cinders were ground into a powder, mixed again, and poured into 96-pound bags.

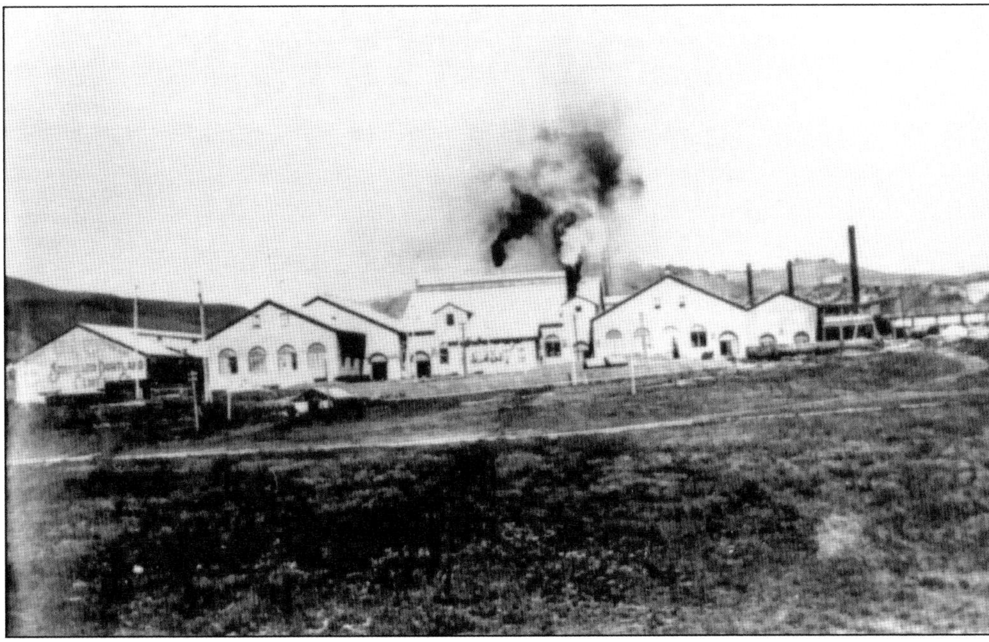

Cement Plant. Cement manufacturers developed their own formulas for the limestone clay mixture. There was no standard formula for Portland Cement until 1917. Regardless of the recipe, it was dusty, dirty work. Conditions were difficult, and 12-hour shifts were normal until the establishment of 8-hour shifts in 1916. The plant operated 24 hours a day. Fine white powder coated everything, hardening to cement whenever it rained or got wet. In 1910, apprentices earned $1.75 per day; by 1927, it had risen to $4. Employee turnover was high. Besides the quarry and the mill, the plant also operated a machine shop and rail yard.

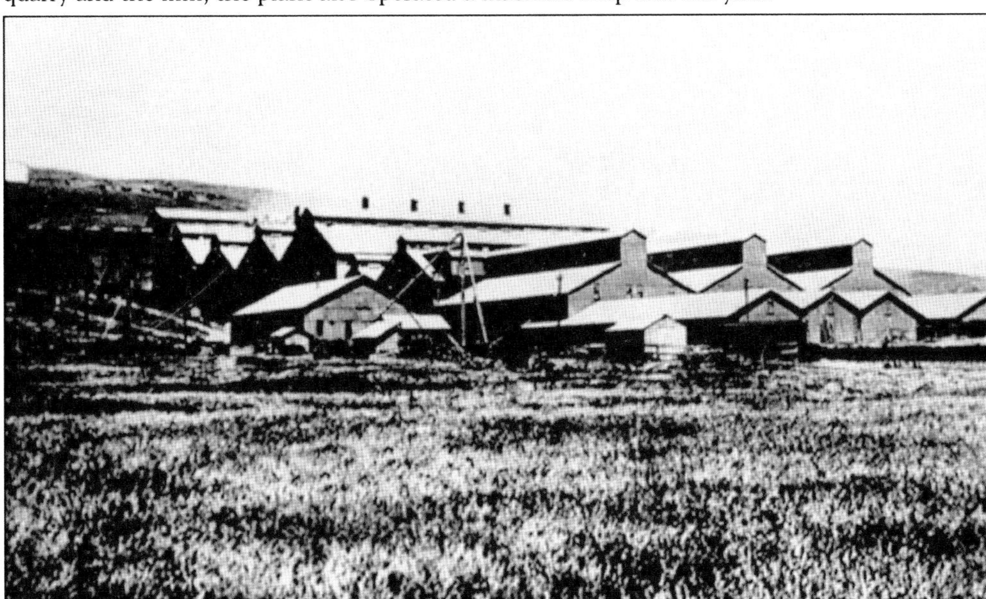

Mill "B," 1915. During the 1910s, the plant grew and prospered. This photo shows Mill "B" sometime after 1915. In its heyday, Cement was one of the largest manufacturing plants on the West Coast.

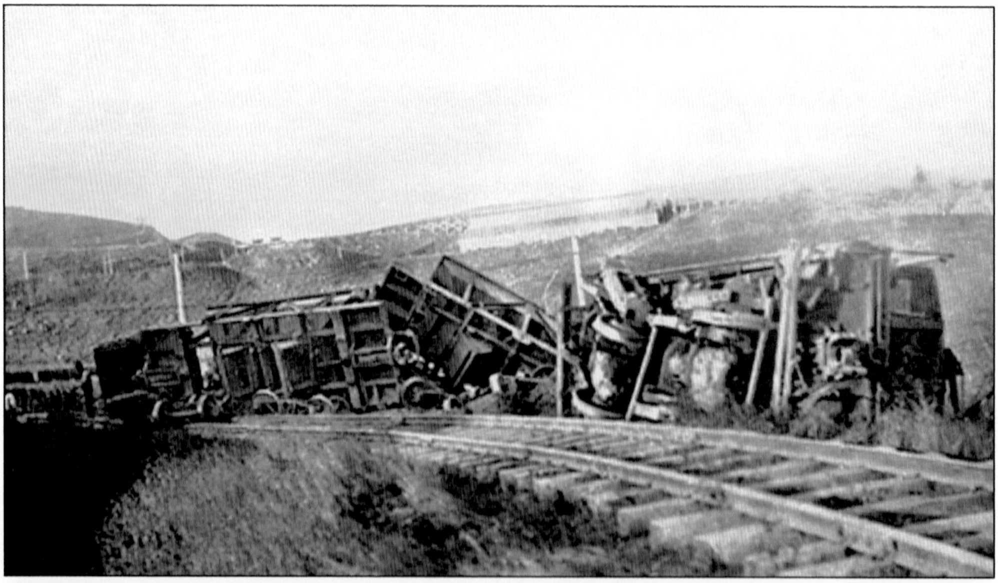

TRAIN CRASH. The Cement, Tolenas & Tidewater Railroad (CT&T) operated three locomotives, two of them electric, connecting the quarry and the different mill operations. The No. 4, a steam engine, ran from Cement to Suisun, crossing the Sacramento Northern and the Southern Pacific tracks. Tracks went down Claybank Road to the Tolenas Depot of the Southern Pacific. In this picture, one of the smaller engines has derailed on a downgrade, pulling the freight wagons off the rail.

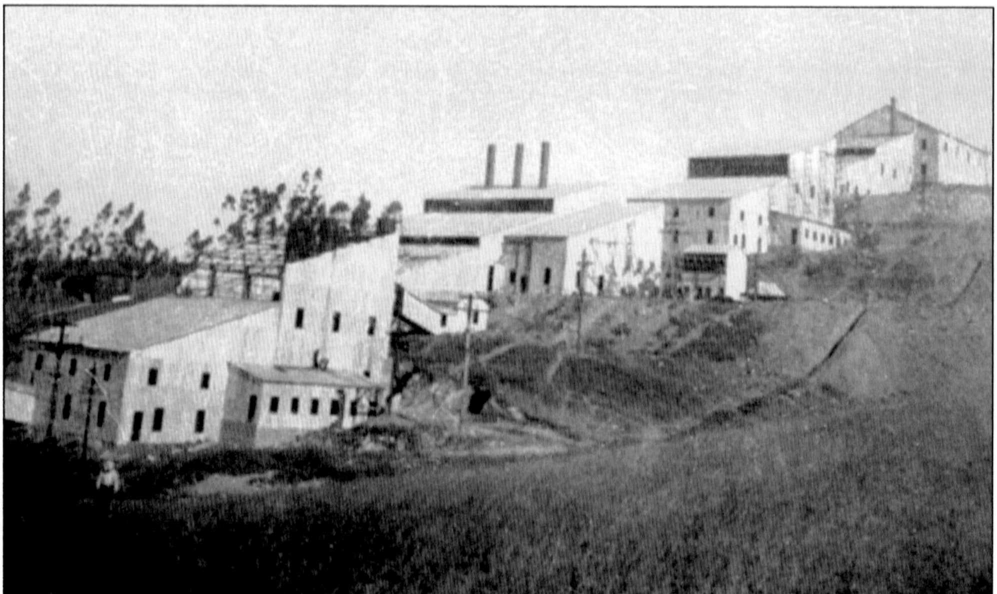

NEW MILL, 1917. The final expansion occurred in 1917 with the construction of the new mill south of town. The new plant could produce up to 6,000 barrels of Golden Gate cement per day. Limestone was brought in from a sister operation near Auburn called Mountain Quarries, via the Southern Pacific Railroad. Eleven short kilns were needed to process the volume of material. The 80,000 barrels of cement produced for Mare Island's dry-dock facilities was among the mill's bigger jobs.

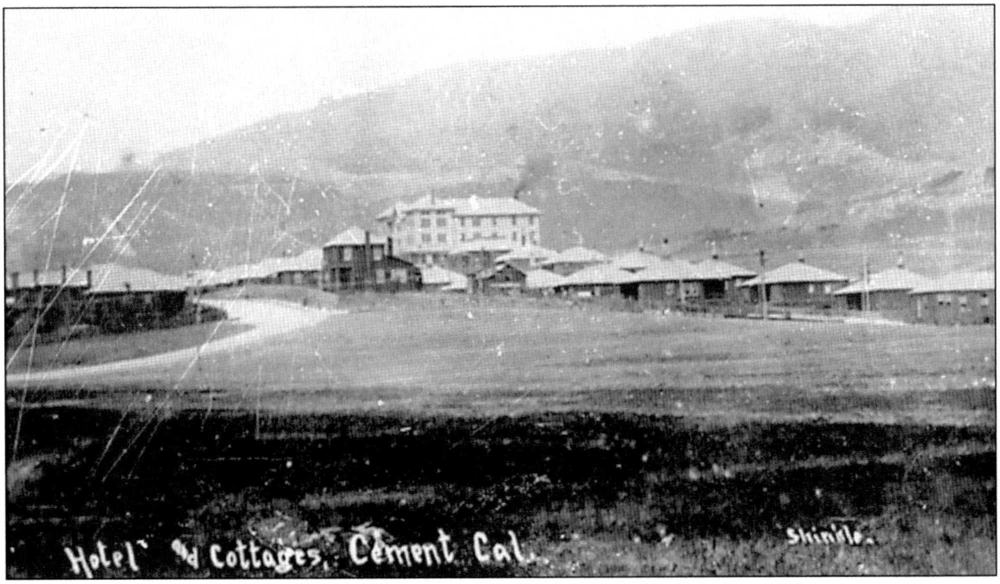

View of Hotel and Cottages. The town of Cement lay east of the manufacturing plant on a hill. Visitors could see rows of houses, topped by the hotel, from far away. Conversely, the town offered a panoramic view of the surrounding area. Several streets were laid out, though never paved. Housing was allocated according to job station. Company officials and foremen lived on one street. Workers and their families, many of them Italian, Portuguese, and Spanish, lived in smaller cottages on the back street. Rent was $12 a month, but electricity, telephone, and light bulbs were supplied free of charge. Water was pumped across the hills from wells in Vacaville. All the houses were painted the same dull red, leading to the comment that the company must have gotten the paint cheap. Bachelors generally lived at the Golden Gate Hotel, where many also took their meals. Others were paid guests at a family table. The Portland Cement Company operated a farm nearby that supplied the company store with fresh meat and dairy products.

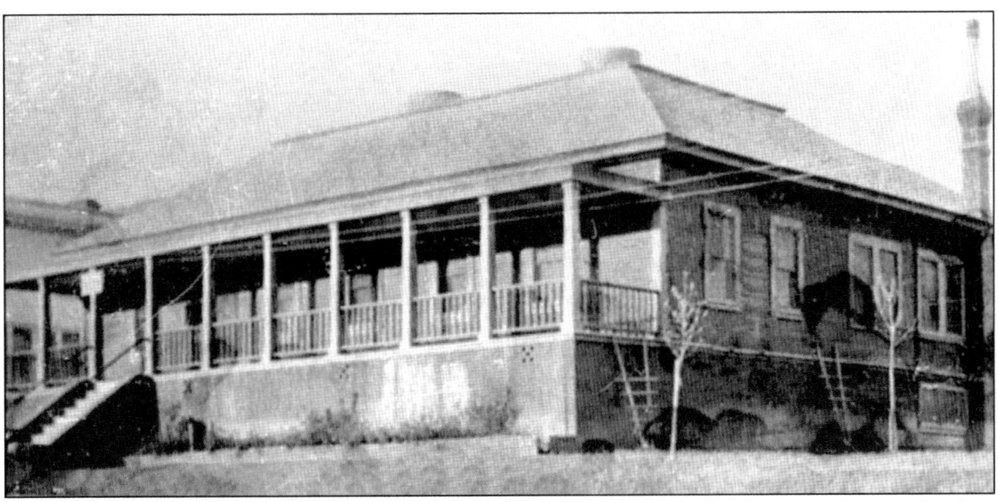

Cement Hospital. Difficult working conditions at the plant resulted in accidents. The fine dust and pollution caused by the use of crude oil in the incinerators caused many respiratory ailments. Medical care was free for company employees and their families. A full-time doctor even made house calls.

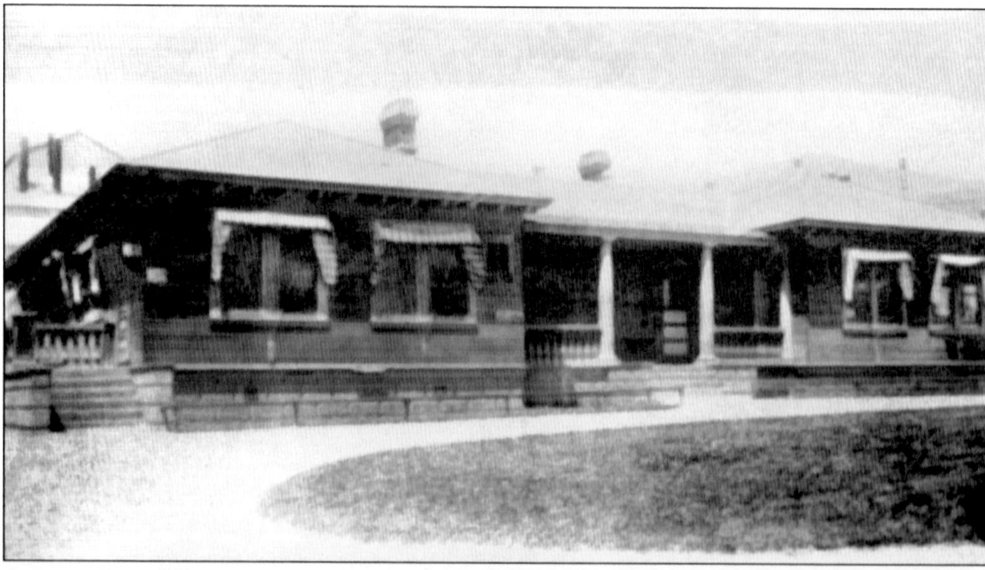

Cement Post Office. Other services included the post office, shown here before 1915. The building was later used as a church and school building. There was a firehouse with volunteer firemen and a grocery store—accepting both regular money and company vouchers—that was famous for its candy counter. Next door was the butcher shop and icehouse. The auditorium served as a church, meeting hall, and theater.

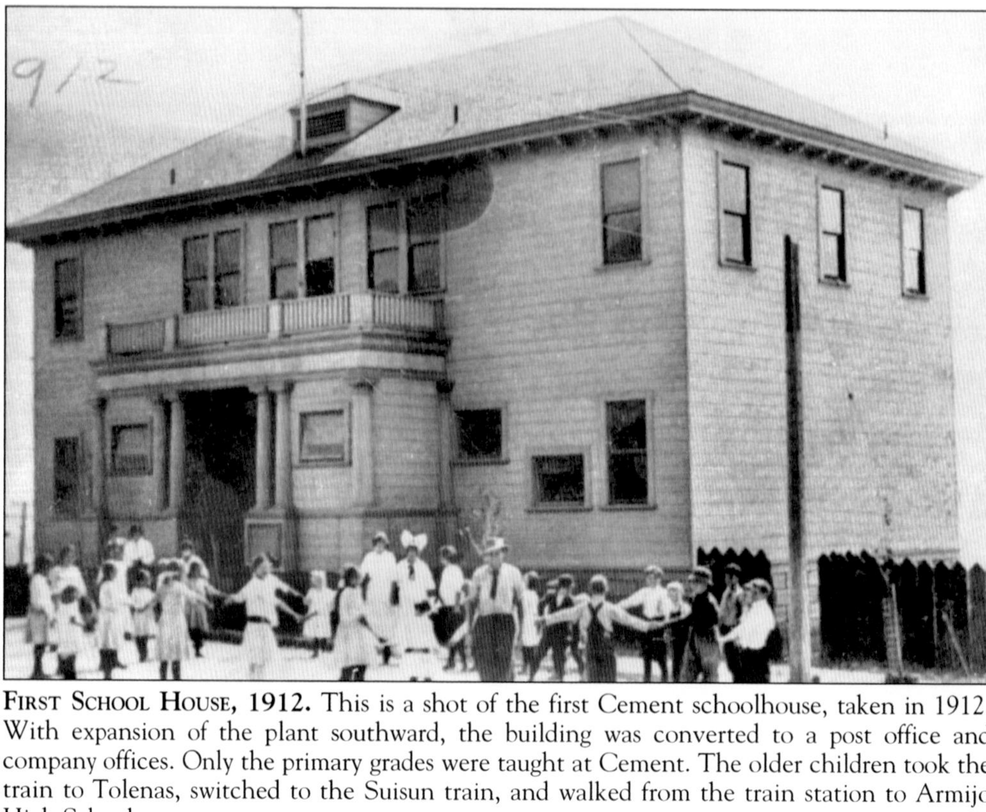

First School House, 1912. This is a shot of the first Cement schoolhouse, taken in 1912. With expansion of the plant southward, the building was converted to a post office and company offices. Only the primary grades were taught at Cement. The older children took the train to Tolenas, switched to the Suisun train, and walked from the train station to Armijo High School.

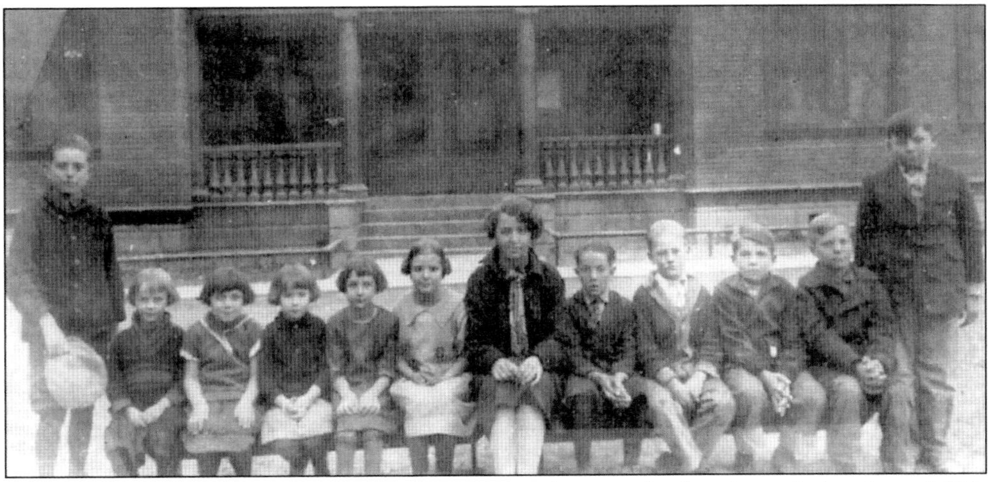

Margaret Jensen and Students, 1927. Two teachers taught first through fourth, and fifth through eighth grades, respectively. During later years, Margaret Jensen taught first through fourth grades. She is shown here with her students in front of the second school building, just before the school and Cement closed in 1927. Her pupils that year were (fourth grade) Malcolm Hubback and Ruth Wright; (third grade) Amy Lefker, Lena Tamborini, and Walter Wright; (second grade) John Esteps, Helen Hoffman, and William Roe; (first grade) Marcia Andrews, Archie Davis, Frank Estepa, Frances Fernandez, Charlotte Griffiths, and Melvin Spidel.

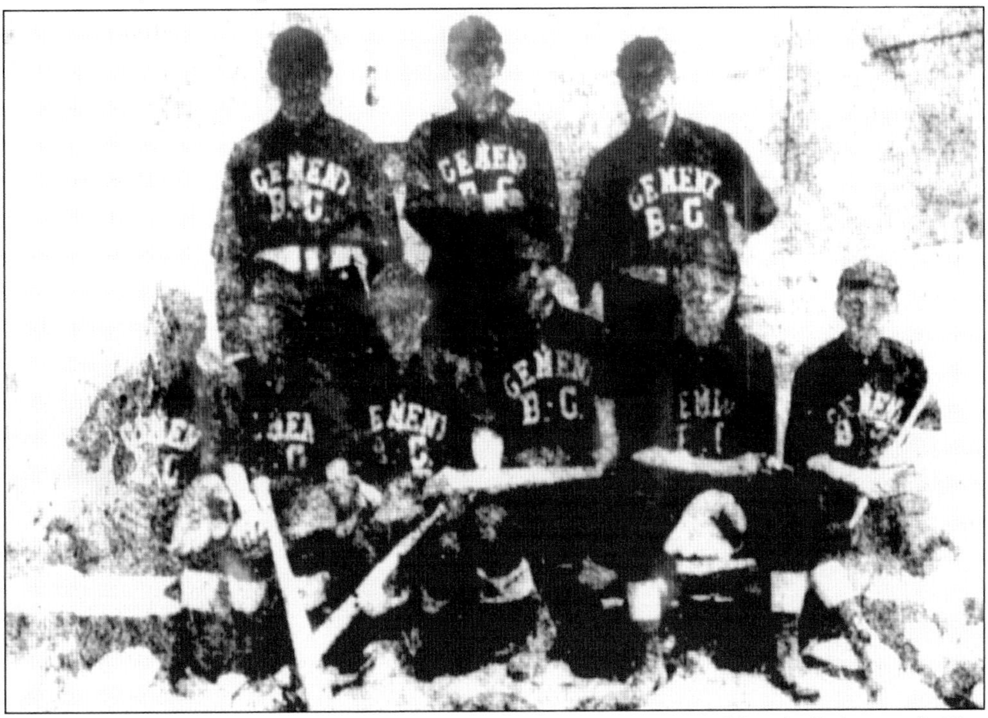

Cement Baseball. The town had its own park, tennis courts, and baseball diamond. The Cement Baseball team played against the Vacaville, Fairfield, and Suisun city teams. Cement also had a competitive bowling team, the "Golden Gate Five." Other entertainments included live theater and movies, annual company picnics, and Fun Day, a big town gathering filled with popular games. July Fourth was celebrated with baseball and other games.

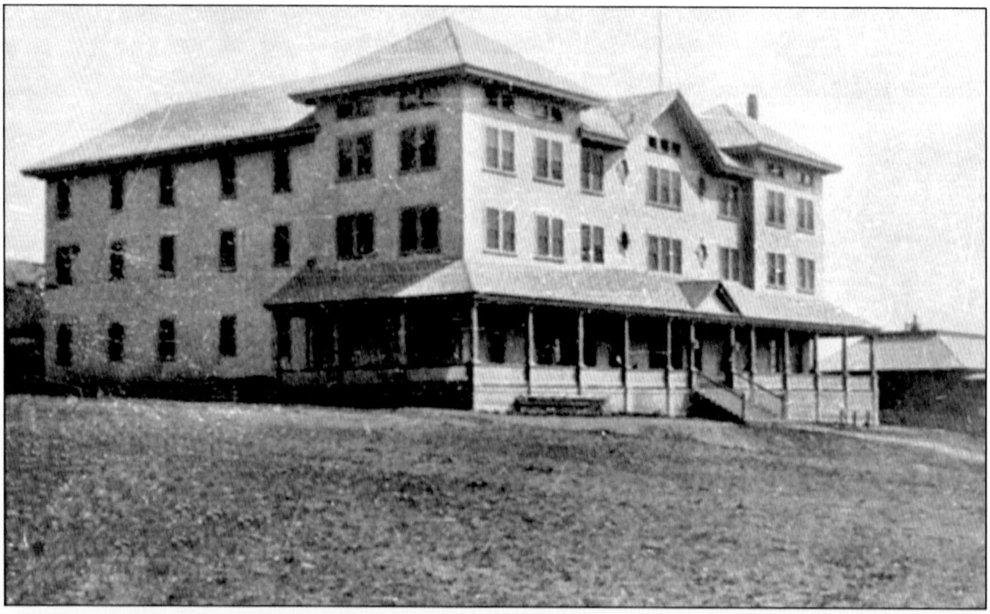

Golden Gate Hotel. The Golden Gate Hotel housed bachelor workers, as well as visiting guests. The three-story hotel could accommodate up to 175 people. It included a kitchen and a large dining room. A fire in 1906 destroyed the building completely.

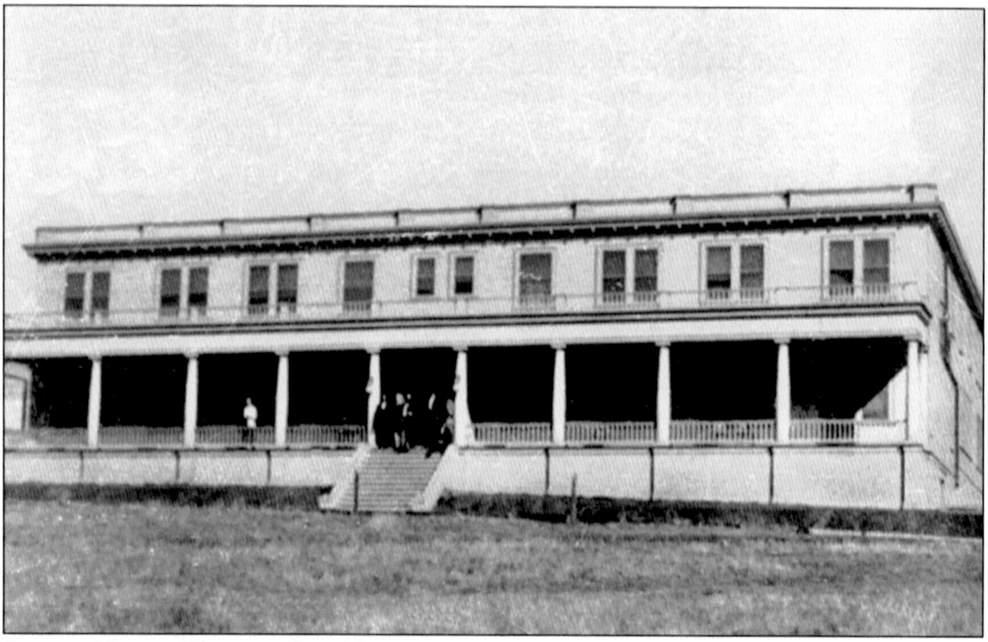

Second Hotel. The second Golden Gate Hotel was a two-story building, fronted by a large veranda. It boasted a barbershop, pool tables, kitchen, swimming pool, tennis courts, rooms with telephone service, a huge ballroom, and a dining room where the annual "Grand Ball" took place. Another popular event was the so-called "Smokers," an annual prize-boxing match that drew thousands of mostly male visitors to Cement.

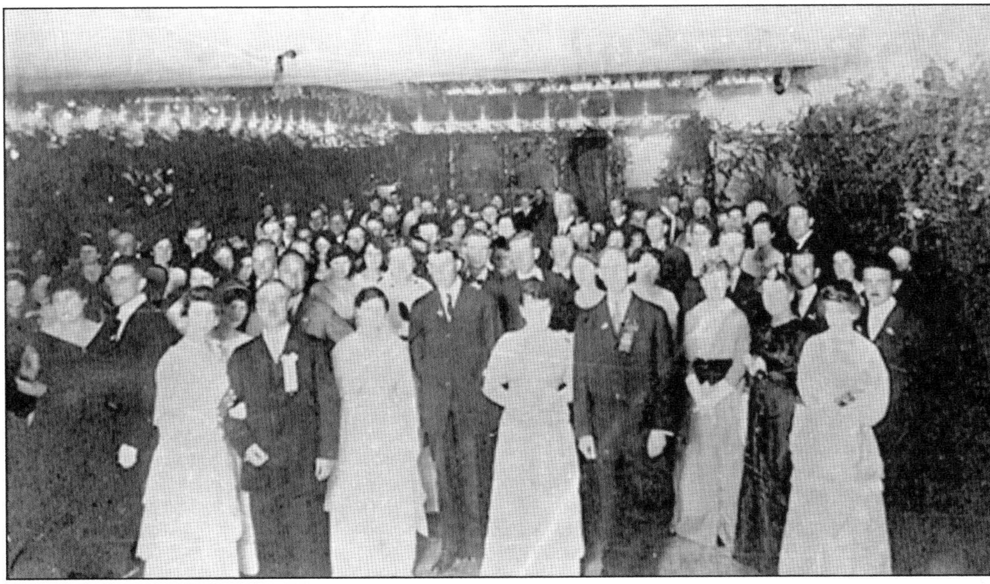

GUESTS AT THE ANNUAL BALL. For 20 years, the annual grand ball was the social event of the area, drawing people from the vicinity and as far away as San Francisco. The price for a couple was $5, which included a full dinner and dancing to a live orchestra.

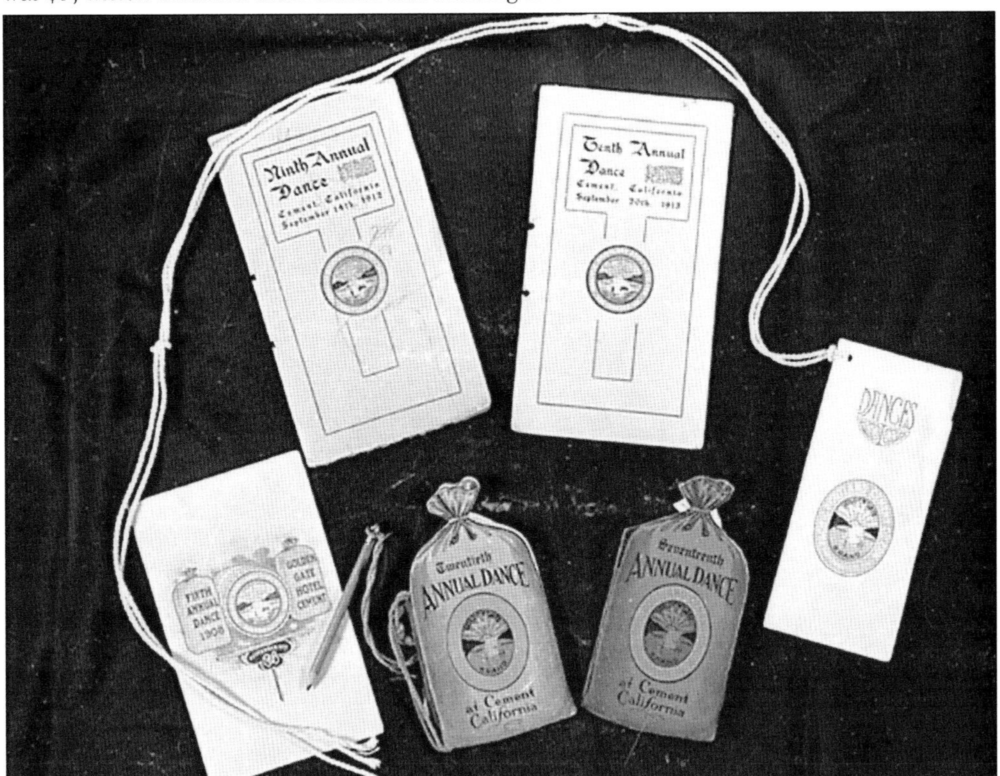

CEMENT BALL DANCE CARDS. This collection shows early invitations to the ball and dance cards in the shape of cement bags. Each lady carried a card listing the dances for the evening. Her dance partners would write their name in pencil next to their chosen dance.

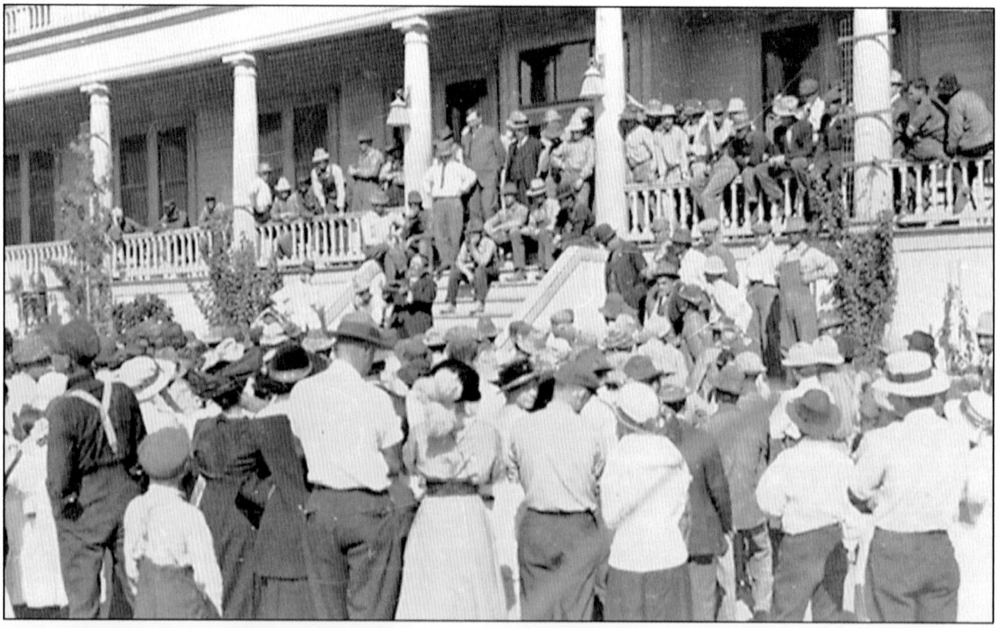

Hiram Johnson. In 1912, California Governor Hiram Johnson campaigned from the veranda of the hotel, drawing a large crowd of residents and visitors.

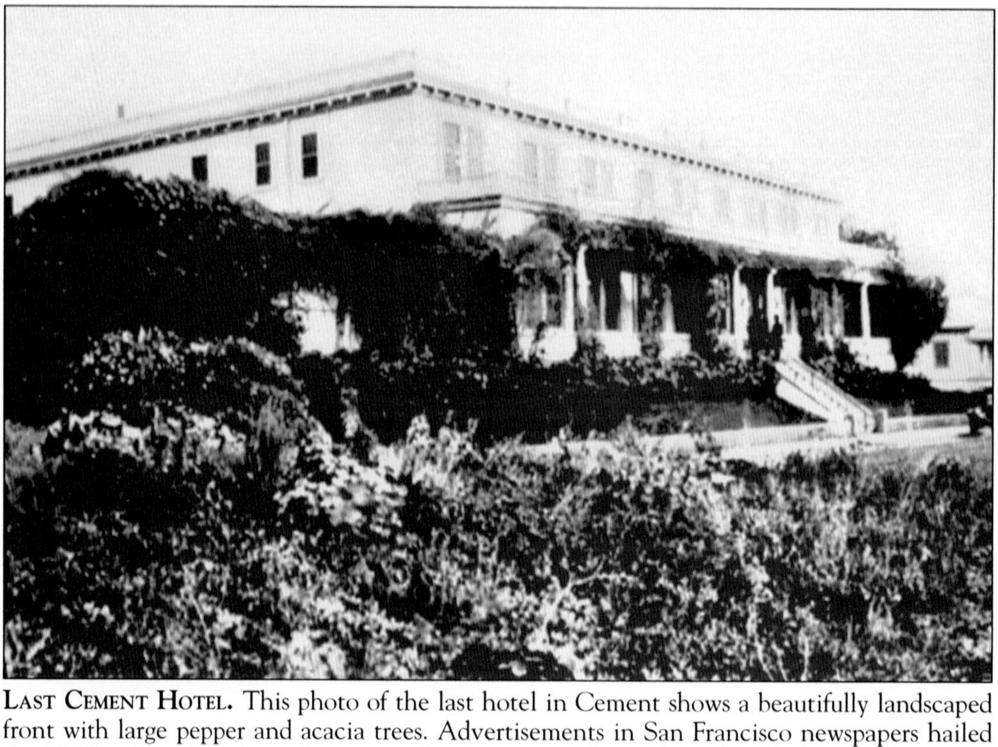

Last Cement Hotel. This photo of the last hotel in Cement shows a beautifully landscaped front with large pepper and acacia trees. Advertisements in San Francisco newspapers hailed the Golden Gate Hotel as a "sensational summer spa." By 1927, rock and clay supplies in the area were exhausted. The Portland Cement Company sold its holdings and closed Cement. Some of the workers' cottages were moved to Fairfield, where many are still lived in. The larger structures, including the hotel, were dismantled and auctioned off.